THE STRANGE CASE
OF
EDMUND GURNEY

BY TREVOR H. HALL

BIBLIOGRAPHY

A Bibliography of Books on Conjuring in English from 1580 to 1850
Mathematical Recreations (1633): An Exercise in Seventeenth Century Bibliography
Old Conjuring Books: A Bibliographical and Historical Study
The Winder Sale of Old Conjuring Books
Some Printers and Publishers of Conjuring Books and other Ephemera, 1800—1850 (with Percy H. Muir)

SHERLOCK HOLMES

Sherlock Holmes. Ten Literary Studies
The Late Mr. Sherlock Holmes
Sherlock Holmes. The Higher Criticism
Sherlock Holmes and His Creator

DOROTHY L. SAYERS

Dorothy L. Sayers. Nine Literary Studies

CRITICAL PSYCHICAL RESEARCH

The Haunting of Borley Rectory: A Critical Survey of the Evidence (with E. J. Dingwall and K. M. Goldney)
The Strange Case of Edmund Gurney
New Light on Old Ghosts
The Spiritualists: The Story of William Crookes and Florence Cook
The Strange Story of Ada Goodrich Freer
(first published as part of *Strange Things* by T. H. H. with J. L. Campbell)

CONJURING

The Testament of R. W. Hull
Nothing is Impossible
Reading is Believing
The Card Magic of Edward G. Brown

HISTORICAL INVESTIGATION

The Early Years of the Huddersfield Building Society
The Mystery of the Leeds Library
Search for Harry Price

The Strange Case of
Edmund Gurney

TREVOR H. HALL
M.A., Ph.D., F.S.A.

With an Introduction
by
ELIOT SLATER
C.B.E., M.D., LL.D.

"There is not a fiercer hell than the
failure in a great object."—JOHN KEATS

DUCKWORTH

Second edition, with new Introduction, 1980

First published 1964

1964, 1980 by TREVOR H. HALL
Gerald Duckworth & Co. Ltd.
The Old Piano Factory
43 Gloucester Crescent, London NW1

ISBN 0 7156 1154 2

British Library Cataloguing in Publication Data

Hall, Trevor Henry
   The strange case of Edmund Gurney.—New ed.
   1. Gurney, Edmund   2. Psychical research—
   Great Britain—Biography
   I. Title
133.9′092′4   BF1027.G8
ISBN 0-7156-1154-2

PRINTED IN GREAT BRITAIN
BY UNWIN BROTHERS LIMITED
OLD WOKING SURREY

CONTENTS

ILLUSTRATIONS

For Marguerite, with love

PREFACE TO THE SECOND EDITION

My publishers have thought it appropriate to republish *The Strange Case of Edmund Gurney* simultaneously with the publication of *The Strange Story of Ada Goodrich Freer* (both with Introductions by Dr. Eliot Slater, C.B.E., LL.D., formerly Editor-in-Chief of *The British Journal of Psychiatry*) for a reason with which I am in entire agreement. Both Gurney and Miss Freer were deeply involved in the activities of the Society for Psychical Research, but were actuated by entirely different motives. I am deeply indebted to Dr. Eliot Slater, whose contributions to both these character studies have added immeasurably to their value and interest.

Gurney, a distinguished and brilliant Victorian man of letters of independent means, the author of *The Power of Sound* and *Tertium Quid*, was happily married and beloved by his friends. Tragically, he was persuaded by F. W. H. Myers to become the first Secretary of the S.P.R. (unpaid) from its foundation in 1882. Gurney, whose life-long, manic-depressive condition demanded his constant immersion in absorbing work, laboured unceasingly for the Society in its efforts to establish that telepathy was a fact in Nature, and that its experimental proof could be a stepping-stone to a convinced belief in immortality. In addition to his dedication to this time-consuming work and his daily duties as Secretary, he was persuaded to become the Editor of both the *Journal* and the *Proceedings* of the Society. Gurney lived in London, but in 1888 he took his own life in mysterious circumstances behind his locked bedroom door at the Royal Albion Hotel, Brighton, where he had been summoned by a letter on the previous day. I believe that what happened in Brighton was the final crisis, the culmination of Gurney's repeated discoveries of fraud in the work to which he had devoted the last six years of his life, and the cause of his suicide at the age of forty-one.

Ada Goodrich Freer, a completely ruthless and extremely attractive woman who effectively concealed both her age and her origins until I was successful in tracing them, joined the Society for Psychical Research in 1888, the year of Gurney's death, and rapidly became a leading member. Sponsored by F. W. H. Myers, she was able to convince distinguished Victorians such as Henry and Eleanor Sidgwick, Lord Bute and Sir Charles Shaw that she possessed supernormal powers, and was able to use the Society effectively for her social advancement and to her financial advantage. She was ultimately caught in fraud, and in consequence left England for Jerusalem at the turn of the century. When she died in 1931 she was 73, although her husband, Dr. Hans Spoer, believed her to be 56 and registered her age as such on her death entry.

It is difficult to imagine two personalities differing so profoundly as those of Edmund Gurney and Ada Freer. Gurney, idealistic, scrupulously honest and a devoted believer in the essential goodness of his fellow-men, owed his death to those very qualities in combination with his total involvement in psychical research and his final complete disillusionment. Ada Freer, shrewd, calculating, fraudulent and fascinating, owed such success as she achieved in her life, directly or indirectly, to her activities in the same subject and the use of her personal attractions. Her importance lies in the fact that a study of her career, following directly as it did the death of Gurney, completes the melancholy history of psychical research in England from the foundation of the Society for Psychical Research to the end of the nineteenth century. Although each story is complete in itself, the fact that they are complementary causes me to welcome the decision of Gerald Duckworth & Co. to make both books available simultaneously.

On the first page of the Preface to the first edition of the present book, I said that during the inquiry that had enabled me to write it I had tried to solve two related mysteries. The first was the enigma of Gurney's death. The second was the riddle of George Albert Smith and Douglas Blackburn, the two young men who in 1882 were presenting a two-person "thought-reading act" at the Aquarium in Brighton, with prices of admission at 1s. 0d and 6d. They were able to persuade the leaders of the newly-formed S.P.R. that their "act", which did not differ from that of many other professional entertainers of the period, relied on genuine telepathy. Since my book was first published in 1964, new information has become available on both these main themes.

In 1965 some new evidence from the past was published, supporting my belief that the fact of Gurney's suicide was concealed by the S.P.R. leaders, and especially by the evidence at the inquest of Dr. A. T. Myers, an S.P.R. member involved in the Smith/

Blackburn experiments and the brother of F. W. H. Myers. *The Diary of Alice James*, privately printed in 1894 in four copies only and unknown to me in that form, was published in 1965 with an Introduction by Professor Leon Edel. Alice James was the sister of William and Henry James. Professor William James held Gurney in the highest regard, and in this letter to his brother about the tragedy (he was writing to Henry James from Chocorua in July, 1888) he said that the sympathetic Gurney understood him better than anyone else, and that in all his thoughts of returning to England Gurney had been the friend from whom he had expected "the most nourishing communion".

Alice James was an invalid, confined to her room. William James returned to England in July, 1889. He had been acutely disturbed by the mysterious circumstances of Gurney's death. He knew people like Sidgwick and Myers extremely well, and we may think that when he arrived in England in the summer of 1889 he would have some questions to ask. We may also be sure that he would visit his invalid sister. On 5 August, 1889 Alice James wrote in her diary:

> "They say there is little doubt that Mr. Edmund Gurney committed suicide. What a pity to hide it; every educated person who kills himself does something to lessen the superstition" (1965 edition, p. 52).

What a pity to hide it! This is a contemporary six-word epitome of one of one of the main themes of my book: that the acute embarrassment of the suicide of the Secretary of the Society for Psychical Research in the midst of his work was purposefully concealed. From whom could Alice James, confined to the sick-room, have been more likely to obtain such information than from her distinguished brother?

In a series of articles in the periodical *John Bull* from December 5, 1908 to 9 January, 1909, Douglas Blackburn revealed that all the experiments in "thought-transference" conducted by the S.P.R. in 1882 and 1883 with G. A. Smith and himself were a hoax so far as the two subjects were concerned, and had been accomplished by wholly natural means. He said that the results of the experiments were produced by a system of codes between Smith and himself, assisted by tricks, coincidences and fortuitous circumstances, and were in no instance genuine. He added that "the mental bias of both Messrs. Myers and Gurney was towards spiritualism, it being the almost invariable rule of the former to give the experiment the benefit of the doubt". The not unamusing account of the reaction of the S.P.R. to Blackburn's disclosure of the truth of the matter is contained in pages 137-49 of the present work.

He made a further published statement three years later in an article "CONFESSIONS OF A 'TELEPATHIST'. Mr. Douglas Blackburn and the Scientists. 30-Year-Old Hoax Exposed. How the Deception was Planned and Worked." This article appeared in the *Daily News* of 1 September, 1911. What is new and important is that at the age of sixty Blackburn told the story of the hoax for the third time in the *Sunday Times* of 16 September, 1917. I am grateful to my colleague of many years, Dr. E. J. Dingwall, for sending me this reference. We may well ask ourselves what possible motive Blackburn could have for these repeated published statements over a period of twenty years that he did not possess supernatural powers of transmitting thought, if he was not telling the simple, common-sense truth.

On pages 132-6 of the present work some account is given of Blackburn's later life and the tributes paid to him in the obituaries after his death in 1929. More important, I quote from reviews of his six outstanding novels about South Africa, and in particular that by Andrew Lang, who coupled Blackburn's *Prinsloo of Prinsloodorp* (London, 1899) with Olive Schreiner's *Story of an African Farm* (London, 1883) as the two great South African classics, "outstanding, unsurpassed in the copious literature of the Sub-Continent". Of Blackburn's *Leaven: A Black and White Story* (London, 1908) the reviewers in *The Academy* and *The Bookman* (the latter by Sir W. Robertson Nicoll) said that the book was written "with a sense of humour and a sense of honour", and that the author is "telling the truth as he sees it, unfalteringly and unshrinkingly". It was in this year, 1908, that the S.P.R. leaders were saying privately (they did not dare to say it publicly) that Blackburn was lying when he confessed that he and G. A. Smith had used simple conjuring methods in their thought-reading act.

I have written briefly about Blackburn's reputation in the literary world simply because I wished to introduce an incident of great interest. In November, 1976, I received a letter from Dr.

Stephen Gray, the senior lecturer in the School of English in the Rand Afrikaans University in Johannesburg, who had written to my publishers to obtain my address. He had some kind things to say about *The Strange Case of Edmund Gurney*, but of greater interest was his revelation of the importance attached today in South Africa to Blackburn's literary achievements, and in his university in particular. "He is from our point of view an immensely important and even unique writer." Dr. Gray went to the trouble of sending me a copy of the lecture he uses on Blackburn and his work, coupled with the information that he is writing a critical study of Blackburn's life and achievements. He asked if we might meet if he came to Yorkshire, and in March, 1977 we spent a day together in my home. I was happy to be of some small assistance, and Dr Gray went away with my notebooks on Blackburn's early life in England, my collection of reviews of his books, and one or two of them (now hard to find) that I had managed to pick up when I was gathering material for *The Strange Case of Edmund Gurney*.

This book was first published in 1964, and has been out of print and virtually unobtainable for many years. In such circumstances, copies of scarce books sometimes have interesting histories of ownership, as the example that has recently come back into my possession will illustrate. An inscribed copy of *The Strange Case of Edmund Gurney*, presented by me to my friend the late Roland Winder of Leeds, was included in Sotheby's sale of his library (Lot 160) on 18 March, 1974, following Winder's death three years previously. It was bought, along with other signed copies of my books, by Dr. M. H. Coleman (whom I do not know) according to the *Price List* of the sale subsequently published by the auctioneers. At a later date the identical inscribed copies were offered for sale in Catalogue No. 8 (Nos. 81, 102 and 103) by a bookseller, R. A. Gilbert of Bristol, at an average price of rather over £7 per book.

By coincidence, at this time my friend and co-author, the late Charles O. Ellison, Emeritus Archdeacon of Leeds, was forming a collection of my books, but still lacked *The Strange Case of Edmund Gurney*, of which I had no second copy. It was duly secured for him from the Gilbert catalogue, and remained in the library of the Venerable Charles Ellison until his death in December, 1978. What had by this time become his complete collection of my books, and some

Sherlock Holmes items, were most kindly bequeathed to me. Only now, on examining what was the original Winder copy at leisure, have I discovered some additions made to it. On the inside of the dust-jacket, which from memory I do not think is the original, is printed the menu of the *Yorkshire Post Literary Luncheon* held on 5 November, 1964, together with my name as "Guest Author". Pasted into the book is a cutting from the *Sunday Telegraph* of 3 January, 1965, "BOOKS OF THE YEAR", an article on 36 books chosen from those published in 1964, in which *The Strange Case of Edmund Gurney* was included. Pasted inside the front cover are two "stills" from the television play adapted from my book by the playwright Ken Taylor, and featured on BBC2 Theatre 625 on Sunday evening, 29 October, 1967. The cast included Richard Todd as Gurney, Anthony Bate as Myers, Ray Brooks as G. A. Smith, John Barcroft as Douglas Blackburn, Lynda Baron as Alice Smith, Diana Fairfax as Kate Gurney and Norman Shelley as Sir James Crichton-Brown.

I have a special reason for listing the distinguished and entirely suitable cast which those responsible at the BBC chose for the play, which entirely satisfied me. I was delighted by the care and expertise with which the Victorian scenes were designed and constructed. I express this appreciation in fairness and goodwill to offset the recording of my disappointment at the way in which the story was altered at the end. One of the most detailed reviews of the book was published in the *Yorkshire Post* on 12 November, 1964. It was by H. Montgomery Hyde, the distinguished authority on the Victorian era, who put the matter succinctly over three years before the play was performed:

> "Between the two World Wars a rumour was current in spiritualistic circles that Gurney and his associates had been secretly engaged in homosexual practices with a number of Brighton youths who had been the subjects for payment of hypnotic experiments, and it has been suggested that blackmail and fear of exposure may have been the cause of Gurney's suicide.
>
> Mr. Hall, quite rightly in my opinion, dismisses this hypothesis".

A similar view of the matter was expressed by Philip Hengist, who reviewed the book in *Punch* on 24 February, 1965:

> "For many years members of the Society for Psychical Research (of which Gurney was the honorary secretary) whispered darkly of homosexuality and blackmail. Mr. Hall thinks differently."

As will be seen from Appendix 1 of this book (pp. 200-6) I was fully aware of these stories of the supposed homosexual activities of the leaders of the Society for Psychical Research with the youthful friends of G. A. Smith in Brighton, and the suggestion that the experiments were a cover for this behaviour. I went to a great deal of trouble and historical inquiry to satisfy myself (and I hoped the reader) that there was no evidence to support these rumours, as the Appendix demonstrates. It was evidently decided, however, that the introduction of the homosexual element would make the play more interesting to viewers, and this was done. Due to the terms of the contract, I could do no more than insist that the announcement of the play in the *Radio Times* contained the phrase, "Based in part on *The Strange Case of Edmund Gurney*, by Trevor H. Hall".

Selby, N. Yorks.   T. H. H.
1979

PREFACE TO THE FIRST EDITION

DURING the inquiry upon which this book is based, I have tried to solve two related mysteries of the Victorian era. The very odd circumstances surrounding the tragic death of Edmund Gurney in a Brighton hotel have remained a much discussed enigma for nearly eighty years. The riddle presented by the activities as a hypnotist and "mind-reader" of Gurney's youthful secretary, George Albert Smith, is one of considerable fascination when the published statements of his partner Douglas Blackburn are considered.

Why the Society for Psychical Research, of which Gurney was a founder and Smith an Associate, has shown such a curious reluctance to examine the whole mysterious affair I do not know. It has invited investigation for over half a century. Most of the early work of the Society on thought-transference, on which all modern experimental psychical research is based, relied entirely upon the integrity of Smith and the assumed reality of his unusual gifts. His large circle of youthful and mainly uneducated male acquaintances in Brighton, used as paid hypnotic subjects by the founders of the S.P.R., has been the subject of speculative gossip for forty years, and in my opinion has long required commonsense discussion.

I have a solution to offer to each of these mysteries, which I hope may be regarded as appropriate and reasonable interpretations of the evidence. It is a matter for the judgment of the reader. Whether or not he accepts my conclusions, he may feel that he has at his disposal in this book a considerable quantity of information, not lacking in interest and even occasional excitement, relating to a very odd series of events in the late nineteenth century.

In the progress of the investigation a large quantity of published material has been examined, and I hope that no important reference to Edmund Gurney and his circle has remained undiscovered. As will be seen, however, the more important conclusions rely upon correspondence and other documentary information hitherto unpublished. Historical inquiry has a peculiar fascination for those with a taste for it. The sense of the past, the indefinable appeal of old books and letters and the pursuit of a clue through the complexities of a large library or a public record office all have an attraction for me which I hope it is within my ability to share with the reader.

It remains my pleasant task gratefully to acknowledge the generous help of my friends who have so willingly assisted in the investigation. Living and working in Yorkshire as I do, it would have been impossible for me to have written the book without their support. Dr. A. R. G. Owen made the detailed examination of the MS. of Henry Sidgwick's "Journal" in the library of Trinity College, Cambridge, for me, and extracted all the quoted information from the files of the Society for Psychical Research. Mr. Frank Beckwith, of the Leeds Library, was tireless in his efforts to find references for me in our extensive collection of Victorian autobiographies and memoirs. Dr. Ronald Mavor of Edinburgh patiently answered all my questions about medical matters.

My especial thanks are due to Dr. Alan Gauld of Nottingham University, who went to much trouble to supply me with all the information at his disposal relating to Edmund Gurney from the letters and papers of F. W. H. Myers. Mr. G. H. Brook afforded me unlimited hospitality and access to the Bagden Hall collection of books and periodicals devoted to psychical research and spiritualism. Mrs. K. M. Vevers, my valued secretary, became greatly interested in the enquiry, made many suggestions and prepared the typescript for the printer.

The investigation could not have been brought to a conclusion in a way that would have satisfied me without the kindness of Miss Helen Gurney, whose vivid memory of events of earlier days has been of inestimable help to me. Her knowledge of the account of the affair by her mother, who knew that there was something very wrong indeed about it, has enabled us to discuss the whole matter in a large correspondence with complete mutual frankness and understanding. The importance of Miss Gurney's knowledge of the letter from Brighton, which reached her father immediately before his death, can hardly be over-estimated, which is equally true of her awareness that her father faced a sudden catastrophe, of a nature unknown to Mrs. Gurney, in June 1888. I am most grateful to Miss Gurney for her permission to publish her information and views, the latter frequently being expressed with an endearing emphasis which is typical of her letters. When she told me, for example, that "Fred Myers was the villain of the piece", as she put it, I felt that my interpretation of the relationship between Gurney and Myers was being vigorously confirmed.

I am deeply indebted to my three close friends and collaborators, Eric J. Dingwall, Herbert E. Pratt and Archie S. Jarman. It was in the Sussex home of Dr. Dingwall, my colleague of many years, that I first started my investigation two years ago, and without his formidable help it is doubtful whether it could have been completed. His weekly letters have contained a fund of information and advice and (most valuable of all) occasional amiable disagreement and correction. Mr. Pratt, the honorary librarian of the Magic Circle and an experienced investigator, has spent many hours at Somerset House, the British Museum and in Brighton gathering information for me, his work being made doubly difficult for him by the unfortunate accident that one of the principal characters in the story had the commonest of British surnames. His keen interest in the case was aroused from the beginning, and our correspondence and discussions have been a constant pleasure to me. Of Mr. Jarman, who to my great good fortune lives in Brighton, what can one say of one's gratitude to a friend, involved in large business affairs, who insists upon giving up weeks of his time to answering the insatiable inquiries of a colleague in distant Yorkshire? On one occasion, of which I am much ashamed, Mr. Jarman spent three whole consecutive days in Brighton Public Library following up an obscure clue, at a time when a heavy cold should have confined him to bed. He refers to this modestly as merely "part of the Jarman service". It is, in fact, the knowledge that help of this devoted quality is available that makes an investigation such as that contained in these pages both possible and rewarding.

Leeds,   T. H. H.
May 1964

INTRODUCTION

by

ELIOT SLATER, C.B.E., M.D., LL.D.

THERE is no mystery so inscrutable to the mind of man as the human personality. Ourselves we know from inside, but can never see how we appear to others. We observe with curiosity, or amusement perhaps, or consternation, the behaviour of others, but can never know how they see themselves. One human being appears to another like a picture that does not "read"; there are always contradictions. Something has gone wrong with the perspective. Inevitably so. Looking on from outside we can only guess the relation between thought and feeling and behaviour, and our guesses make no sense, or in the event are proved to be mistaken. We see only surfaces. We lack the double focusing, the stereoscopic viewing from without and from within, which would reconcile the contradictions.

Edmund Gurney shows us a succession of portraits, but it is hard indeed to see the man behind. Who is it that now and again, from deep within him, moves to the control centre to throw everything into disarray? To divert him suddenly from one path to another; to destroy career and life style again, again and yet again; and at last to destroy the man himself and its own secret ego within?

Gurney was born into a distinguished, brilliant and wealthy family, one of nine brothers and sisters. His talents and education made him a scholar at Trinity College, Cambridge, a Prizeman, and finally a Fellow. He had a keen analytic mind, great energy and indefatigable endurance. He completed an enormous body of work. His books, *The Power of Sound*, *Tertium Quid* and *Phantasms of the Living* are all of great compass. The last, a book of 1300 pages, was compiled at a time when the author was heavily engaged as the honorary secretary of the Society for Psychical Research, and the editor of both its periodicals, the *Journal* and the *Proceedings*.

It is perhaps because these books were so large that they failed to make the impact they should have deserved. If he had spared himself he might have spared his readers and have won more appreciation. One suspects that there was an element of obsessionality in his persistent tireless drive. And there must have been a temperamental softness that weakened his power to use the blue pencil. The huge labours that went into *Phantasms of the Living* would have had happier results if they had been spent in vain, if the book had never found its way into print. It was published in 1886, and by the autumn of 1887 it had become totally discredited. For hardly one of the seven hundred or so ghost stories could documentary accreditation, though often claimed, be actually produced. "Where are the Letters?" asked a reviewer; and Gurney's co-editors, Myers and Podmore turned tail and ran. Gurney had to face the music alone. His self-esteem, throughout his life a tender plant, was dealt a wound that did not heal. The Society was made to look ridiculous. The high spiritualist cause for which he worked was brought into contempt. It may well have been the case that his co-editor Podmore was given the task of validating the documentation, and didn't do it. Podmore was a poor pathetic creature who ended his life penniless, disgraced and drowned. But was it not Gurney's duty, even with confidence in his colleague, to see that vitally necessary work had actually been done before going into print? Gurney's secretary, George Albert Smith, was a most engaging and plausible young man. But he had probably been previously caught out by Gurney in trickery, and then forgiven, and actually taken into employment in a position of trust. No serious seeker after truth can be *that* forgiving. Let him trust his cheque-book to a twister, but not his data-sheets! The third editor, Frederic Myers, styled himself "minor poet and amateur savant". As a research worker he was as untrustworthy as Podmore and Smith. One may ask then, how was it that Gurney, a man of honour, worked in intimate collaboration with three dishonest ones.

Gurney was regarded by all his acquaintance as a man of elevated character. George Eliot took him as her model for Daniel Deronda. Lady Battersea called him "one of the elite", Ellen Harrison "the most lovable and beautiful human being I have ever met". Frederic Myers recorded his "profound sympathy for human pain . . . for sorrows not his own" (a spontaneous sympathy one finds in some depressives). He made warm and friendly contacts readily and with ease. He was, in fact, an extreme extravert. He himself recorded his great dependence on the sense of union with his friends. He would find it painful to be called on to check their statements. His wonderful belief in the goodness and honour of others was testified to by Podmore: "I have never met anyone with such an absolute belief in goodness and truth as common human attributes" (see p. 26). Gurney never tried to deceive others, and never tried to excuse himself. He faced the critics when exposure came, and even tried to shield his false friends.

In fact we can find in his saintliness the causes of his ruin. The emotional ties that bound him to his associates robbed him of independence and the will to stand up for himself when he was being exploited. His lack of realism about others led him into disastrous misjudgments. A plausible rascal, relying on his determination to see only the best, could abuse him again and again. Furthermore his great intellectual talents were not founded on a solid basis of common sense. Smith and Blackburn were actually urged to hold hands, in order to get good strong thought transference going between them (p. 102). Myers said that, even to the end of his life, Gurney was never fully convinced that psychical events could not be explained by normal thought processes, even in ones we did not fully understand. From his initiation to his death, he seems to have been aware of "the inherent rottenness of the evidence on which the huge fabric of modern Spiritualism has principally rested" (p. 41). Keeping such opinions to himself must have been a constant strain, and ruthless candour would at least have given him the comfort of spiritual integrity.

For a man with such brilliant gifts, Gurney's career was a succession of disasters. It was he himself who made it so, and the manic-depressive tendencies were not mainly responsible. His education in classics and mathematics won him a scholarship to Trinity College, Cambridge. There he shared the Porson Prize in Greek verse with a classicist who later became Editor-in-Chief of the Loeb Classical Library. He took fourth place in the first class honours list of the Classical Tripos. And in 1872, at the age of twenty-five he was elected to a Fellowship of his College. He had already reached the peak of a brilliant career, and if he wished to he could rest on his laurels. His Fellowship, and the other University and College engagements which would naturally come his way, would provide him for the rest of his life with congenial and challenging work, gracious living in one of England's loveliest settings among men of the most varied intellectual distinction. He threw it all away. He gave up classics where he had succeeded for music where he failed. There was no reason for it. Music had been a passion since boyhood. He could have kept it like that, on a non-professional basis, and it could have rounded and enriched his emotional life. But we have to take the hyperthymic mood state of the manic-depressive into account. He had had depressive phases while an undergraduate which had held him back for two missed years of residence. Now came the flow of the tide. Gurney, the extravert, so understanding of others, had no understanding of himself. He was more intelligent, more gifted, handsomer, more socially charming than anyone else he knew; and since boyhood all his aspirations had been crowned with success. One suspects that under that becoming modesty of manner there lived the most enormous arrogance. There was not anything he wanted to do that he could not do. He had excelled in one discipline; and his faith in himself told him that he could excel also in another and better loved one. His fanatical will took over.

But despite his utmost efforts he found that both mastery of the piano and musical composition were beyond him. How should it have been otherwise? These things are separate and distinguishable gifts of great rarity. Did he imagine that he had only to work for it and he would be given top prize in any lottery on which he set his heart? But the disappointment need not have been crushing. With his passion for scholarship he could have made an intellectual career for himself as a musical theorist. His book *The Power of Sound* appeared in 1880 when he was thirty-three. Though it won no general acclaim, it was a pioneering work and was highly praised by one authority. It was bulky and made difficult reading. It seems to have created more impression in Germany, where scholars are more tolerant of bulk and appreciate a philosophic approach. A modest man might have been well enough pleased with his achievement, and have gone on with the working out of his ideas and the improvement of their presentation.

Gurney considered but rejected the plan of a second edition. A moderate success could not be enough for him. There must be some pathway by which he could scale the heights. He retreated again, and found himself at the foot of the valley, facing the ascent of other peaks. His misconceived attempts at the professional mastery first of medicine (1877–80) and then of the law (1881–2) both ended in miserable failure and were abandoned. These should have been happy and relaxed years. He married in 1877, and his daughter was born in 1881.

Kate Gurney was a lovely and most loving wife. They married when he was thirty and she was twenty-three. No doubt he loved his wife and daughter; but with his obsessive drive to achieve the tasks he took in hand, he showed but small consideration for his family. Kate Gurney had many dark days and hours of loneliness while he pursued his obsession. Victorian husbands generally regarded their own affairs as pre-eminent, to which their wives should willingly be handmaids; and in this respect Gurney was not exceptional. But if he had been able to show his wife more love and seek her companionship, she might have been able to pilot him through the ebbs and flows of his manic-depression. If he had been able to discuss his plans with her she might have got him to see their unwisdom. But in that male-dominated world he never did.

As Dr. Hall rightly points out in many places, Edmund Gurney was the subject of manic-depression. That means that the spontaneous ups and downs of mood to which we are all subject to some degree, reached in him high plateaux or Stygian gulfs. The plateaux were more extended than the gulfs, and most of his life Gurney spent in a higher mood state then merely normal good spirits. To this we can attribute his fantastic capacity for long and enduring hard work, his willingness to undertake nearly impossible work loads, his misjudgments of the work called for by particular tasks, allowing too much energy for quantity and too little for quality, and his lack of critical self-appraisal. Those immense works would have been so much more effective if they had been critically pruned. With a colder appraisal of the situation and of his own capacities, he could have cut his losses at many times to those of a trial run. 1882 saw the foundation by Barrett, Myers and Sidgwick of the Society for Psychical Research.

Gurney was persuaded to undertake three duties, each of them arduous: the general secretarial work and management of the Society's affairs, the editing and management of the Society's *Journal*, and the editing and management of the *Proceedings*. This meant, with his own extensive writings, devoting his whole time at high pressure, to doing enough work for three men. His personal and family life must have been practically obliterated.

The depressions, from which he also suffered, as a rule exercised a much less pernicious influence on his life than the manic enthusiasms. At times they may have protected him from his constitutional tendency to engage in ill-judged ambitions. The danger came when objective failure stared him in the face, and, co-incidentally, his high mood ebbed. It seems clear that this was the state of affairs by the end of June 1888. If Dr. Hall's reconstruction is correct, Gurney's eyes had been opened to the fourth successive failure of his ambitions: music, medicine, the law, and now psychical research. He had been duped by his trusted secretary. The high enquiry into possibly supernatural potentialities of the human mind had proved empty and fraudulent. Nevertheless a man of his ability but cooler temperament, taking a dispassionate view, would see that all was not lost. The fraud had not disproved the possibility of telepathy. The mistakes of the past, once they had been recognised, could be guarded against and need not be repeated. A new enquiry, better controlled, might yet yield results. A battle had been lost, but not a war. He himself was intact with his powers and resources. Too true! Unfortunately Gurney could not judge the situation rationally. An irrational element within him, long dormant, had taken control, and he was being rushed down a headlong path to destruction.

The coroner's verdict was accidental death. The reader who carefully considers the facts collected by Dr. Hall and his analysis will surely agree that the coroner and his jury were wrong. An interested witness had suppressed part of the truth and had suggested what was false. In fact, the dead man had deliberately taken his own life, by the inhalation of chloroform, in a staged situation, which he himself had carefully planned. At once we are struck by a glaring contradiction—the careful planning of the suicide and the suddenness of the crisis, the well-considered course of behaviour and the ill-considered impulsive motivation that triggered it off. The contradiction may be resolved if we take contingency planning into account. We know from Myers that Gurney had "often wished to end all things". With suicide a recurring thought he may well have thought out how, in the last necessity, it might be carried out with least distress to his family and least damage to his character and reputation. The general lines of the plan—the chloroform, the hotel bedroom in another town, the elimination of personal items of identification, and the unposted letter to his doctor friend—all this might have been worked out years before it was, in the end, put into effect.

In depressive illness the greatest risk of suicide arises at the beginning of a depression or when recovery is on its way; at the heart of the illness the lassitude, anergia and paralysis of the will are too great for action. When he dined with Cyril Flower on the Thursday Gurney was in a good, perhaps even a euphoric, mood. The mood was shattered by the arrival of a letter. When he left his home for Brighton in the morning, his wife was aware that something was amiss. If there had been confidence between these two, the tragedy might still have been avoided. He told her nothing, and she never saw him alive again. However disastrous the news he was given in Brighton that Friday, there must have been other ways of dealing with the situation than the one he chose. Suicide, in the circumstances, lacked any rational justification. If it had been rational, one would have to stigmatise it as cruel, irresponsible and wicked. He had a loving wife and a little girl of six, and to both of them he owed a husband's and a father's love and protection. It is not possible that a man of Gurney's kindness and sympathetic disposition could have inflicted such a cruelty upon them, if he had been able to think of them at all. In the comfortless hotel bedroom late that Friday night and in the small hours of Saturday, the shadows must have closed in and in on him, until he could think only of his despair and the need to end it. At the time, in the strictest sense, he was insane.

Edmund Gurney won his scholarship at Trinity College, Cambridge, in 1866. He soon made a number of friends, among them Frederic Myers. Myers was a poet, and though his lustre is somewhat tarnished now, at that time he must have been a brilliant figure. He was four years older than Gurney, who no doubt felt overshadowed by him. Gurney remained under his influence for the whole of his life, and that influence was an evil one.

Frederic William Henry Myers, 1843–1901, poet and essayist, rates seven columns in the *Dictionary of National Biography*, contributed by his friend Arthur Sidgwick. Arthur Sidgwick, Frederic Myers and John Addington Symonds were all linked by homosexual relationships, according to the biography of the last-named by Phyllis Grosskurth (1964). According to the *Dictionary*, Frederic Myers was a scholastic star of the first magnitude. He had learned the whole of Virgil by heart before he had passed school age. In Cheltenham College he won prizes for both Latin and English poems. He went to Trinity with a scholarship in 1860, and subsequently gained further College scholarships, two University scholarships, and six University prizes for English and Latin poems and Latin essays. He was elected a Fellow of Trinity in 1865 and was a classics lecturer for four years. He then gave up his lectureship to join the permanent staff of school inspectors.

There were some shabby episodes that Sidgwick does not mention. In 1863 Myers submitted an entry for the Camden Gold Medal for Latin verse, and won it. It was quite quickly discovered that he had stolen no fewer than 31 of his hundred or so lines from Oxford prize-winning poems of the years 1806, 1807, 1812, 1818, 1827, 1830, published in *Musae Oxonienses*. There was a storm in the pages of the *Cambridge Chronicle and University Journal*, and Myers was compelled to resign the prize. Very strangely, no further action was taken by the University or College authorities; and two years later he was elected to his Fellowship in 1865, as if he was not a disgraced man. In *Fragments of Inner Life*, an autobiographical sketch privately printed in 1893, this is how he describes the episode:

"Jugend ist Trunkenheit ohne Wein",—and few have known either the delight or the folly of that intoxication more fully than I. On the sensual side of my nature I shall not dwell. Of the presumption of those early years I take as an example one braggart act. Having won a Latin prize poem, I was fond of alluding to myself as a kind of Virgil among my young companions. Writing again a similar poem, I saw in my bookshelves a collection of Oxford prize poems, which I had picked up somewhere in order to gloat over their inferiority to my own. I laid this out upon my table, and forced into my own new poem such Oxford lines as I deemed worthy of preservation. When my friends came in, I would point to this book and say, "Aurum colligo e stercore Ennii"—"I am collecting gold from Ennius's dung heap",—a remark which Virgil used to make with more valid pretensions. My acquaintance laughed; but when my poem was adjudged the best, a disappointed competitor ferreted out these insertions; and the Master of Trinity, although he roundly asserted I had done nothing illegitimate, advised me to resign the prize. Many another act of swaggering folly mars for me the recollection of years which might have brought pure advance in congenial toil."

What is astonishing about the whole story, what is indeed psychopathological, is not so much the original crime as the later exculpation. The first was merely a betrayal of scholarship, an attempted cheating of his rivals, an attempt to gain honour by dishonourable means. The later defence is more clearly symptomatic of a personality that has grown corrupt. In 1893 he was a man of fifty; his standards of conduct were now an integral part of him. With wisdom, he might have confessed to the disgrace, and purged his soul. With mere worldly-wisdom he would have contrived to forget the whole story and hope everyone else would too. But that was not the way he saw it. The trouble with Myers was that he substituted soggy poetry for the hard prose of life. So he drags up to the light of day something which was mean-spirited, sneaking and clandestine, to glorify it as a "braggart act" of "staggering folly". He probably felt that those words were the right one. To such a character words do not have their ordinary meaning.

Little is known of the sexual aspects of Myers's life. In *Fragments of Inner Life* he writes "on the sensual side of my nature I shall not dwell". In 1866 John Addington Symonds wrote in a letter that he, Arthur Sidgwick and F. W. H. Myers were "three of not the least intellectually constituted members of our Universities assailed by the same disease". Yet a great part of his life was spent in running after young women. His great love affair was with Anne Marshall, the wife of his cousin Walter Marshall, two years younger than he, who was 31 when she took her life in 1876. He courted her unremittingly from 1873 to 1876, and says that he "looked upon her face 426 times". As he was living in Cambridge, and she on the banks of Ullswater this would seem to imply that he visited her practically every vacation for days, and for many week-ends before returning to Cambridge for a working week. She had a family of five children by her husband. The last of her pregnancies was in 1872, before Myers came on the scene. One assumes that after that marital relations ceased. Early in 1876 she separated from her husband and moved into a smaller house in the same grounds with her children. Matters had reached a critical state at that time. The long courtship reached "self-surrender" for Anne, and for Walter Marshall a nervous breakdown.

Myers was a poet, and he poured out his heart in poetry which may have been very moving to Anne, but which now seems distastefully lush. Arthur Sidgwick in his memoir praises "the compressed force, the ardent feeling, the vivid and finished expression, and above all, the combined imaginativeness and sincerity of his best work." One does not feel much of the "sincerity" in *Fragments of Inner Life*. His poems are embellished with verbal gems: "emprize", "fjeld and fjord", "wildered", "list" (for "hear"), "pent", "empery", "deep-weltering", "dove-green, dove-purple", "faery", "evanish", and others. These mannered phrases impress one with their artificiality, their insincerity. One has the feeling that, as far as Myers was concerned, it was all sex in the head. The voice of normal sexuality is far different: "Roses and lilies her cheeks disclose; But her ripe lips are more sweet than those. Press her, caress her, with blisses her kisses dissolve us in pleasure and soft repose." One doubts whether there was anything much in the way of pressing and caressing between Frederic and Anne, and when physical expression of love is transmuted into poetry, one cannot look for an aftermath of soft repose.

The hypothesis one has to consider is this. Myers was, basically, a homosexual. Whatever he says, he was incapable of a passion based on normal sexuality. In his relations with women he substituted for it the shallow courtship of a philanderer, which

I*a*. Royal Albion Hotel, Brighton, *c*. 1880

I*b*. Gurney's home at 26 Montpelier Square, London

IIa. F. W. H. Myers's home, Leckhampton House, Cambridge

IIb. "Geordie", preparing for a séance, by J. S. Smith, c. 1894

From the collection of Dr. E. J. Dingwall

would commit him to nothing but give him opportunities for high-flown poetic self-display. The indications are that Anne fell a victim to this make-believe. Myers has a poem, "Honour", in which the lovers say "between us two there is God". That is the way he would have had it. But he was on a slippery slope; and one day in April 1876 the pair of them slipped too far. Myers tells us almost explicitly that sexual intercourse took place on only that one single but fatal occasion:

> If but one hour Love showed thro' perilous storm
>   His heaven-ascending form;
> If to our hearts his hallowing whisper came
>   With earthquake mixt and flame;
> If o'er our brief bliss hung with boding breath
>   Madness, Despair and Death;
> And yet these could not mar it, had not power
>   To spoil one sacred hour . . .

One cannot have much doubt what Myers was referring to with "one sacred hour". But he lied. Madness, despair and death did indeed mar it. That was, most likely, some time in April 1876.

> I spake; she listened; woman-wise
>   Her self-surrendering answer came . . .

This tells us that the courtship was conducted in words, and not in kisses; and the affected archaism of "spake" tells us what kind of words. By May, Anne had discovered she was pregnant. When she died in August the pregnancy was four-and-a-half months gone.

> For ere the fourth moon, August-bright,
>   Had rounded o'er the glimmering plain,
> Beyond the clear-obscure of night,
>   Her lovely life was born again.
> Calm in the calm . . .

When he wrote those lines was Myers thinking of the new life in her womb? One can't be sure. Myers fudges everything he writes. The story is one of horror and tragedy, to which somehow he successfully closes his eyes, passing it off with hysterical *belle indifférence*. He slips away from the emotional impact, leaving Anne to bear it alone.

Archie Jarman (*Dr. Gauld and Mr. Myers*, 1964) describes the situation thus:

"So how did Myers react when the dismaying news of pregnancy was established in May? Perhaps he would have been ready to marry her, together with the five children, had Walter Marshall been ready to give her a divorce. But Marshall, approached and furiously refusing, perhaps caused the 'intense trouble in May', and suffered his own mental breakdown. What alternative was there? A compromise perhaps acceptable to Anne was that she and Myers should set up home elsewhere . . . Presumably Myers was not agreeable to this makeshift . . . It may be thought that she pleaded this course with Myers, but he, realising that this scandalous situation would jeopardise his whole future, decided that he could not endure the dilemma further. By August the matter had crystallised. There had probably been discussions, perhaps quarrels, emotional scenes, arguments and the shedding of tears . . . But in spite of her acute distress, which was grieviously obvious to her father and others . . . Myers left her. In any circumstances this is difficult to understand. When her need was most desperate (whatever its origin) Myers forsook her for the Norwegian fiords."

Anne went into a state of stony depression. About a fortnight later, on the night of 29 August 1876, after stabbing herself in the throat with scissors, she flung herself into Lake Ullswater. Next day her mutilated body, clad in a nightdress, was taken from twelve feet of water. Of this bloody and frenzied suicide Myers wrote:

> Her lovely life was born again:
>   Calm in the calm her spirit fled,
> With faery softness stole afar,
>   By Love unknown beguiled and led
> Past dream and darkness, sea and star.

It is difficult to see what meaning, if any, is carried by these opaque lines; but one has the strong impression that, in writing this nauseous rubbish, Myers found consolation.

Myers is supposed to have been extremely upset by Anne's death, and to have turned to the hope of life after death that he might yet win her forgiveness. To the present writer it does not seem that Myers ever had, for any of his acts, any simple honest motivation. He relished the idea of being a great lover, and could play-act the part, but ran away when called on to prove his truth. He deserted Anne when she was in extreme torment of mind, when she was in desperate need of his love, so often sworn. He moved out with a callous heartlessness that not even a good friend could have shown. One feels reasonably confident that he was profoundly relieved to be quit of the whole business. As for the "mourning years" about which he wrote, it seems likely that they were as make-believe as all the other transports of his soul. He found other young women to pursue in 1877, 1878, and 1879. He married in 1880.

Myers started to take an interest in mesmerism and spiritualism in 1871, and became one of the founders of the Society for Psychical Research in 1882. The Society was immediately successful, and by 1886 had seven hundred members and associates. He devoted the main part of his energies to it for the rest of his life. He had a decisive influence on Edmund Gurney. He induced him to take part in séances with disreputable mediums, much against the grain. Myers records that Gurney "sat in the *cénacles* of those happy believers, an alien, formidable figure, courteous indeed to all, but uncomprehended and incomprehensible by many". It was Myers who induced him to undertake the whole administrative and editorial responsibilities of the S.P.R., who persuaded him into preparing the huge collection of ghost stories, *Phantasms of the Living*, but would not stand by him when that work was attacked. It was Myers who involved Gurney in the phony telepathic experiments at Brighton. Himself an uncritical enthusiast, he implicated Gurney in sins against the truth, which proved a crushing burden when Gurney realised what he had given his name to. Arthur Sidgwick concludes his memoir on Myers with the words: "All who knew him agree that he was a man of rare and high intellectual gifts, original, acute, and thoughtful; subtle in insight, abundant in ideas, vivid and eloquent in expression; a personality at once forcible, ardent and intense". He was also a cold-hearted egoist, who loved no one but himself. He was a liar and a coward, and he ran out on his friends when they were in trouble.

In Dr. Hall's scrupulously researched history the reader will find portrayed in detail the drama of the relationship between these two men and the contradictions within the characters of each of them that make that relationship so complex and obscure. Dr. Hall gives us also a vivid picture of a wealth of other personalities, and how they impinged on one another. He throws a strong light on the hopes and fears of the last quarter of the nineteenth century, the fears of death and the hopes of life eternal. Many mysteries remain unresolved, above all the mystery of why Gurney allowed himself to fall such a victim to his unscrupulous friend. Arthur Sidgwick gives us a notion of the superficial brilliance of the deceptive but more dominant one of the pair. But there are many witnesses to be heard, and there is more than one complex story to be unfolded. No judgments we make on the personalities of our fellow men can be written down as an absolute truth; everything is always provisional, till further facts emerge. But we are not absolved from doing the best we can with what we have.

CHAPTER ONE

DEATH BY THE SEA

DURING the early evening of Friday, 22 June, 1888, a gentleman named Edmund Gurney, whose home was in London, arrived at the Royal Albion Hotel at Brighton, the Sussex coastal resort. He had not booked a room in advance, and was not known at the hotel.[1] He dined alone in the coffee-room, and afterwards asked a waiter for a glass of water as he went upstairs to bed about ten o'clock. At two o'clock on Saturday afternoon, as Gurney had failed to respond to repeated knocking, first by a maid and then by the hotel manageress, his bedroom door, locked on the inside, was broken open.

Gurney was found dead in bed. A sponge-bag was over his face, his mouth and nostrils being covered by it. A small bottle, containing a very small quantity of colourless fluid, was found by the bed. Gurney was forty-one, and was survived by his wife and a young daughter.

The following obituary of Gurney appeared in *The Athenæum*:[2]

"We regret to announce the death by misadventure[3] of Mr. Edmund Gurney, author of 'The Power of Sound' and other works. The deceased, who was born about 1847, was the son of the Rev. Hampden Gurney, sometime Rector of Marylebone, and was educated at Trinity College, Cambridge, of which college he became a Fellow. His large work, above mentioned, on the philosophy of music, may be said to have attained a standard position, and it has been more discussed

---

[1] Gurney had been a frequent visitor to Brighton, but usually stayed in lodgings, probably at the house of a Mrs. Margaret Alice Smith.

[2] 30 June, 1888, p. 827.

[3] The verdict at the inquest was not universally accepted. The Countess of Oxford and Asquith, for example, in her book published nine years before the death of Gurney's widow, said without qualification that he committed suicide. *The Autobiography of Margot Asquith* (London, 1920), p. 142. F. W. H. Myers, in an unpublished note written in 1891 and now found among his papers, wrote that Gurney "often wished to end all things" and was only sustained by his work for the Society for Psychical Research.

in Germany than in England. Its singularly acute exposure of many current fallacies in musical theory and criticism was combined with much original and constructive thought and deep musical feeling. Mr. Gurney was also the principal author of 'Phantasms of the Living',[1] and was widely known as the energetic hon. secretary of the Society for Psychical Research, of which society, indeed, he may be said to have been the mainspring. Mr. Gurney's latest publication, two volumes of essays, collected under the title of 'Tertium Quid',[2] was recently noticed in these columns. The deceased suffered from obstinate sleeplessness and occasional neuralgia, prompting recourse to opiates, though he was in full social and literary activity. He succumbed to an overdose of chloroform, incautiously taken when alone at an hotel at Brighton. The body was identified by a letter, found in his coat, inviting a friend to join him in the business on which he had visited Brighton. He was a man who attracted very strong attachments, and he will be deeply mourned."

Gurney was a remarkable man by any standards. Over six feet in height, he was thin and loosely built; upright of bearing and swift of step. His features are described by those who knew him well as seeming to be moulded for haughty fastidiousness, yet whose expression was either one of kindly humour or sympathetic tenderness or, on occasions, one of absorbed melancholy. Jane Ellen Harrison, lecturer in classical archaeology at Newnham College, Cambridge, said that "Edmund Gurney was, I think, the most lovable and beautiful human being I have ever met".[3] George Eliot, who met Gurney at Cambridge in 1873, used him as the prototype of the high-souled Daniel Deronda in her novel of that name. She confessed that she was so impressed by Gurney's good looks that for some days she could think of nothing else, afterwards discovering "that his mind was as beautiful as his face".[4] His friend Walter Leaf, the classical scholar and banker,

---

[1] Edmund Gurney, Frederic W. H. Myers and Frank Podmore. Two volumes, London, 1886.
[2] Two volumes, London, 1887.
[3] J. E. Harrison, *Reminiscences of a Student's Life* (London, 1925), p. 55.
[4] *See* Ethel Sidgwick, *Mrs. Henry Sidgwick. A Memoir by her Niece* (London, 1938), p. 108, and Oscar Browning, *Life of George Eliot* (London, 1890), p. 116. In view of the contents of Appendix I, in which the insinuation by G. A. Smith that there was

thought him one of the handsomest men he had ever met, and a master of subtle dialectic and of wit and humour in conversation.[1] Lady Battersea said that Gurney "was one of the elect, both in mind and character" and recalled in her memoirs that both she and her husband (formerly Cyril Flower, M.P.), "had been much struck by the very able and original mind of Mr. Gurney, and by the beauty and charm of his young wife".[2] William James said that the Brighton tragedy was "one of Death's stupidest strokes" and a cruel blow to him, for the sympathetic Gurney understood him more than anyone else, and in all James's thoughts of returning to England (he was writing to Henry James from Chocorua in July 1888) Gurney had been the Englishman from whom he had expected "the most nourishing communion".[3]

Frederic W. H. Myers, the poet, wrote of Gurney's "commanding stature and noble presence which gave the impression of so much force and fire", of his "characteristic qualities; on the one hand the depth, the force, the refinement of emotion; on the other hand the trenchant dialectic, the logic which pierces like a dividing sword through the tangle of sentimental fallacies with which all aesthetic criticism is still painfully encumbered", and of his "profound sympathy for human pain, the imaginative grasp of sorrows not his own, which made the very basis and groundwork of his spiritual being."[4] Dr. Eric J. Dingwall, in an appreciation of Gurney written sixty-seven years after his death, said:

"Through his death, not only did the Society for Psychical Research lose one of its greatest figures, but England lost a man of genius whose breadth of vision, idealism, sympathy

a homosexual connexion between Gurney's co-author Frank Podmore and the youths at Brighton who were the subjects of Gurney's hypnotic experiments is examined, I think it fair to say now that I believe Gurney himself to have been perfectly normal. He seems to have been as attracted to women as they were to him. His friend Lord Esher recorded, for example, that in Cambridge in 1873 a Miss Huth "took Gurney's heart by storm" during a casual meeting. *Journals and Letters of Reginald, Viscount Esher* (4 vols., London, 1934–8), i, p. 8.
[1] Charlotte M. Leaf, *Walter Leaf: 1852–1927. Some Chapters of Autobiography. With a Memoir.* (London, 1932), p. 95.
[2] Lady Constance Battersea, *Reminiscences* (London, 1922), p. 206.
[3] *The Letters of William James. Edited by his son, Henry James.* (2 vols., London, 1920), i, pp. 279–80.
[4] F. W. H. Myers, "The Work of Edmund Gurney in Experimental Psychology", *Proceedings*, Society for Psychical Research, 1888–9, v, pp. 360–1.

and tolerance were qualities which were an inspiration to all those who were privileged to meet him.''[1]

It was, appropriately enough, whilst staying with Dr. Dingwall in May 1962 at his house in Sussex, the county in which Gurney met his tragic end, that I first became interested in the mystery of Gurney's lonely death in Brighton seventy-four years previously. I read a copy of *The Athenæum* obituary in Dr. Dingwall's library, together with a somewhat similar account in the spiritualist newspaper *Light*, also of 30 June, 1888. In the latter periodical it was said of the purpose of the last journey of Gurney's life that ''he went on Friday of last week to Brighton on some business connected with Psychical Research''. It is noteworthy that this explanation was offered nowhere else, so far as I am aware, and was certainly not mentioned in the quite detailed accounts of the inquest. In fact, the reason for Gurney's solitary visit to Brighton on 22 June, 1888, has remained undiscovered. It is, however, certain that it was quite different from that which had regularly brought him to Brighton during the previous five years, although I do not think that this has ever been appreciated before.

Gurney's work in Brighton for the Society for Psychical Research during the years 1883 to 1888, which is fully described by him in his many and detailed reports in the *Proceedings* of the S.P.R., was concerned with experiments in hypnotism and in alleged thought-transference under hypnosis. The experiments took place in Brighton because the subjects were a group of working-class youths who lived in that town, introduced to the Society by a young man of eighteen (in 1882), George Albert Smith, formerly of Brighton, who became Gurney's paid private secretary from 1883 until his employer's death in 1888.

Smith had been a seaside entertainer in Brighton, giving paid stage performances in hypnotism and alleged mind-reading, before he was employed by Gurney and the S.P.R., and he was additionally used by Gurney, who could not himself hypnotize, as the sole operator in all the Brighton experiments. Smith always accompanied Gurney to Brighton on these occasions. As the only hypnotist available to the Society, and the introducer of the

---

[1] E. J. Dingwall, "The Work of Edmund Gurney", *Tomorrow*, New York, 1955, iii, No. 2, p. 52.

youthful subjects, he was of course the central and indispensable figure in the whole of this work. Smith was on his honeymoon in the Isle of Wight[1] at the time of Gurney's death, and it is therefore quite clear that the latter's solitary visit to Brighton on 22 June, 1888, was not to continue with the experimental work which had been the sole purpose of Gurney's numerous earlier stays in that town. It is, indeed, rather curious that Gurney's last journey to Brighton should have been made during the very period when his secretary-cum-hypnotist was preoccupied elsewhere.

On the evening of Thursday, 21 June, 1888, Gurney dined at the House of Commons with his friend Cyril Flower, M.P. (afterwards Lord Battersea). When he returned to his home at 26 Montpelier Square he found a letter awaiting him asking him to go to Brighton, which he did on the following day. Mrs. Gurney never knew who wrote the letter, which Gurney took with him on his last journey.[2] It is reasonable to suppose that the suggestion that he went to Brighton for some reason connected with psychical research was an assumption made by Mrs. Gurney, in the absence of any specific explanation offered by her husband regarding either the purpose of his sudden departure from London, or the identity of his correspondent. Mrs. Gurney would be unlikely to appreciate that the temporary absence of G. A. Smith in the Isle of Wight meant that no experiments with the Brighton boys were possible, and that the reason for the sudden summons to Brighton was clearly not that which had consistently taken Gurney and Smith there on earlier visits.

Quite apart from Gurney's failure to tell his wife who the letter was from, it seems quite obvious that the summons and the visit were not for any everyday purpose, on the very reasonable assumption that Gurney went to Brighton to meet his mysterious correspondent. This unknown person did not give evidence at the inquest (and presumably was not discovered by the police) despite the extreme likelihood that he or she was the last person to see

[1] George Albert Smith, private secretary, married Laura Eugenia Bayley at the Ebenezer Chapel in Ramsgate, Kent, on 13 June, 1888. As the enquiry progresses, the reader will hear a great deal more about G. A. Smith, who was one of the most interesting and bizarre characters in the history of psychical research.
[2] This information, hitherto undisclosed, has been given to me by Gurney's daughter, Miss Helen May Gurney. The matter of the dinner engagement was confirmed in evidence given at the inquest.

and talk to Gurney alive, apart from the staff of the Royal Albion Hotel.

In *The Athenæum* obituary I noticed a significant sentence which will not have escaped the attention of the reader:

> "The body was identified by a letter, found in his coat, inviting a friend to join him in the business on which he had visited Brighton."

The obituary in *Light* slightly amplified this information. The identification of Gurney's body was made by means of "an unposted letter, found in the coat pocket". The unnamed addressee of the letter was referred to as "a colleague", and the undisclosed objective which had brought Gurney to Brighton was described as an "inquiry". Curiously enough, no mention whatsoever of this letter was made in any other accounts of Gurney's death that I have seen, and in these I include the four long reports of the inquest which appeared in the local newspapers.[1] It is remarkable that the text of the letter was not disclosed at the inquest. As the reader will discover, even eighteen years later certain persons, with what I hope to show was an interest in concealing the truth about Gurney's death, found it expedient to suppress information that might have led to speculations about the mysterious letter, and to the same chain of reasoning which enabled me to discover to whom it was written, and why it was written.

The fact that the letter was addressed to a friend but was found "unposted" in Gurney's pocket points to the fact that it was sealed and ready for posting. Why then was it not posted? We can, I fancy, dismiss with certainty the idea that Gurney simply forgot to do so. It was (ostensibly at least) a letter asking his colleague to join him in a matter of first importance connected with the matter which had brought Gurney to Brighton, and the desirability of his friend receiving it as soon as possible would be at the forefront of Gurney's mind as he wrote it. He would normally have posted it as soon as it was written.

---

[1] *Sussex Daily News* and *Brighton Examiner* of 26 June, 1888; *Brighton Gazette* of 28 June, 1888, and *Brighton & Hove Herald* of 30 June, 1888. To this curious circumstance must be added the fact that enquiries at the office of the Coroner at Brighton, the Clerk of the Peace at Lewes (Brighton was not a County Borough in 1888) and the Public Records Office in London show that the official account of Gurney's inquest seems no longer to exist.

The only other everyday explanation that readily suggests itself is that Gurney wrote it too late to catch the last post, and intended to send it on the following day. This is, I think, also untenable, for a very good reason. The letter was addressed (to anticipate a little) to a London doctor and was written on a *Friday*. Obviously, if Gurney's colleague was to obey the unexpected summons to come to Brighton at short notice, he could only reasonably be expected to leave his professional appointments to do so *over the week-end*, and to do this he would have to receive the letter on Saturday morning at latest. Gurney would be fully aware of this when he wrote the letter, and it is hard to believe that he would have written it on Friday at all if it could not be posted in time to reach London by Saturday morning. He would have sent a telegram instead.

It can, incidentally, reasonably be inferred that Gurney had the opportunity to write and post the letter in Brighton earlier on Friday had he so wished. There is good evidence to show that it was a short note and would, on the face of it, have taken only a few minutes to write. It was obviously written in Brighton, for only in that town could the "business on which he had visited Brighton" have progressed to a point where Gurney could make the unforeseen decision that he urgently needed the assistance of a colleague living in London, from where he himself had journeyed alone earlier on Friday. But this local activity must have been completed before early evening, when Gurney presented himself unheralded at the Royal Albion Hotel,[1] to dine alone in the coffee-room and then go to bed. Clearly his business for the day was over by then. It is reasonable to suppose, therefore, that Gurney had already made the discovery or elicited the information upon which his decision to send for his friend was based before he settled down in the hotel, and that he could therefore have written the note earlier. One is left with the curiously contradictory impressions (a) that if the letter was to serve its ostensible purpose it could,

---

[1] There is no reason to suppose that Gurney necessarily intended to stay at the Royal Albion Hotel when he set off from London. The fact, indeed, that he was not known at the hotel and had not booked a room in advance, rather suggests the opposite. He may well have intended to follow his normal habit of going to his customary lodgings until he decided at some point during the progress of the inquiry (whatever it was) that it was necessary for his purpose to spend the night in accommodation where he was not known.

and should, have been written and posted before Gurney arrived at the hotel in the evening, and yet (b) that the letter was in fact written in the evening, probably in the hotel, where it was found, and possibly even after Gurney had retired to his room, and therefore (c) that when Gurney wrote it, he knew full well that he was doing so too late for it to be of use for its supposed purpose.

It has been suggested to me that whilst the two everyday explanations already discussed are admittedly untenable, there is a third possibility. Gurney might have written the letter in good time to catch the London post, and then decided that there would be no point in sending it. This seems at first sight a possibility, although it would involve our acceptance of the considerable coincidence that Gurney's death occurred, in circumstances that were certainly not commonplace, within a matter of hours of his decision urgently to summon a friend to Brighton, and shortly afterwards reaching the opposite conclusion. But, like the other explanations, it will not do, for a reason which overshadows the whole incident and to my mind removes all possibility of the solution of the riddle being a simple one, and which I have left until the last.

As has been said, Gurney had been a frequent visitor to Brighton, but had invariably stayed in lodgings where he was known. Why, on this last journey to Brighton, did he choose a large hotel where, in the event, his body could only be identified by the opening of an unposted letter found in his pocket? If he had signed the hotel register,[1] why had he not given his address? This was curious in itself, but what can only be regarded as incapable of normal explanation is that no other method of identification was available, and that Gurney, an eminent Victorian and man of letters "in full social and literary activity", and the "energetic hon. secretary of the Society for Psychical Research", had about his person no visiting cards, diary, wallet, letters addressed to himself,[2] bills or other papers which would have immediately revealed who he was. The reader can confirm for himself the extreme oddness of this circumstance by examining the contents of his own pockets as he reads these lines.

---

[1] The registers of the Royal Albion Hotel are not now available prior to 1920.
[2] It will have occurred to the reader that one letter, at least, which should have been in Gurney's pocket was the one urging him to come to Brighton.

If the reader thinks that this means that before his death Gurney deliberately removed from his pockets and hid or destroyed in Brighton all the items by which he could normally be identified, his first inevitable inference will be that this was part of a purposeful preparation for suicide, and that the verdict of accidental death was wrong. Since Gurney clearly could not hope that his body would remain unidentified indefinitely, the reader's second inference may well be that the purpose of this action, and the writing and placing of the deliberately unposted letter in his pocket, was probably a device contrived by a mind of considerable subtlety to ensure the sequence of events which actually resulted. When the tragedy was discovered, the person with whom the authorities urgently communicated with the request that he come to Brighton to identify the body *was the addressee of the letter and not Mrs. Gurney*. Whether there were other reasons is a matter for the later consideration of the reader, but he may well think it significant, for example, when he reads the account of the inquest, that it was the evidence of the addressee of the letter which secured the somewhat surprising verdict of accidental death.

To whom was the letter addressed? Gurney had gone to Brighton "on some business connected with Psychical Research". He had spent much time there previously on similar activities. The last six years of his life had been devoted to immense labour for the Society for Psychical Research, and at the time of his death he was not only Hon. Secretary but also Editor both of the Society's *Journal* and *Proceedings*. It seemed therefore almost certain that the "colleague" and "friend" to whom the letter was addressed would be a leading member of the Society. Gurney's special friends on the Council of the S.P.R. were Professor Henry Sidgwick, Professor William F. Barrett and Frederic W. H. Myers (who with Gurney were the Society's principal founders in 1882), Frank Podmore (Gurney's collaborator, with F. W. H. Myers, in *Phantasms of the Living*) and Frederic Myers's brother Dr. Arthur T. Myers. It seemed, therefore, extremely likely that it would be one of these five persons whose name and address was on the envelope of Gurney's letter, and who would therefore be summoned by the police to Brighton on Saturday, 23 June, to identify the body. Probability would incline slightly to either Podmore or Dr. A. T. Myers, both of whom lived in London and were within easy reach of Brighton, whereas Barrett's home was in Dublin and Sidgwick and F. W. H. Myers lived in Cambridge.

Both the *Journal* and the *Proceedings* of the S.P.R. were entirely (and possibly significantly) silent about the circumstances of Gurney's death. I recalled, however, that Henry Sidgwick, professor of moral philosophy in the University of Cambridge and the first President of the S.P.R., had kept a "Journal" or diary of events in his life, from July 1884, which was reproduced in the biography written by his brother and widow and published after Sidgwick's death.[1] As in the case of nearly all *published* material over which past and present members of the S.P.R. have been able to exercise any control Sidgwick's "Journal" as printed in the *Memoir* contains no information of significance related to the matter before us. The original MS. of the "Journal" has, however, recently been presented to the Library of Trinity College, Cambridge, and I was able to examine it there.

To my very considerable surprise, on comparing the original "Journal" with the printed version published by Sidgwick's widow (herself a leading and active member of the S.P.R.) and brother, I found that two suppressions had been deliberately made, and that both were directly concerned with the mystery of Edmund Gurney's death. The first, to which I shall return later, would, if it had been published, have revealed to the reader of the *Memoir* that Sidgwick himself "had painful doubts" about the correctness of the verdict of accidental death at the inquest. The second was the entire omission of Sidgwick's entry for 31 July, 1888. It is of great interest, for he recorded in retrospect the sequence of events by which Gurney's death became known to his friends in London and Cambridge:

"Edmund Gurney died in a hotel in Brighton on Friday night, 22nd June. Arthur Myers was telegraphed for on Saturday morning: on Saturday evening and Sunday the calamity was communicated by him to one or two relatives and friends. Nora [Mrs. Sidgwick] and I and Fred Myers learnt it (from Arthur M.) on Sunday. The inquest took

[1] Arthur and Eleanor Mildred Sidgwick, *Henry Sidgwick, A Memoir* (London, 1906).

place on the Monday: but the news was not generally known in London till the Tuesday."

It is, of course, now obvious that the friend and colleague whose name and address were on the unposted letter was Dr. Arthur T. Myers,[1] a member of the S.P.R. Council. It was to him that the telegram was sent by the Brighton police when the body was found on Saturday. He had a busy week-end, for after receiving the telegram on Saturday afternoon (Sidgwick was clearly mistaken about Saturday *morning*, as the body was not discovered until 2.00 p.m.) he went to Brighton to identify the body, presumably returning to London on Saturday evening to break the news to Mrs. Gurney. On Sunday, he set out for Cambridge to see F. W. H. Myers, after which the two brothers, as we shall see later, called upon Henry Sidgwick and his wife.

Dr. Myers was a sick man; he suffered from both epilepsy and Bright's disease. As he was to go to Brighton again on Monday, as the principal witness at the inquest, it is difficult to understand why he made the physical effort of the journey to Cambridge on Sunday between his two visits to Brighton, unless it was urgently necessary for him to consult with his brother before the inquest. If it was simply a matter of informing him of Gurney's death, a telegram or even a letter written on Sunday would have sufficed. It might be thought, moreover, that since Gurney had devoted the last six years of his life to the Society without any material reward, and had indeed died whilst presumably engaged upon his duties, it would have been more seemly if the S.P.R. leaders had spent that Sunday in London with Gurney's widow, rather than conferring amongst themselves in Cambridge. We can only conclude that the conference, and the omissions from the published version of Sidgwick's "Journal" eighteen years later, were considered to be expedient and necessary.

Any suspicions which may have formed in the reader's mind that there was something very odd about Gurney's death and what appears to have been the concern of the S.P.R. leaders permanently to conceal certain aspects of it, will be confirmed or dissipated by the account of the inquest which follows. The

---

[1] As the reader will discover, Dr. Myers had been intimately involved in the hypnotic experiments with the Brighton youths.

reader's interest will no doubt be directed at any unusually active and prominent part played by Dr. A. T. Myers,[1] and especially at the immediate readiness or otherwise of the jury to agree upon a verdict of accidental death.

[1] There is a striking similarity between the lives and deaths of Arthur Myers and Edmund Gurney. Both obtained firsts in classics at Trinity College, Cambridge, and both later turned to medicine, studying for the M.B. examination at Cambridge and at St. George's Hospital, London. Both were members of the Council of the Society for Psychical Research. It was said in the obituary of Dr. Myers, who only survived Gurney by five years, that "the main direction and management of the experimental or other work that has been done in the department of hypnotism in connection with our Society has—since Edmund Gurney's death—been in his hands". (*Journal*, S.P.R., February 1894, p. 197.) Both men died from an overdose of narcotics. Both, before their deaths, had been involved in hypnotic experiments with G. A. Smith and the Brighton youths.

CHAPTER TWO

A BRIGHTON INQUEST

Mr. A. FREEMAN GELL, a solicitor and the Deputy Coroner for Brighton, presided over the inquest held at the Town Hall during the afternoon of Monday, 25 June, 1888. As Dr. Myers did not identify Gurney's body until Saturday afternoon at earliest the inquest seems to have been arranged with considerable expedition, in view of the intervention of Sunday. Indeed, as we have learnt from the unpublished entry in Sidgwick's "Journal" already quoted, even the fact that Gurney was dead was not generally known in London until Tuesday, 26 June.

As I have said earlier, the official record of the inquest is for some reason no longer available, and we must therefore rely for our published information upon the four fairly detailed accounts published locally in the *Sussex Daily News*, *Brighton Examiner*, *Brighton Gazette* and *Brighton & Hove Herald*. The only other document known to me which provides some additional facts is an unpublished letter from Dr. A. T. Myers to his brother in Cambridge,[1] written on the same day as the inquest and presumably too late to catch the post, preceded by a telegram to say that a verdict of accidental death had been obtained. "I wish", wrote Dr. Myers, "my telegram could have given you some of the relief I felt when I wrote it."

We shall probably never know any more about how Gurney spent the last evening of his life, for the inquest provided no new facts. He dined alone in the coffee-room of the hotel, and then went to bed.

> "The following day [said the *Brighton Gazette*] he did not appear downstairs and a maid knocked on the door of his bedroom. She, however, obtained no answer. Later on she

---

[1] I am indebted to Dr. Alan Gauld for my knowledge of this letter. The fact that Dr. Myers felt it necessary to anticipate it by a telegram seems to me to be of crucial significance. I think it unfortunate that my request to be allowed to reproduce the letter in full has been refused.

THE STRANGE CASE OF EDMUND GURNEY

again knocked and, obtaining no answer, she informed the manageress. The door of the room was found to be locked and that lady ordered it to be broken open. The deceased was found to be lying on his left side, dead. He had a small sponge bag over the lower portion of his face and near the bed was a bottle containing a clear fluid, supposed to be chloroform."

This account was amplified on one or two points by the *Brighton & Hove Herald*. Gurney's room was broken open and his body found at 2.00 p.m. The sponge-bag was pressed by the dead man's right hand over his nose and mouth. Under it was some cotton wool. The bottle contained a few drops of colourless, odourless fluid, said the newspaper report, which seemed curiously at variance with the conclusion that it was chloroform. The *Brighton Examiner* confirmed that the fluid in the bottle was without smell. The testimony of Mr. Charles Burland, a surgeon, who made a post-mortem examination, did nothing to resolve the mystery. Mr. Burland said that he sealed the bottle himself, but as the contents had not been analysed he had no idea what it contained, according to the report in the *Brighton & Hove Herald*. This oddly inadequate testimony was apparently not questioned by the Coroner.

In his unpublished letter to F. W. H. Myers, Dr. Myers said that the bottle contained a very small quantity of oily liquid, which was the residue of something which had been dissolved in the chloroform. The bottle was unlabelled, and Dr. Myers's conclusion seems to have been that Gurney had used a bottle which previously contained hair-oil, when purchasing the chloroform.

Dr. Myers was the most important witness. He had arrived in Brighton at 1.08 p.m., he wrote to his brother, "and at once saw Heathcote[1] and told my version of the story to him", before the proceedings began. He told F. W. H. Myers that his evidence had been regarded as "completely decisive and satisfactory", adding that the jury had not been "inquisitive or inconvenient". He said that a memorandum which had been prepared had been useful, as had the letters obtained from Henry Sidgwick and Cyril Flower. It is for the reader to judge the extent by which Mr.

---

[1] Charles Heathcote was the Stipendiary Magistrate at Brighton in 1888.

Burland and the Deputy Coroner were influenced by what Dr. Myers had to say at the inquest, and possibly before it.

Dr. Myers's testimony was principally reported by the *Brighton & Hove Herald*:

"Dr. A. T. Myers of 9 Lower Berkeley Square, [London] said he had been an intimate friend of the deceased for nineteen years and as a friend he had sometimes advised Mr. Gurney professionally. Deceased had for many years been subject to sudden and severe fits of neuralgic pains, generally about the head and face, and had been a bad sleeper. In order to relieve this pain and sleeplesssness he had, himself, given him large doses of morphia without it producing as much effect as it would in most people.

He had also administered chloral and belladonna to him. Deceased had often discussed with him the use of chloroform in small doses for the relief of pain. Witness had often spoken of the danger of it and he had no certain knowledge that he had ever used chloroform. Deceased had gone through a medical education for three years. He had no reason to believe that the deceased intended to make away with himself. On Thursday Mr. Gurney had dined with Mr. Cyril Flower at the House of Commons who had written to the witness saying 'I have rarely seen him in better health and spirits and his conversation was brilliant'. "

According to the *Brighton Gazette* Dr. Myers said that he was definitely of the opinion that the death was caused by an accident, whilst he was reported in the *Brighton Examiner* as stating that he "was convinced that Mr. Gurney had taken accidentally a larger dose than was his custom and was suffocated". This forthright opinion seems to have had its effect upon the next witness, Mr. Charles Burland,[1] whose testimony was reported in the *Brighton & Hove Herald*:

[1] Charles Burland was a young man who had qualified in 1884 as a L.R.C.P. and L.R.C.S. In 1886 he was a ship's doctor with the P.O. & S.S. Co. In 1887 he started in practice at 11 Conduit Street in London, about half a mile from Dr. Myers's address in Lower Berkeley Street. Burland had no professional connexion with Brighton, and the name Burland does not appear in street directories of that town between 1884 and 1890, from which it must be assumed that his presence in Brighton at the time of Gurney's death was for some temporary purpose.

THE STRANGE CASE OF EDMUND GURNEY

"With Mr. Blaker and Mr. Hodgson he [Mr. Burland] had made a post mortem examination. All the organs were healthy and there was nothing to indicate the reason for sudden death. As to the cause of death he could merely conjecture, after hearing that the deceased was addicted to anaesthetics, that he had died from suffocation from inhaling too large a quantity of chloroform. No trace of that drug was met with in the post mortem but it would not be likely to leave any trace and if the bottle did contain chloroform it had evaporated."

The witness added that death had occurred "several hours previously" to the discovery of the body. The account of Mr. Burland's evidence in the *Brighton Examiner* added that the postmortem examination showed that the body was well-nourished and that all the organs were healthy. The heart was, however, distended with fluid blood, and the stomach was congested.

The reader will have observed that Dr. Myers said that "as a friend he had sometimes advised Mr. Gurney professionally", which suggests that he was not Gurney's regular physician. One would have thought that corroborating evidence from his own doctor regarding Gurney's supposed addiction to a surprising variety and quantity of drugs would have been helpful to the Deputy Coroner and the jury.[1] But no such testimony was offered.

The only other evidence came from a brother of the dead man,

---

[1] It seems probable that the drugs to which Dr. Myers said Gurney was addicted were identical with those that he was in the habit of taking himself. It is a remarkable fact that on 10 January, 1894, Dr. Myers himself died of an overdose of narcotic taken to procure sleep. His brother and Mr. G. W. Prothero both gave evidence at the inquest that "there was no reason to suppose that he designedly took an overdose", and spoke of the "deceased's good spirits and to arrangements he had made for the future". According to the medical evidence Dr. Myers had been in the habit of taking narcotics for sleeplessness, and the symptoms of his death were consistent with narcotic poisoning.

Dr. Myers had been an epileptic for eighteen or nineteen years, a condition relieved by belladonna and the other sedatives mentioned by Dr. Myers in relation to Gurney's alleged neuralgia. He also suffered from Bright's disease. His obituary in the S.P.R. *Journal* made no mention of narcotics, and simply stated that he died "after two days' illness", presumably a euphemism for the fact that after he had been found insensible on the morning of 9 January, artificial respiration was unsuccessfully applied for thirty-two hours. (*News of the World*, 14 January, 1894, and *Borough of Marylebone Mercury*, 20 January, 1894). If the reader thinks it probable that Dr. Myers took his own life he will be struck by the coincidence that at the inquest on Leopold H. Myers, the son of F. W. H. Myers, the verdict was that of suicide by a self-administered narcotic.

Alfred Gurney, who like almost everyone else concerned in the case had been a member of the Society for Psychical Research since its formation in 1882. He said that he believed that his brother took opiates to relieve neuralgia and sleeplessness. The reader may think that this testimony, given for not unworthy reasons, may well have been heavily influenced by the informative and persusasive Dr. Myers, who revealed in his letter to F. W. H. Myers that he had a talk with Alfred and Harry Gurney[1] at the Royal Albion Hotel. Dr. Myers added the later curious comment in the circumstances that it came as a great relief to him that both brothers of the dead man "thoroughly believed in the verdict of the Jury".

One wonders what the Gurneys and the jury would have thought if they had learnt that Gurney's private secretary, George Albert Smith, who had worked in daily contact with him for five years and was so employed at the date of Gurney's death, had no knowledge that his principal suffered from neuralgia at all. Their opinion might have been different, too, had they known that the dead man's intimate friend Henry Sidgwick had "painful doubts" about his alleged accidental death, and that F. W. H. Myers was to record privately three years later the fact that Gurney "often wished to end all things", a desire only kept at bay by his belief in his work for the S.P.R.

Even in the absence of this information, and certain other facts to be discussed, Mr. Freeman Gell understandably encountered difficulty with the jury, a circumstance which was reported in the *Brighton & Hove Herald*:

> "At the end of the evidence the deputy coroner asked the jury whether they would care to have the stomach and contents of the bottle analysed; he added that he did not think that any good could come of it. After a short and far from edifying discussion, in the course of which the foreman (a Mr. Nye) conducted himself very strangely, the jury decided that death was accidental and that it was due to deceased inhaling an overdose of chloroform to relieve pain."

The *Brighton Gazette* recorded that it was only after a long consultation that the jury returned a verdict of accidental death.

---

[1] Henry G. Gurney was also a member of the S.P.R.

17

Against these reports must be set Dr. Myers's private comment that the jury had not been inquisitive or inconvenient. Clearly some difficulty was encountered, for the foreman, who was named, would obviously have objected strongly to what was said in the *Brighton & Hove Herald* if it was untrue. And the *Brighton Gazette* confirmed that a long consultation was necessary. On the other hand, Dr. Myers had no need to lie to his brother in a private letter. It is reasonable to assume, perhaps, that Dr. Myers meant that against the background of what was being attempted the jury were not *unduly* inquisitive and inconvenient. However that may be, the recorded verdict was that Edmund Gurney was "Accidentally suffocated by an overdose of chloroform taken to relieve pain". A final oddity of this curious inquest was the fact that, according to the death certificate, the no doubt flustered Deputy Coroner incorrectly recorded the date of death as Sunday, 24 June.

I turn now to the other part of Henry Sidgwick's "Journal" which was suppressed by his biographers in *A Memoir*. A transcription follows of Sidgwick's entries of 25 and 29 June (which followed each other, the diary not being written every day) with the sentences in italics which were omitted in the published version. The biographers did something else. To the entry for 25 June was added the truncated entry for 29 June, the later date not appearing in the published version at all, presumably in order to give the deliberate impression that Sidgwick wrote everything on 25 June and, as the reader can see for himself, to conceal what would otherwise have been an obvious omission:

> "June 25. Alas! Alas! F. and A. Myers came yesterday to tell us the terrible news of Edmund Gurney's sudden death. It happened at Brighton on Friday night from an overdose of chloroform, supposed taken for neuralgia or insomnia: he is known to have been suffering lately from obstinate sleeplessness. Quis desiderio[1] . . . I can write no more journal this month. . . .
>
> "*June 29. One more line. I have just come back from the funeral. Arthur Myers, with whom I have had more than one*

---

[1] "*Quis desiderio sit pudor aut modus, tam cari capitis?*" Horace, *Odes*, 1, xxiv. (What shame or measure should there be in grief for one so dear?)

talk, tells me that at the inquest on Monday there was a slight suggestion that it might be suicide: but it was easily and at once overborne by the evidence on the other side. I have myself had painful doubts:—but the evidence is very strong that he was making plans vigorously for the future up to almost the very day of his death. We saw him last on Tuesday 19th; he seemed to us well and in good spirits. Fred Myers feels it terribly, but we too—Nora and I—do not know how we shall do without him."

Sidgwick's use of the expression "supposed taken for neuralgia and sleeplessness" is very suggestive. He himself seems to have had no knowledge of Gurney's alleged sufferings from neuralgia, and one wonders whether it was Dr. Myers who told him about Gurney's sleeplessness. The indication that Sidgwick found Dr. Myers's information new to him is supported by the surprising fact, supplied to me by Dr. Alan Gauld, who has access to the papers of F. W. H. Myers, that there is no indication whatsoever among the correspondence of the S.P.R. leaders that Gurney was in the habit of taking opiates, or that he suffered from neuralgia. Sidgwick's "painful doubts" speak for themselves.

The verbal evidence of George Albert Smith, Gurney's private secretary, to Dr. Eric J. Dingwall many years after these events that he never knew that his employer had ever suffered from neuralgia at all, is of great interest in view of the fact that he was in daily contact with Gurney for five years to the time of the latter's death. There is confirmation of Smith's statement in one of Gurney's own published accounts of his work. A paper "Recent Experiments in Hypnotism" had been read by Gurney to the Society for Psychical Research on 2 December, 1887, and afterwards published in the Society's *Proceedings*.[1] In it he said, "During the past autumn and winter [i.e. 1887] I have carried out a long course of hypnotic experiments at Brighton, with the invaluable assistance of Mr. G. A. Smith (designated in this paper as S.) who was throughout the hypnotizer". On p. 13 of Gurney's paper the following paragraph appeared, being the entirety of a short section of the paper sub-titled by Gurney, "Removal of Pain by Suggestion".

[1] *Proceedings*, S.P.R., 1888–9, v, pp. 3ff.

"Parsons [one of the Brighton youths who were invariably the subjects] one evening complained a good deal toward the latter part of the evening of headache and toothache. Before leaving, S. hypnotized him and assured him that they would speedily vanish, and that he would in a few minutes be free from pain. He was then woke, and the few upward passes and light touches, usually performed at the end of hypnotic experiments, were gone through. After this process Parsons volunteered the information that he not only felt quite awake, but that his pains had gone, and he cheerfully departed. Questioned on a subsequent evening, he said that he had no return of them."

The fact that nowhere in his paper, written a few months before his death and containing this paragraph, did Gurney mention his own alleged neuralgia seems to me strongly to suggest in itself that G. A. Smith's statement was true and that the testimony of Dr. Myers was correspondingly false. We know what Dr. Myers had to say at the inquest about the severity of Gurney's supposed sufferings, and the extreme lengths to which he was alleged to have gone to relieve them. Had there been any truth in this, Gurney's supposedly chronic indisposition could no more have been unknown to his colleagues in the S.P.R., with whom he was in constant contact, than it could have been outside the knowledge of his private secretary, G. A. Smith. Had Gurney suffered from neuralgia, he could not possibly have included, in a scientific paper to be printed in the *Proceedings* of the Society, a claim that an experiment in the cure of facial pain by hypnosis had been highly successful, *without saying whether he had asked Smith to try to give him similar relief, and with what result.* Without such an explanation, Gurney would be in the same position as a man with bronchitis trying to sell a patent cough mixture.

There is another thing. F. W. H. Myers was to write later in his obituary of Gurney that the dead man's work for the Society, apart from his daily duties as Hon. Secretary and Editor of both the *Journal* and the *Proceedings*, had included virtually the whole of the immense burden of producing the monumental *Phantasms of the Living* (two vols., London, 1886), "the trouble—the tedious trouble—to get census-papers filled up by over 5,000 persons taken at random", and the writing of "fifty autograph letters in a day, sometimes as many as sixty—involving some eight or nine hours of close application" over a period of three years.[1] In 1887 his two-volume work, *Tertium Quid*, was published. To all this had to be added Gurney's constant work and experiments in connexion with the hypnotic state and his voluminous and meticulous reports on this subject, which formed a major part of the contents of the five volumes of the Society's *Proceedings* from 1882 to 1888. His friend Professor G. Croom Robertson, in the *Dictionary of National Biography*,[2] wrote:

> "The other special inquiry of his later years was into hypnotism, which about that time had come at last to be recognized as a matter of serious scientific import. Nothing has so far been done in England to equal, or elsewhere to surpass, his work in this field, whether in the way of carefully devised experiment (which, however, he required the help of an operator to carry out), or of acutely reasoned interpretation."

Is it conceivable that all this could have been accomplished in the short space of six years by a man suffering so acutely from neuralgia that, according to the evidence given at the inquest, he was in consequence in the habit of taking quantities of depressive drugs such as morphia, chloral, belladonna and chloroform?[3] Obviously it is not, just as it is now obvious that the only real suggestion that Gurney did suffer from neuralgia was made for the first time after his death by Dr. Myers, the whole of whose testimony is therefore exceedingly suspect, massively contradicted as

---

[1] F. W. H. Myers, "The Work of Edmund Gurney in Experimental Psychology", *Proceedings*, S.P.R., 1888–9, v, pp. 370–2.

[2] Vol. xxiii (London, 1890), p. 358. Croom Robertson and Gurney were intimate friends, and the former's personal knowledge of Gurney may be regarded as authoritative. Both were members of "The Sunday Tramps", a companionship of writers and philosophers who took long walks together on Sunday afternoons. A group of the "Tramps", calling themselves "The Scratch Eight", formed an inner society to dine together and talk philosophy. The members were Gurney, Croom Robertson, Shadworth Hodgson, F. W. Maitland, F. Pollock, Carveth Read, James Sully and Leslie Stephen. (F. W. Maitland, *The Life and Letters of Leslie Stephen*, London, 1906, p. 363.) Gurney was a frequent contributor to the periodical, *Mind*, of which Croom Robertson was Editor.

[3] It is of great interest to record that Mrs. Gurney, according to her daughter's letter to me, totally disagreed with Dr. Myers's evidence in regard to her husband's alleged use of drugs.

it is, moreover, by the facts and other opinions which have been assembled and which point unmistakably to the conclusion that Gurney committed suicide.[1]

It seems to me that only in the latter circumstances do the odd events at the inquest, the disappearance of all Gurney's personal papers from his pockets, the unpublished views of F. W. H. Myers, Henry Sidgwick and G. A. Smith and the other remarkable features with which the whole affair bristles, become readily understandable. This conclusion is supported, too, by the urgent visit of Dr. Myers to Cambridge before the inquest and the curious phrases in his communication to his brother, by the incidents of the mysterious summons to Brighton and the unposted letter, and by the determined efforts of the S.P.R. leaders to suppress the fact that their Hon. Secretary took his own life.

Whether Gurney actually used chloroform is not proved but seems fairly certain, when it is remembered that when Gurney's body was found the sponge-bag was over his mouth and nostrils. The opiate was obviously inhaled. I think also that the bottle was uncorked when found, for Mr. Burland said in his evidence, it will be recalled, that if the bottle had contained chloroform this had evaporated. What, then, was the very small quantity of oily fluid left in the bottle which, as Dr. Myers said in his letter to his brother, "was smeared over the glass quite unlike chloroform"? I see no reason to suppose that Dr. Myers was not right in his surmise to his brother that Gurney had probably used his hair-oil bottle.

This assumption is strongly supported, in my view, by Gurney's use of his sponge-bag which, like his hair-oil bottle, would be with his other toilet requisites in his over-night case. It would seem that in his extremity Gurney used what came readily to hand, presumably emptying his hair-oil bottle before buying the chloroform in Brighton.[2] If the reader has any doubts about the whole of this inference, let him consider all the implications of the alterna-

[1] Miss Gurney has told me several times in correspondence, with permission to quote her, that her mother was convinced that Gurney died because he faced a catastrophe, the nature of which was not known to her. As Mrs. Gurney never knew either the contents or the author of the letter from Brighton, it is reasonable to suppose that her conviction was based on Gurney's demeanour when he opened the letter on the evening of 21 June, 1888, and during his remaining hours in London before he set off to Brighton on the following day.

[2] No prescription was, of course, necessary for the purchase of chloroform in 1888.

tive. If Gurney was regularly inhaling chloroform to relieve unbearable neuralgic pains and insomnia, as Dr. Myers suggested
at the inquest, and therefore took the equipment he habitually used
for this purpose with him to Brighton, is it conceivable that a
fastidious man like Gurney could find no more suitable and convenient articles than a bottle containing the remnants of hair-oil
and his sponge-bag? Can we really believe, moreover, that a man
with medical training[1] could administer to himself the quantity of
chloroform which Gurney evidently did, without realizing that he
was inviting the fatal result which actually occurred? Finally, on
the mere question of probabilities, can we reasonably accept the
coincidence that on the occasion when Gurney was alleged by Dr.
Myers to have taken an accidental overdose he did so after disposing of all papers in his pockets which would normally have
enabled him to be identified? Can we believe, moreover, that this
was done by chance behind a locked door in a strange hotel, in a
town to which he had been summoned by a letter the contents of
which he did not reveal to his wife, but which according to her
convinced impression heralded a catastrophe of some kind?

Does the evidence given at the inquest throw any additional
light upon the mystery of the unposted letter, ostensibly summoning Dr. Myers to Brighton? I think it does, inasmuch as we
now at least know with some certainty two things which the letter
did *not* contain. First, for reasons which are sufficiently obvious,
it certainly did not say directly that Gurney was about to take his
own life. Secondly, it is now evident that it contained no information regarding the nature and programme of the inquiry in
Brighton in which it was ostensibly suggested Dr. Myers should
join. Had Gurney indicated what he proposed was to be done in
Brighton during the day or two following Friday, 22 June, this
would, of course, have been good evidence that he was not con-
templating suicide. We may be quite sure that had there been
anything of the sort in the letter the persuasive Dr. Myers would
have made the most of it in support of his evidence that there was
no reason for suicide and that death was accidental. But Dr. Myers
was silent about it. Obviously what Gurney had written was of no
help in countering the suggestion of suicide. It is very difficult to

---

[1] Gurney had passed the second M.B. examination at Cambridge and had studied
and worked in St. George's Hospital in London.

understand why the actual text of the letter was not revealed at the inquest.

It will be recalled that in his evidence Dr. Myers quoted a letter he had received from Cyril Flower, M.P., with whom Gurney had dined at the House of Commons on the Thursday evening. Mr. Flower had written to Dr. Myers to say that he had rarely seen Gurney in better health and spirits. It seems quite clear from the dates that this letter was written for production at the inquest on Monday at the suggestion of Dr. Myers, for the reader will recall from Sidgwick's "Journal" that the news of the calamity was not communicated "to one or two relatives and friends" until Saturday evening. Dr. Myers, in his letter to his brother, made it plain that he had Flower's letter in his possession on Monday at Brighton.[1] Gurney may, of course, have been in good health and spirits on the day before his visit to Brighton, but on the other hand what Mr. Flower wrote may have been coloured, for what seemed to him worthy reasons, to avoid a verdict of suicide.[2] F. W. H. Myers was an intimate friend of Cyril Flower, as the latter's widow recorded in her memoirs,[3] whilst Gurney and his wife had been frequent guests of the Flowers at their country house, Aston Clinton, in Buckinghamshire. It is of great interest to discover that Lady Battersea, as Mrs. Flower later became, did not think that Gurney's condition had been good during the months before his death, as her reference to his expended strength makes clear:

"It was a serious pen, and he [Gurney] wrote seriously upon the theory of music in connection with the happiness of human life; then being infected by the enthusiasm of his friends, Mr. Myers and Mr. Sidgwick, he gave himself unreservedly to the problems of psychical research, that perplexing and elusive subject, and devoted his time, his pen, and alas! his strength, to that which seemed always evading his grasp. It was a sad ending to what had promised to be a fine career."[4]

[1] Dr. Myers's letter to F. W. H. Myers also stated that he had produced a letter from Henry Sidgwick. This was clearly obtained during Dr. Myers's visit to Cambridge on the Sunday, and was for the same purpose as that written by Mr. Cyril Flower.
[2] It may be remembered, too, that the letter summoning Gurney to Brighton was not read by him until after he had taken leave of Flower.
[3] Lady Constance Battersea, *Reminiscences* (London, 1922), p. 205.
[4] *Ibid.*, p. 206.

Gurney's close friend G. Croom Robertson, Professor of Philosophy of Mind and Logic at University College, London, also told a different story in the *Dictionary of National Biography*[1] where he wrote that Gurney "continued busy with the subject to the last, through a year or more of nervous exhaustion that went on ever increasing", whilst Gurney himself wrote to F. W. H. Myers in an unpublished letter six months before his death that the only thing to which he could cleave "in the depths—and in the heights if there are any" was the sense of union with his friends. Myers, in an unpublished note written in 1891, wrote that Gurney "often wished to end all things" and was only sustained by his belief in his work for the S.P.R.[2]

Gurney, as we know from the evidence of the post-mortem, was entirely free from any physical disease. He was of independent means and his estate was proved at the equivalent today of about £80,000. He had clearly no problems in regard to either physical, health or money. By the terms of his will, moreover, his wife, Kate Sara, was the sole executrix and beneficiary of his estate from which it is reasonable to suppose that he and his wife were on excellent terms. Mrs. Gurney was an attractive woman. George Eliot, with whom the Gurneys were on friendly terms, described her as Gurney's "graceful bride",[3] whilst Lady Battersea was much struck with her beauty and charm.[4] William James wrote of Gurney's "lovely wife".[5] Mrs. Gurney's loyalty and affection towards her husband, despite his preoccupation with his work for the S.P.R., are also recorded by Lady Battersea:

> "His wife had to encounter many dark days, also hours of unavoidable loneliness, in spite of which her devotion to her husband never flagged."[6]

Gurney's marriage was blessed by a young daughter. There is nothing to suggest that he was anything but most fortunate in his domestic circumstances.

Gurney was socially accomplished, and it is said by those who

---

[1] *Op. cit.*, p. 358.
[2] I am indebted to Dr. Alan Gauld for my knowledge of this letter and note.
[3] G. S. Haight, *The George Eliot Letters* (London, 1956), vol. vi, p. 398.
[4] *Op. cit.*, p. 206.
[5] *Op. cit.*, p. 279.
[6] *Op. cit.*, p. 206.

knew him that his brilliant powers of conversation and amiability of temperament gave his personality a singular charm which made him universally popular wherever he went. He was, moreover, a man who attracted strong friendships by reason of his love for his fellow-men; his wonderful belief, as Frank Podmore wrote to F. W. H. Myers after Gurney's death, in "the goodness and honour of others, of all whom he knew. I have never met anyone with such an absolute belief in goodness and truth as common human attributes, at least in his friends. It warmed my heart often just to hear him speak of other people."[1]

Gurney, by reason of his ample private means, had always been in the enviable position of being free to choose what work, if any, he cared to undertake. He took no salary from the S.P.R. and his devotion to psychical research, which was a labour of love, seems to have been complete during the last six years of his life. The congeniality of his work for the Society, of which he had been a founder and its most active officer from the beginning, must have been increased by his intimate friendships with its fellow leaders.

Gurney should have been the happiest of men. Why, then, did the life of this noble, handsome and brilliant man, endowed, it would seem, with every advantage Providence could bestow, end so tragically? What was the secret the S.P.R. were still determined to keep eighteen years after Gurney's death? Why did his wife have to endure "dark days"? What was the hitherto undisclosed purpose of his solitary journey to Brighton on that Friday in June three-quarters of a century ago, and what was the nature of the inquiry he had to make?

---

[1] I am indebted to Dr. Alan Gauld for my knowledge of this unpublished letter.

CHAPTER THREE

FAILURE OF A MUSICIAN

EDMUND GURNEY was born on 23 March, 1847, at Hersham, near Walton-on-Thames, Surrey. He was the third son of the Rev. John Hampden Gurney (1802–62), author and divine, who later in the year of Gurney's birth became Rector of St. Mary's, Marylebone, London, an incumbency which he held until his death. It is an odd coincidence that Gurney, in common with his friends and fellow-founders of the Society for Psychical Research, Henry Sidgwick and Frederic Myers, was the son of an Anglican clergyman and was to become a classical scholar and Fellow of Trinity College, Cambridge. Gurney was a member of a distinguished, brilliant and wealthy family. His grandfather, for example, was Sir John Gurney (1768–1845), a judge and a Baron of the Exchequer. His uncle, Russell Gurney, Q.C. (1804–78), was the Recorder of London, a Privy Councillor and Member of Parliament for Southampton.

At the age of ten Gurney had the misfortune to lose his mother, from whom he probably inherited his intense passion for music. His father's death occurred five years later and Gurney, in company with his eight brothers and sisters, came under the guardianship of his uncle, Russell Gurney. He had in the previous year been sent away to school at Blackheath, where he stayed until he was seventeen.

Gurney is described at this time as an exceedingly handsome and attractive boy, working diligently and successfully at both classics and mathematics, but demonstrating already the absorbed preoccupation with music, sadly coupled with an inability to master the art in a way that satisfied him, which was to dominate his life. Coming events cast their shadows, and it is noteworthy that even as a schoolboy Gurney was practising assiduously on the violin with, however, a lack of success.

From the beginning of 1864 Gurney read with a private tutor at Hatfield Broad Oak, in Essex, and although his enthusiasm for music continued to be his principal interest, he nevertheless gained a scholarship at Trinity College, Cambridge, in the spring of 1866 and went into residence in the October of the same year. His academic success demonstrates Gurney's remarkable diligence and intellectual acuity and, at the same time, the curious division of his personality upon which F. W. H. Myers was to remark in his obituary of Gurney:

> "Edmund Gurney's intellectual nature offered one of those cases, so to say, of double foci, of juxtaposed but scarcely reconciled impulses. . . . I mean that while his instincts were mainly aesthetic, his powers were mainly analytic. His dominant capacity lay in intellectual insight, penetrating criticism, dialectic subtlety. His dominant passion was for artistic, and especially for musical sensation. For a long time it seemed as though, by some strange irony, Nature had heaped upon him gifts which he did not care to use, only to deny him the one gift of musical inventiveness—or even of executive facility—which would have satisfied his inborn, ineradicable desire. During his boyhood, during all his college days, music was his strong preoccupation. Called upon to choose between classical and mathematical studies, he chose classics almost at hazard, and worked at them, one may say, in the intervals of his practice on the piano. In spite of this divided interest, and of a late beginning—for he came up to Cambridge ill-prepared—his singular acuteness in the analysis of language, his singular thoroughness in leaving no difficulty unsolved, secured him high honours and a Trinity Fellowship. Few men have attained that position by dint of studies which formed so mere an episode in their intellectual life. He quickly returned to music, and for years continued a struggle for executive skill which at last became obviously hopeless."[1]

At Trinity Gurney shared the Porson Prize (for the best translation in Greek verse) with Thomas E. Page, who later became Editor-in-Chief of the Loeb Classical Library. In 1871 Gurney was placed fourth in the first-class list of the Classical Tripos and his Fellowship of his college soon followed in 1872. He is described

---

[1] *Op. cit.*, p. 360.

by his friend Professor G. Croom Robertson as being successful at Cambridge in athletic sports, to which he brought a large and finely developed frame, and attracting friendships by his peculiar warmth and closeness of sympathy.[1] Those friends were, as we have seen, men like Walter Leaf and Cyril Flower, and included F. W. Maitland, Henry Jackson, Gerald Balfour, R. C. Jebb, Frederic and Arthur Myers, Arthur Lyttelton, S. H. and J. G. Butcher and Lord Esher.[2] But it is Professor Croom Robertson who shows us for the first time the edge of the shadow which was already taking its sinister shape even at this early stage:

> "Gurney's undergraduate course had been lengthened by broken residence,[3] caused by a depression of body and mind which was apt with him to follow upon moods of high enthusiasm and consuming activity."[4]

F. W. H. Myers said the same thing in rather less plain and understandable terms, when he wrote that in spite of "the impression of so much force and fire" Gurney nevertheless "suffered from a constitutional lassitude which often made all effort distasteful."[5] I shall have more to say, as we examine Gurney's life, about this pronounced manic-depressive aspect of his personality, but it is desirable to record in its place this early evidence of it.

Gurney's friend, Walter Leaf, confirmed in his autobiography that at this period of his life Gurney's thoughts and aspirations were wholly devoted to music. He had all the instincts and perceptions of a musician, and it was his ambition to adopt music as a profession, as he told the Master of Trinity, the sharp-tongued Thompson, when he was admitted to his Fellowship:

> " 'Well, I suppose it is better than dancing', replied the Master. Gurney was naturally furious at what was, under the circumstances, an unpardonable and gratuitous insult. But Thompson had neither manners nor mercy if he saw his way to a sharp epigram. In order to carry out his plan, and obtain

---

[1] *Op. cit.*, p. 356.
[2] Reginald, Viscount Esher, *Ionicus* (London, 1923), pp. 58–9.
[3] Gurney was an undergraduate for five years before obtaining his bachelor's degree in 1871.
[4] *Op. cit.*, p. 356.
[5] *Op. cit.*, p. 361.

the necessary training as a pianist, Gurney went to live at Harrow, and put himself under John Farmer,[1] working with unwearied energy at his piano, and at the same time studying the theory of music. In theory he obtained a fair proficiency; but Nature, alas! had denied him the manual dexterity needed to make even a fair performer; and after a courageous fight he at last had to abandon the struggle."[2]

It seems probable that during this period Gurney was already preparing, gradually and subconsciously at least, to gather the material for his book *The Power of Sound* which he was to publish in 1880. As Professor Croom Robertson was to remark, "The notion of writing a book which should include, with a strict investigation of the musical art, an impassioned plea for its civilizing function, seems to have taken shape gradually".[3] Be that as it may, Gurney was already studying psychology, philosophy and the physics and physiology of sound, in the intervals of his many hours each day spent over the piano and violin, all this activity being made possible by his easy financial circumstances and consequent freedom from any necessity to adopt a profession that would be financially rewarding. But this enthusiasm and immense labour was clearly interrupted at intervals by the depressive phases of his indisposition. Lord Rayleigh wrote to F. W. H. Myers in May 1875 to say that he had met Gurney and was distressed at his "wretched condition", adding that he was of the opinion that Gurney should relinquish his study of psychology.[4]

It would seem that by the time Gurney left Harrow in 1875 he knew that he would never make any notable mark in music either as a composer or executant. As Lady Battersea recorded in her memoirs, Gurney was told, presumably by John Farmer, that he would never surmount the technical difficulties that the piano offered. "This made him very unhappy for a time, and he might

---

[1] John Farmer was the famous music-master at Harrow School, who took private pupils. It seems to me indicative of Gurney's intense sympathy for others that he looked forward, even during this early period, as Croom Robertson has recorded, to his hoped-for musical prowess being put "to social account in efforts towards brightening the joyless lives of the poor". Cf. Gurney's essay "A Permanent Band for the East-End" (*Tertium Quid*, ii, pp. 96–118).

[2] *Op. cit.*, pp. 96–7. Leaf said that Gurney had no interest at all in psychical research at this period.

[3] *Op. cit.*, p. 357.

[4] I am indebted to Dr. Alan Gauld for my knowledge of this unpublished letter.

possibly, had he sought other advice, have been encouraged to continue on the path he had chosen. But he submitted, and his pen came to the rescue. It was a serious pen, and he wrote seriously upon the theory of music in connection with the happiness of human life."[1]

In December 1875 Gurney suffered a deep personal sorrow. Three of his four sisters were tragically drowned in the Nile whilst on holiday in Egypt.[2] Two had been his closest sympathizers in his musical appreciation, whilst the youngest was "the very darling of his heart", as F. W. H. Myers wrote to George Eliot in January 1876. Writing about music was, however, a palliative, as Lady Battersea said, and by 1876 Gurney was settled in London, contributing his first article "On Some Disputed Points in Music" to the *Fortnightly Review* in 1876, and from that time on, in different periodicals, he offered proof that the deepest feeling for musical effects was not inconsistent with a rigid scientific analysis of their conditions. The writing of *The Power of Sound* was definitely commenced by the middle of 1879, and appeared before the end of 1880.

Whether it was, as Professor Croom Robertson has suggested, that the book was beyond the grasp of common readers, or that musical experts resented the excess of scientific speculation, or that professional theorists found the exposition over-discursive, the merits of the book were not at once recognized. The *Spectator* conceded with restraint that it was a book "which disputants on every side will need attentively to ponder", and that psychologically, physiologically and aesthetically "it is a book which makes a distinct forward step". The *Athenæum*, however, offered the stricture that with all his depth and keenness of observation "the author adds little or nothing to what every musician of ordinary attainments must know as a result of his own experience. The problem of the effect of musical phenomena on the mind is not made lighter by the manner in which it is here approached."

[1] *Op. cit.*, p. 206.
[2] *Pall Mall Gazette*, 30 December, 1875, and *The Times*, 31 December, 1875, and 10 January, 1876. Gurney's sisters were drowned on 23 December, 1875, when their boat was overturned by a sudden squall as they passed Gobel el Jagr, the Mountain of the Bird. Their uncle, the Right Hon. Russell Gurney, with whom they were on holiday, was in a separate boat.

Others, however, thought differently. Professor Croom Robertson wrote:

> "It stands in truth without a rival in its class, not only for varied interest and philosophic breadth of view, but also for positive scientific insight into some, at least, of the aspects of music. Gurney's own feeling was stronger for melody than for anything else in music; and as melodic charm is that which most directly appeals to the common people, who were to be refined, it was in melody most of all that he sought the secret of its unique power. Of melody, no one else has written with the same penetration. Nor is his treatment less masterly when he deals with the relation of music to the other arts, and more especially poetry, which had hardly less hold upon him than music itself."[1]

Whichever of these judgments was right there is no doubt that the writing of *The Power of Sound* was, for Gurney, in a sense little more than a palliative to his deep sense of failure in 1875 that he was not able to compose, nor even to master the musical technique upon which he had so early set his heart. As he himself was to say twelve years later in "The Psychology of Music", the concluding essay in his book *Tertium Quid*:

> "I linger round a subject which has been to me, for as long as I can remember, both a central interest and—from the lack of natural facility and early training—a chronic torment. How many people, I wonder, fully realize the significance of a lifelong craving for a particular outlet of expression, in one to whom the mechanical means, lavished on numbers who set no special store by them, are denied? Perhaps the experience is common enough—part of its poignancy is that it is almost always bound to be dumb. . . . One thing, at any rate, is tolerably certain: that had the facility and the training been mine, and had I become a master of the art instead of being dragged at its chariot-wheels, I should have troubled myself but little, and others less, with speculations respecting it. And in that case I should have been incomparably the richer, and the world not much the poorer."[2]

[1] *Op. cit.*, p. 357.
[2] *Tertium Quid* (2 vols., London, 1887), ii, pp. 300–1.

Gurney himself, moreover, reached the conclusion that the book had largely been written in vain. He said in "The Psychology of Music", in which he replied to his critics, that "so strange a thing is authorship that even the failure of a book does not preclude the desire that its positions should be made as intelligible as possible". He said that his response "might, no doubt, have found a more appropriate place in a second edition of the work itself; *might*, but for one sufficient reason—the practical certainty, namely, that the work itself will never reach a second edition. . . . Its bulk got it at once stamped as 'ponderous', and it has been supposed to be an esoteric treatise, comprehensible only to experts. After seven years, an impression of this sort is not likely to get corrected."[1]

On 5 June, 1877, Gurney, at the age of thirty, married the beautiful twenty-three year old Kate Sara Sibley.[2] George Eliot, writing to Mme Eugene Bodichon on 2 August, 1877, said of Miss Sibley, "She was very poor before her marriage and had worked in an exemplary way both to help her mother and educate herself—her father having lost his property and left his family destitute".[3] However this may be, Miss Sibley's father was a witness to the marriage and was described as a solicitor, a profession not commonly associated with destitution. The newly married couple set up house in fashionable Clarges Street in Mayfair, and their social life seems to have been quite full. Gurney was, for example, meeting Ellen Terry and going to the opera with Lord Esher. He and his wife were lunching with George Eliot, visiting the Sidgwicks in Cambridge and were frequent country-house guests of Mr. and Mrs. Cyril Flower in Buckinghamshire.[4]

It seems to me to be of the highest significance that Gurney found even the bliss of the early months of his marriage, the pleasant, leisurely life of the social round and writing about music entirely inadequate for his psychological needs. Within six months of his marriage he embarked upon a course of medical instruction. This may have been stimulated in the first instance by his assiduous

[1] *Ibid.*, p. 251.
[2] In spite of secret interference by F. W. H. Myers, according to a letter from Miss Helen Gurney to me.
[3] *Op. cit.*, p. 396.
[4] *See* Reginald, Viscount Esher, *Extracts from Journals, 1872–1881* (Cambridge, 1908), G. S. Haight, *The George Eliot Letters*, vol. vi (London, 1956), and Lady Constance Battersea, *Reminiscences* (London, 1922).

study of some aspects of physiology as he prepared the material for *The Power of Sound*. But there can be no doubt that the principal motivation was that to a personality of Gurney's manic-depressive type complete absorption in immense, demanding and congenial intellectual labour of some kind was necessary if existence was to be tolerable. As F. W. H. Myers was to say of Gurney's turn from music to medicine:

> "He could not bear to live without hard work; yet toil was so irksome that he could not willingly undertake it for a merely personal end. Since, then, artistic delight had failed him, he had to appeal to a still deeper, a still more potent stimulus. That stimulus he drew from his moral nature, on which I have not yet touched;—from the profound sympathy for human pain, the imaginative grasp of sorrows not his own, which made the very basis and groundwork of his spiritual being. . . . And now, in the ruin of artistic hopes, this human sympathy, this deep desire to better the lot of suffering men, became and remained his dominant, almost his only motive."[1]

The reader may think, as Professor Croom Robertson said with more brevity than Myers, that Gurney plunged into the study of medicine for two reasons which were vital to him. First, this new interest attracted him because of his intense sympathy with all suffering, coupled with the practical anticipation that he might equip himself professionally to help to relieve it. Secondly, he rather desperately hoped that medicine would provide him with the new and absorbing interest which he so urgently needed after the collapse of his musical aspirations and with the necessary outlet, when the manic phase was upon him, for what Professor Croom Robertson described as his "moods of high enthusiasm and consuming activity". Be that as it may, before the end of 1877, the year of his marriage, he was working hard at his new profession at University College, London, from where he moved a year later to Cambridge. There, among his many friends in the University town, he followed the regular M.B. course, completing two of its three examination stages in two years, working as we might

[1] *Op. cit.*, p. 361.

expect and as F. W. H. Myers wrote, with "unusual thoroughness, unusual penetration".[1]

In the autumn of 1880 he returned to London and entered at St. George's Hospital upon the practical training necessary for the final examination at Cambridge. Tragically, by the early part of 1881, Gurney found it quite impossible to continue with clinical work and surgical dressing. His extreme sensitivity to suffering of every kind made hospital work intolerable to him. As F. W. H. Myers wrote, Gurney found that he could do no other than "leave the bandaging of the actual physical wounds of poor humanity to men who perhaps sympathized with the sufferer less, but who fastened the bandages better."[2] To his intense sorrow, he had to put his medical ambitions aside, as he had his musical aspirations.

In desperation, Gurney now turned to the law. There was a strong legal tradition in the family, for, as we have seen, his grandfather and uncle had been respectively a judge and the Recorder of London. Just as his marriage had offered no solution to his problems in 1877, so the exciting prospect of the birth of his first and only child, Helen May, on 20 November, 1881, at 26 Montpelier Square, Knightsbridge, London, to where the Gurneys had now moved, provided no adequate relief. Gurney entered as a student at Lincoln's Inn in May 1881, and read first with a special pleader and then with a conveyancer. At first he worked with his usual ardour and absorption, but he discovered in a year that legal study did not satisfy his inquisitive and over-active mind sufficiently to keep the demon of depression at bay, and he relinquished his new profession. He was now thirty-five, and his position was an acute one. He had failed to establish himself in three professions in succession, music, medicine and law, and was now without an occupation of any kind. Yet his psychological structure was such that during his manic phases intense intellectual effort was vitally necessary to his acute and penetrating mind and immense energy if life was to be bearable. To what could he turn in this extremity, knowing, as he must have been aware, that this might well be his last chance?

Fate ordained for Gurney that in 1882, his year of crisis, the Society for Psychical Research was formed. How he became

[1] *Op. cit.*, p. 362.
[2] *Op. cit.*, p. 362.

involved with the S.P.R. from its first establishment is a curious story. Chance, as I hope to show, played little part in it, and it was due to the persuasive influence of F. W. H. Myers, who had been trying unsuccessfully to interest him in spiritualism since 1874, that Gurney took the fatal step in 1882 that was to end in tragedy six years later.

CHAPTER FOUR

THE MEDIUMS AND THE S.P.R.

W HEN Edmund Gurney went up to Trinity College, Cambridge, in October 1866 to read for the Classical Tripos, Frederic W. H. Myers (1843–1901) was already a young Fellow and classical lecturer there. The two men became intimate friends for the remainder of Gurney's life, despite the four years' difference in their age. It is reasonable to suppose that the undergraduate Gurney would be much influenced by Myers by reason of the latter's position in the College and by the attributes of Myers himself, "abundant in ideas, vivid and eloquent in expression; a personality at once forcible, ardent and intense".[1] Myers was already on terms of friendship with Henry Sidgwick (1838–99), another classical lecturer and Fellow of Trinity,[2] with whom Gurney also became intimately acquainted during his years at Cambridge, and who was to become, in 1882, the first President of the Society for Psychical Research.

Myers had been intensely interested in spiritualism for many years before the S.P.R. was founded, and before he met Gurney. Lady Battersea, who with her husband had known Myers intimately, openly described him as a spiritualist in her memoirs:

"A poet when we first knew him, as the years went on he became an ardent Spiritualist, and one of the first members of the Society for Psychical Research."[3]

The views of impartial contemporaries in Cambridge do not seem

[1] This assessment of Myers was by Arthur Sidgwick in the *Dictionary of National Biography*. (Supplement, vol. iii, London, 1901), p. 218. There can be no doubt about Myers's influence over Gurney. Miss Helen Gurney has told me in her letters that Myers even insisted upon joining Gurney and his bride on their honeymoon in 1877, on the grounds that Gurney had made an earlier promise to take Myers on holiday to Switzerland with him that year (presumably at Gurney's expense), a promise which Myers insisted Gurney must implement. Miss Gurney wrote, "My mother did not resent this from my father—he was utterly unworldly and she could expect and allow for his idiosyncracies. But she felt that Fred Myers knew *quite* enough of the world to refrain from going on the honeymoon. *He went!*"

[2] Sidgwick exchanged his classical lectureship for a lectureship in moral philosophy in 1869, and became a professor in the latter subject in 1875. He married Eleanor Mildred, the sister of the Right Hon. A. J. Balfour, both of whom became prominent S.P.R. members, in 1876. [3] *Op. cit.*, p. 205.

to have differed from those of Lady Battersea. Sir Richard Jebb, later to occupy the Greek Chair at Cambridge, said in a letter to the future Lady Jebb, written on 25 November, 1873, from Trinity College, that for the first time in his life he had assisted at a séance as a result of a visit from Myers, who "is interested in spiritualism at present". Jebb added that he was inclined to think that the whole thing was "deliberate imposture", whilst he had no doubt whatever that two preposterous faked spirit messages addressed to him during the sitting were "imposture pure and simple".[1]

Lady Caroline Jebb herself described the spiritualist activities of Myers and Sidgwick in Cambridge during this period in a letter to her sister, saying that life was being varied by "a set of spiritual séances, the most arrant nonsense and imposture in my mind, but it amuses these great geniuses who think they can see some distance into a mill stone. Henry Sidgwick and Fred Myers, the latter the author of a poem called 'St. Paul', are the head of the investigation as they call it, but they both seem as easy to delude and as anxious to believe as any infant." Lady Jebb distinguished the greater credulity of Myers from that of Sidgwick when she remarked only of the former, "Fred Myers is a complete convert to the existence of spirits able to materialize themselves through the presence of a medium, and he now spends all his time in sitting in these séances, most of which are failures".[2] It has to be conceded, in regard to these strictures, that Lady Jebb disliked and distrusted Myers, whom she regarded as having "an insidious nature", and that she was herself firmly opposed to spiritualism. On the other hand, her antipathy towards Myers seems mainly to have arisen from her disapproval of his sensual hankering after young women rather than his interest in mediums.[3] Lady Jebb

[1] Lady Caroline Jebb. *Life and Letters of Sir Richard Claverhouse Jebb* (Cambridge, 1907), pp. 167–8.
[2] Mary R. Bobbitt, *With Dearest Love to All. The Life and Letters of Lady Jebb* (London, 1960), pp. 110–11.
[3] *Ibid.*, pp. 87, 141 and 153. According to Lady Jebb, writing to her sister in June 1878, the mother of Eleanor, the youngest and most attractive daughter of the Bishop of Meath, was so afraid of Myers's attentions to the girl that she declared that if there was no other way of keeping Eleanor from Myers's influence, she would leave London altogether. In a letter to her sister in August 1879 Lady Jebb said that Myers was in America, and that she was sure that he had gone there with many ideas of amusing himself with the young ladies of that country. She added, "*He* does not see that his girth is wide, his hair thin, his thirty-five years fully printed on face and figure, and that the only kind of person fitted to *attract* him, would scorn him".

was not, incidentally, alone in her distrust of Myers. Jane Ellen Harrison, lecturer in classical archaeology at Newnham College, Cambridge, recorded in her memoirs that to her Myers "always rang a little false".[1]

Sir Joseph J. Thomson, O.M., the Master of Trinity College from 1918 to 1940, described in his reminiscences how, at the persuasion of Myers, he sat at a considerable number of séances, saying that "at all but two of those I attended nothing whatever happened, and in the two where something did there were very strong reasons for suspecting fraud".[2] Sir Joseph, moreover, hinted that Myers's enthusiasm was such that he was not beyond giving the medium a helping hand if this became necessary. Describing a séance with the medium Eusapia Palladino, who was staying with Myers in Cambridge at the time, Sir Joseph said that it was part of the programme of the séance that a melon was to be transported by the spirits from a small table which was placed near to that round which the participants in the séance, including Myers and the medium, were sitting clasping hands in complete darkness. Sir Joseph said that a considerable time passed during which nothing happened:

"Then Myers, who thought it good policy to encourage mediums at the commencement of a séance, jumped up and said he had been hit in the ribs. The circuit was thus broken and it was perhaps a minute before it was re-formed. . . .

Myers admitted he was a sensualist in his privately-printed *Fragments of Inner Life*. Miss Helen Gurney has told me in her letters, moreover, that Myers hotly pursued Kate Sibley before her marriage to Gurney, adding that Myers "by a series of lies tried to prevent my father from proposing to her—and her from accepting him if he did".

[1] *Op. cit.*, p. 55. Further examples of this aspect of Myers's personality may be found on pp. 106–8 of *Four Score Years* (Cambridge, 1943), the autobiography of G. G. Coulton, the Birkbeck lecturer in ecclesiastical history at Trinity College. Coulton describes the scandal at Cambridge in 1863 in regard to Myers's literary kleptomania in using twenty-five lines which were not his own composition in the prize poem for Latin verse in that year. Richard Shilleto (1809–1876), of Trinity College, the foremost Greek scholar of his day, said that the offence with which Myers was charged was without parallel in Shilleto's thirty-five years at Cambridge, adding that this "foul blot" tainted the name of the University. (*Cambridge Chronicle and University Journal*, 29 August 1863). Coulton also records the statement of Henry Lee-Warner, who regarded Myers as "a queer fellow", and who on returning to his room in St. John's College unexpectedly on one occasion discovered Myers reading his letters.

[2] Sir J. J. Thomson, *Recollections and Reflections* (London, 1936), p. 147.

What had happened was quite obvious: while the circuit had been broken and Eusapia was free she had reached out, got the melon, sat down and put it on her lap, intending to kick it from her lap on to the table."[1]

Lady Battersea wrote that Edmund Gurney's embracing of psychical research was a result of his "being infected by the enthusiasm of his friends, Mr. Myers and Mr. Sidgwick",[2] but this was an over-simplification of what occurred. There is no doubt that Gurney was finally influenced in this regard by Myers,[3] but it would seem that the persuasions of the latter were not at first successful. In May 1874 the first definite seeds of the future Society for Psychical Research were sown, according to Mrs. E. M. Sidgwick and Arthur Sidgwick, in their biography of Henry Sidgwick:

> "The investigation of spiritualism had been going on to some extent during these months, but in May [1874] Myers seems to have proposed something more systematic and persistent—in fact, a sort of informal association for the purpose, with a common fund."[4]

Gurney was pressed to join, but courteously said that he could offer no more than his sympathy in the project. Sidgwick's biographers remarked, with more tragic significance than they would admit, upon the curious fact "that Edmund Gurney, who soon after became, and remained to the end of his life, one of the most important collaborators in the movement, hesitated at first about joining in it".

Gurney's initial reluctance was understandable. As Mrs. Sidgwick herself recalled, it was the printed accounts in 1874 by William Crookes, in a spiritualist paper of the period, of the alleged materialization of "Katie King" by the notorious medium

---

[1] *Op. cit.*, p. 149. According to the notes taken at the time, no mention was made of Myers getting up or being touched. He did, however, claim that his chair was being taken away from him.

[2] *Op. cit.*, p. 206.

[3] Between Myers and Sidgwick, also, the former seems to have been the instigator. Sidgwick's biographers record, from his correspondence with Myers, that it was Myers who proposed the "informal association" in 1874 to experiment with mediums, that Sidgwick asked for time to give the matter consideration, and finally wrote to Myers consenting to give his co-operation. (*Op. cit.*, p. 288.)

[4] *Op. cit.*, p. 288.

Florence Cook (in whom, it might be thought, nobody of sane mind could believe) that first aroused the interest of the investigators in so-called physical phenomena.

"Our attention had been called to this branch of the subject by Mr. Crookes's experiments with Miss Cook, accounts of which were published in this same year."[1]

What arguments Myers finally used to bring the hesitant Gurney into the project I have been unable to discover, but the fact that in 1874 Gurney, after his first sensible lack of enthusiasm, was persuaded by his friend to dabble in spiritualism is stated by Myers himself in his obituary of Gurney:

"His practical concern with such matters was of gradual growth. It began with a form of research—if research it could be called—strangely at variance with his previous companionships or habits of thought. He attended (and here I must confess to some persuasion on my own part) during the years 1874–8, a great number of Spiritualistic *séances*. He sat in the *cénacles* of those happy believers, an alien, formidable figure, courteous indeed to all, but uncomprehended and incomprehensible by many. What knowledge, what opinions he gained in this long ordeal he never made known to the world, nor shall I here attempt to say."[2]

It does not seem unreasonable to suppose that Gurney's polite silence about the séances Myers had persuaded him to attend in these early days arose from the fact that he was unfavourably impressed by what he had observed, and that Gurney's courtesy and respect for his friend's enthusiasm did the rest. Be that as it may, for four years, during which he married and began his study of medicine, Gurney was initiated into the seedy darkened rooms and shifty frauds of spiritualism, under the euphemism of psychical research. It would be tedious and unprofitable to discuss the

[1] E. M. Sidgwick, "Results of a Personal Investigation into the Physical Phenomena of Spiritualism", *Proceedings*, S.P.R., 1886–7, iv, p. 48. An account of Florence Cook's mediumship and William Crookes's participation in it may be found in *The Spiritualists* (London, 1962) by the present writer.

[2] *Op. cit.*, p. 364. Myers's statement that Gurney never made known his final opinion of spiritualism was quite untrue. In 1887, a year before his death, Gurney had pointed to "the inherent rottenness of the evidence on which the huge fabric of modern Spiritualism has principally rested". (*Tertium Quid*, i, p. 266n.)

surprising dalliance of the future leaders of the Society for Psychical Research with such notorious frauds as Frank Herne,[1] Charles Williams and A. Rita,[2] "Dr." Henry Slade,[3] Mary Showers[4] and Edward Bullock[5] during this period, except to say that it is remarkable that the investigators could find no more useful way of spending their time. When the careers of these impostors and the available photographs of some of the "materializations" are examined, it seems impossible to believe that persons who were not actually mentally deranged could even momentarily consider that the "phenomena" might be genuine.

Perhaps the solution to the problem lies in the credulous and obsessive wish of the future members of the S.P.R. to believe and, above all, in their entire lack of knowledge of deceptive methods. W. Stainton Moses,[6] one of the first Vice-Presidents of the Society, for example, wrote in *The Medium and Daybreak* of 24 August, 1877, stating his conviction that the leading stage illusionists of the period were actually mediums using their supernormal powers to entertain paying audiences. He wrote, "Given mediumship and shamelessness enough so to prostitute it, and

[1] For an account of the exposure of Herne in Liverpool in 1875 in what the spiritualists themselves described as "imposture of the grossest kind", *see* my *The Spiritualists*, p. 12, n. 2.

[2] For details of the exposure of Williams and Rita in flagrant trickery in Amsterdam in 1878 *see The Spiritualists*, p. 10, n. 3. The mediums were intercepted in an attempted flight from the house and searched by the angry spiritualists. The equipment for the impersonation, consisting of muslin, false beards, false wigs and other paraphernalia was discovered on the persons of both mediums.

[3] Slade was exposed by Sir Edwin Ray Lankester (1847–1929), the zoologist, in 1876 (*The Times*, 16 September, 1876) and fled to the Continent in fear of arrest and imprisonment. J. W. Truesdell gives an amusing account of Slade's later trickery and exposure on pp. 143–59 and pp. 276–307 of *The Bottom Facts concerning the Science of Spiritualism* (New York, 1883). In 1885 Slade was also caught in fraud by the Seybert Commission, appointed to investigate spiritualism by the University of Pennsylvania, whose report was published in 1887.

[4] For an account of the exposure in fraud of Mary Showers by Serjeant E. W. Cox in 1874, *see The Spiritualists*, pp. 76–8. Miss Showers later made a written confession in 1875 that the whole of her "phenomena" were accomplished by imposture and the occasional use of an accomplice, as recorded in my *Florence Cook and William Crookes. A Footnote to an Enquiry* (London, 1963).

[5] The investigators had four séances with Bullock in the summer of 1876. He is scarcely worth discussion. Mrs. Sidgwick herself said that no phenomena occurred when "the conditions were not sufficiently favourable for fraud", and that Bullock "was not really a skilful performer, and that he may have acted wisely in his own interests when he gave up the career of medium and took to that of exposer of Spiritualism, as he did six or seven months later". (*Op. cit.*, pp. 54–5.)

[6] Stainton Moses was not only an original Council member and Vice-President of the Society for Psychical Research, but was also a leading spiritualist of the period and a physical and mental medium.

conjuring can, no doubt, be made sufficiently bewildering. It is sheer nonsense to treat such performances as Maskelyne's, Lynn's [two famous professional magicians of those days, both of whom published books on conjuring] and some that have been shown at the Crystal Palace, as 'common conjuring'." When an amateur conjurer, Mr. S. J. Davey, using the simplest of trickery, reproduced as an experiment some popular mediumistic effects and invited the "sitters" to describe what they had seen, Alfred Russel Wallace, whose name was included in the first list of S.P.R. members, refused to believe that Mr. Davey had obtained his results by conjuring and accused him of being a medium.[1] Coming to later times and beliefs, it is of interest to record that in their book Bernard M. L. Ernst and Hereward Carrington gave an account of a slate trick shown by Harry Houdini, the famous magician and escapologist, to Sir Arthur Conan Doyle.[2] Doyle "came to the conclusion that Houdini really accomplished the feat by psychic aid and could not be persuaded otherwise". Can it be that Andrew Lang was right when according to Edward Clodd he remarked that "it looked as if psychical research does somehow damage and pervert the logical faculty of scientific minds"?[3] Lang himself had been a President of the S.P.R.

I have tried to deal with a sample of the more patently obvious frauds with whom Myers and his friends were involved as briefly

[1] *Journal*, S.P.R., March 1891, p. 43. Cf. Dr. Richard Hodgson, "Mr. Davey's Imitations by Conjuring of Phenomena sometimes attributed to Spirit Agency", *Proceedings*, S.P.R., 1892, viii, pp. 253–310. A. R. Wallace also publicly stated his implicit belief in the infamous medium "Dr." W. F. Monck, who in 1876 was exposed in Huddersfield by an amateur conjurer named H. B. Lodge. The medium fled to an upstairs room and escaped through a window with the aid of sheets. Amongst his luggage were found the usual impedimenta of fraudulent mediumship, including "spirit hands", masks, muslin, etc., together with a number of obscene letters from women with whom Monck had carried on intrigues under the cloak of spiritualism and the convenience of dark séances. Monck was arrested, tried and sentenced to three months' imprisonment (the maximum penalty) as a rogue and vagabond. When giving evidence on oath in the subsequent Colley v. Maskelyne libel case, in which the question of the genuineness or otherwise of Monck's mediumship was an ingredient, Wallace said that very few mediums had been caught in fraud, adding, of the Huddersfield exposure, "Monck was not caught in the act of trickery. Monck was a guest on the occasion, and a demand was made that he should be searched, and he departed through the window". (*The Times*, 27 April, 1907.)

[2] *Houdini and Conan Doyle* (London, 1933), pp. 245–9. Cf. also the chapter "The Riddle of Houdini" on pp. 1–62 of Doyle's *The Edge of the Unknown* (London, 1930), in which the great spiritualist and S.P.R. member expounded at length his conviction that Houdini was a powerful medium who had prostituted his gift to obtain fame and fortune as a professional conjurer.

[3] Edward Clodd, *Memories* (London, 1916), p. 211.

as possible. It is of obvious importance, however, to examine in rather more detail the activities of the investigators, who were to be joined by Mrs. Sidgwick in 1875, in connexion with the two young mediums whom they regarded as the most important in their enquiry and where, moreover, there is some published evidence indicating that Myers, unlike Mrs. Sidgwick, stated his belief in their genuineness. Mrs. Sidgwick, writing in retrospect of these events, said:

> "I now come to what was by far the most important series of experiments we have made, those with Miss Wood and Miss Fairlamb (now Mrs. Mellon), of Newcastle, who, I believe, first developed as mediums for materialization in the summer of 1874."[1]

Miss C. E. Wood and Miss A. Fairlamb (afterwards Mrs. J. B. Mellon) were both young girls in their 'teens whose mediumship developed under the wing of the Newcastle Spiritual Evidence Society, just as Florence Cook's first steps towards fame had been taken through the Dalston Association of Enquirers into Spiritualism. Miss Wood's materialized "spirit" was an Indian infant named "Pocha", whilst Miss Fairlamb produced at least two familiars, the childlike "Cissie" and, appropriately enough in view of his Tyneside provenance, the bearded "Geordie". The reader who is sufficiently interested to know what these alleged visitors from the hereafter looked like should turn to Plate VI of Harry Price's *Fifty Years of Psychical Research* (London, 1939), where he will find a photograph of "Geordie".[2] I have little doubt that he will consider that a remark by W. H. Salter[3] in regard to the ridiculous alleged materialization "Bien Boa", an Arab Chieftain produced by the fraudulent medium Marthe Béraud, who later recommenced her somewhat tarnished career under the pseudonym "Eva C.", is extremely applicable to "Geordie". He wrote with restraint:

> "The souls of the departed may conceivably inhabit forms

---

[1] *Op. cit.*, p. 48. It is a curious coincidence that Miss Wood and Miss Fairlamb discovered their profitable powers as materializing mediums immediately after the widely publicised séances of Florence Cook, endorsed in print by William Crookes, in the spring of 1874.

[2] For a unique photograph of "Geordie" preparing for a séance, see plate IIb.

[3] A former president of the S.P.R., and its Hon. Secretary for many years.

resembling Bien-Boa; if so we must endure the prospect with fortitude."[1]

Alfred Russel Wallace recalled in his memoirs Myers's interest in Miss Wood and Miss Fairlamb and his apparent belief in the genuineness of their phenomena:

"I think I must have met him [F. W. H. Myers] first at some *séances* in London, and he asked me to call on him at his rooms in Bolton Row, Mayfair. I think this was in 1878. I spent several hours with him, discussing various aspects of spiritualistic phenomena. He told me a great deal about the long series of experiments with the celebrated Newcastle mediums, Miss Wood and Miss Fairlamb, both under twenty, and whose powers had been discovered only two years previously, who were engaged for twelve months by Professor Sidgwick, Mr. Gurney, and himself, for a long series of *séances* in Newcastle, in London (at Mr. [A. J.] Balfour's house in Carlton Gardens) and in Cambridge at Professor Sidgwick's rooms. He showed me several MSS. books full of notes of these *séances* of which he was the reporter, and drew my attention to some which I read through. In addition, he described to me the complete tests which were applied in order to render it certain that the phenomena were not produced by the mediums themselves. . . . When talking to me about the remarkable *séances* with the two Newcastle mediums, the entire series of which he attended and recorded very carefully in the notebooks he shewed me, he laid great stress upon the extremely rigid precautions that were taken against the possibility of imposture, and conveyed to me the impression that he himself was quite convinced of the genuineness of the whole series."[2]

[1] W. H. Salter, *Zoar* (London, 1961), pp. 68–9. A photograph of Bien-Boa may be found on p. 507 of Professor Charles Richet's *Thirty Years of Psychical Research, being a Treatise on Metapsychics* (London, 1923). It seems almost impossible to believe that Richet could have been deceived by the blatant and confessed trickery of Marthe Béraud, but the fact remains that he stated in his book that the materialization was unquestionably genuine. It is extremely odd that he supported his endorsement of the medium by detailed published accounts which demonstrate to any sane person exactly how the fraud was accomplished. (Cf. also *Pall Mall Magazine*, December 1906, and *Annals of Psychical Science*, October 1906, p. 207.) Richet was elected President of the Society for Psychical Research in 1905.
[2] Alfred Russel Wallace, *My Life, A Record of Events and Opinions* (two volumes, London, 1905), ii, pp. 334–7.

Myers's fellow-investigators were evidently not so credulous. In her account of the affair Mrs. Sidgwick conceded that she was not present during the first series of materialization séances arranged by Myers, Sidgwick and Gurney in Newcastle in January, February and March 1875, nor during six sittings in London in April of the same year, apparently in Myers's rooms. However, writing of the further séances which immediately followed these, held in Mrs. Sidgwick's own house (she was then Miss Balfour and was living at 4 Carlton Gardens, S.W.) the narrator seemed very dubious in regard to what was taking place. A white figure, which Mrs. Sidgwick thought might have been a doll or mere drapery, appeared at the doorway of the medium's cabinet. During the "phenomena" the investigators were subjected to various distractions, including what appears to have been a temporary loss of sanity by Miss Wood, who suffered "the delusion that she had shot someone and was in gaol".[1] A doctor who was consulted offered the opinion that Miss Wood's trance was a pretence, as she refused to allow him to feel her pulse.

Further sittings followed in July 1875, also in Carlton Gardens, and resulted in Mrs. Sidgwick asking leave to search Miss Fairlamb. "This she sharply and decidedly declined. She was reminded that she had agreed to be searched, but she said that was before and not after the séance."[2] The impression made upon Mrs. Sidgwick was not favourable. She added, however, that "as some friends of the mediums at Newcastle offered a more or less plausible explanation of the refusal to be searched, another series of séances was held with them through a period of three weeks, in August and September 1875 at Cambridge. The results were again inconclusive, and in some respects suspicious."[3]

One might have thought that this would have been the end of the investigators' interest in Miss Wood and Miss Fairlamb, but Mrs. Sidgwick records in her account that in the following October Myers (apparently alone) had some further séances with the two girls at Newcastle which were encouraging, according to his account of them. As a result of this temporary rehabilitation of the young mediums, the investigators held a final series of materialization séances in Newcastle. Miss Wood and Miss Fair-

[1] *Op. cit.*, p. 50.
[2] *Op. cit.*, p. 52.
[3] *Op. cit.*, p. 52.

lamb had by this time quarrelled, and sat separately. Of the sittings with Miss Wood Mrs. Sidgwick said that the signs of fraud "were palpable and sufficient", and that she was "not surprised to hear a few months later that a more aggressive investigator had violated the rules of the séance, and captured Miss Wood personating the 'spirit'."[1] The collateral sittings with Miss Fairlamb produced no more satisfactory results.

What opinion Edmund Gurney formed of this time-consuming nonsense we can only imagine, particularly in view of the later careers of the two mediums concerned. In 1882, the year of the formation of the Society for Psychical Research, Miss Wood was finally exposed in gross fraud in Peterborough. "Pocha", her Indian child control, was found to be the medium on her knees, partially undressed and covered with muslin which she endeavoured unsuccessfully to conceal about her person.[2] Miss Fairlamb, by then Mrs. J. B. Mellon, was exposed in Sydney by Thomas Shekleton Henry, an architect interested in spiritualism, on 12 October, 1894. Mr. Henry caught Mrs. Mellon kneeling on the floor, to give the impression in the virtual darkness of the small figure of "Cissie", wearing a mask and a shroud of white muslin around her head and shoulders. When the gas was turned up, the false beard used for the impersonation of "Geordie", more muslin and various articles of Mrs. Mellon's clothing were discovered in the "cabinet". Mr. Henry prepared a written statement which he declared before Mr. A. Dean, J.P., whilst another sitter, Mr. C. L. Wallis, declared his own independent account of the exposure before Mr. A. Sinclair, J.P. Six other sitters prepared signed statements corroborating the accounts of the exposure by Mr. Henry and Mr. Wallis, all of which are reproduced in Mr. Henry's book.[3]

[1] *Op. cit.*, p. 53. Cf. the seizures of Florence Cook's various materializations by William Volckman and Sir George Sitwell, described on pp. 27–30 and 132–4 of *The Spiritualists*.
[2] See Frank Podmore, *Modern Spiritualism* (London, 1902), ii, p. 113, his *Studies in Psychical Research* (London, 1897), pp. 26–7, and the spiritualist newspaper *Light* of 16 September, 1882. Cf. the identical way in which Miss Wood's former partner produced the child-like form of "Cissie".
[3] *Spookland. A Record of Research and Experiment in a Much-Talked-of Realm of Mystery, with a Review and Criticism of the So-called Spiritualistic Phenomena of Spirit Manifestation* (Chicago, 1902), pp. 43–54. Photographs of "Cissie" and "Geordie", sufficient by themselves instantly to convince the most naïve person of the patent fraud of the whole affair, are reproduced as the frontispiece and on p. 35 of Mr. Henry's book.

It is of interest to read that Mrs. Mellon claimed to Mr. Henry and his friends before the exposure that she had been subjected to tests by "scientific men and learned societies throughout Great Britain; had referred myself and all inquirers here, to tests given before Professor Sidgwick, Mr. Myers, Mr. Balfour, Professor Stewart and many other well-known men in London and Oxford [sic] and particularly before the Psychical Research Society of London some years ago".[1] Equally interesting is the statement by Mr. Henry that when the exposure was made he was assaulted by some of the spiritualists present, and his necktie torn off, just as William Volckman had lost part of his beard at the hands of the infuriated believers when he caught Florence Cook in imposture twenty years earlier.[2]

It is difficult to believe that a man of Gurney's character and intellectual capacity could have been anything but highly critical of palpable frauds like Miss Wood, Miss Fairlamb and the rest of the sorry characters who were the subject of investigation during the years 1874 to 1878. His courtesy, and what Frank Podmore described, as we have seen, as his "absolute belief in goodness and truth as common human attributes, at least in his friends", probably caused his silence on the subject, of which Myers wrote. However this may be, it would seem that after this experience, Gurney showed little further interest in the physical phenomena of spiritualism after 1878.[3] Indeed, his activity in psychical research seems largely to have evaporated during the next three or four years, and in this understandable loss of interest his example seems to have been followed by Henry Sidgwick, who is recorded by his biographers as having written to J. A. Symonds on 4 September, 1881, to say that his readiness to look into the phenomena of spiritualism was only then reviving once more. His biographers added that this renewal of Sidgwick's lost interest was mainly due to some experiments by William F. Barrett which seemed to show thought transference as a reality.[4]

---

[1] Op. cit., p. 43.
[2] The Spiritualists, p. 28.
[3] Professor C. D. Broad quotes Sidgwick, Gurney's co-investigator, as writing to Roden Noel on 24 June, 1878, "I have not quite given up Spiritualism, but my investigation of it is a very dreary and disappointing chapter in my life." Proceedings, S.P.R., 1938, xlv, p. 138.
[4] Op. cit., p. 358. John Addington Symonds, the classical scholar, author and translator, was one of Sidgwick's most intimate friends, despite his scepticism in regard to

William (later Sir) Fletcher Barrett (1845–1926) was Professor of Experimental Physics at the Royal College of Science at Dublin from 1873 to 1910. He was an indefatigable believer in the miraculous. At a meeting of the British Association in Glasgow in 1876, presided over by his friend Alfred Russel Wallace, Barrett read a paper entitled "On Some Phenomena associated with Abnormal Conditions of the Mind". Barrett's paper was primarily concerned with mesmerism and alleged thought-transference in the mesmeric state and more briefly with the so-called physical phenomena of spiritualism. At the conclusion of his address, Barrett urged the appointment of a committee of scientific men for the investigation of the phenomena of mesmerism and spiritualism.

Little enthusiasm was shown and no action was taken, although Barrett's suggestion was supported by A. R. Wallace, William Crookes and some others. However, as Edmund Gurney was to write ten years later "the discussion in the Press to which the paper gave rise led to a considerable correspondence, in which Professor Barrett found his first hints of a faculty of thought-transference existing independently of the specific mesmeric *rapport*".[1] These speculations arose in connexion with the favourite Victorian parlour pastime called the "willing game" in which the performer tried to pick out an object or perform some action selected by the rest of the company during his temporary absence from the room. This amusing diversion is described in numerous books and pamphlets on conjuring and party games of the period. It was accomplished by the rest of the company helping the performer by indications that he was "getting warmer" or "getting colder", by the use of a confederate or by the expedient of a simple form of what professional "mind-readers" such as Washington Irving Bishop and Stuart Cumberland made famous as "muscle-reading", and which I shall discuss later.

Barrett found it extremely difficult to account for successful results in this party game on any natural grounds and considered that "the facts pointed in the direction either of a hitherto un-

psychical research. Writing to H. F. Brown on 16 November, 1882, for example, Symonds said that he was sending to the S.P.R. some original documents in connexion with a dream, adding, "It is all bosh. At least the interpretation they will put upon the occurrence of a dream, partitioned between you and me and Mrs. Stevenson and Henry Somerset, is sure to be nonsense." H. F. Brown, *Letters and Papers of John Addington Symonds* (London, 1923), p. 149.
[1] *Phantasms of the Living* (London, 1886), 1, p. 13.

recognized sensory organ, or of the direct action of mind on mind without the intervention of any sense impressions".[1] In a letter published in *Nature* of 7 July, 1881, he made it clear that he had been interested for a number of years in proving the existence of thought-transference, and that some examples of results allegedly obtained during the playing of the "willing game" offered the most favourable chance of doing so. He said in his book:

> "One of these cases which seemed quite inexplicable on any theory of muscle-reading, and which was personally investigated [by Barrett] during Easter 1881, was that of the children of the late Rev. A. M. Creery, a respected clergyman in Buxton. This case is historically of importance, for it led to the first clear evidence of thought-transference in the normal state of the percipient."[2]

Myers and his friends took no part in the initial experiments with the Creery girls, but it seems clear that it was Barrett's visit to Buxton at Easter 1881 that led to the formation of the Society for Psychical Research a year later. Barrett said in his book that the results obtained by him in Derbyshire opened up an entirely new field of scientific inquiry. Further investigation, in his opinion, lay outside the scope of any existing scientific organization, and it therefore seemed desirable to form a new society to carry on the inquiry started by him and publish the results obtained. After consultations with F. W. H. Myers and some others, a conference was convened by Barrett on 6 January, 1882, at the rooms of the British National Association of Spiritualists, and the Society for Psychical Research was founded on 20 February, 1882. Henry Sidgwick consented to be the first President of the Society. Barrett wrote:

> "This resulted in the foundation of the Society for Psychical Research in January 1882, [*sic*] an investigation of the evidence on behalf of thought-transference being the first work undertaken by the Society. The special committee appointed for this purpose consisted of Mr. F. W. H. Myers, Mr. E. Gurney and the present writer.

---

[1] W. F. Barrett, *Psychical Research*, New and Revised Edition (London, 1921), p. 52. Barrett was quoting from his letter to *Nature* in July 1881.
[2] *Ibid.*, pp. 53–4.

A preliminary account of the results obtained at Buxton with the Misses Creery was published as a joint article by Gurney, Myers and myself, in the *Nineteenth Century* for June 1882; this therefore marks a not unimportant date in the history of psychical research."[1]

Myers went rather further than Barrett in the importance he attached to the proof of thought-transference in regard to the formation of the Society. He wrote, in his obituary of Gurney:

"The Society for Psychical Research was founded, with the establishment of thought-transference—already rising within measurable distance of proof—as its primary aim, with hypnotism as its second study, and with many another problem ranged along its dimmer horizon."[2]

There is no difficulty in understanding the leading part which Barrett played in the formation of the Society and its stated purpose of proving thought-transference. He had attained the objective at which he had aimed six years earlier, as we have seen. Myers's enthusiasm, however, seems to have been based on other considerations. It is hardly necessary to document the suggestion that Myers's dominating interest in middle and later life was his desire to prove survival. His writings, especially his poetry, and above all his book published two years after his death, *Human Personality and Its Survival of Bodily Death* (London, 1903) all demonstrate this beyond any doubt. It seems to me that there can be no doubt that one of the ingredients in this obsessive desire was the tragic suicide of Anne Eliza Marshall, the wife of Myers's first cousin, in 1876.

The story of Myers's passionate three-year affair with Mrs. Marshall, which ended in her death, has been published by Mr. W. H. Salter[3] and Mr. A. S. Jarman.[4] Whether Myers was involved to a greater extent than he admitted is a mystery that can now probably never be solved, but there can be no doubt from his own writings that the dead Anne Marshall dominated his mind to the end of his own life. Despite his pursuing of young women in 1877, 1878 and 1879 and his marriage to Eveleen Tennant in 1880, he

---

[1] *Op. cit.*, p. 55.   [2] *Op. cit.*, p. 365.
[3] "F. W. H. Myers's Posthumous Message", *Proceedings*, S.P.R., 52, pp. 1–32.
[4] "Failure of a Quest", *Tomorrow*, Vol. 12, No. 1, pp. 17–29.

was still completely obsessed by the memory of Mrs. Marshall when he wrote his privately printed *Fragments of Inner Life*, with elaborate precautions that it should not be read, even by his family and friends, until after his death. In his sealed message given to Oliver Lodge in 1891, moreover, not to be opened until after his death, he named Hallsteads, in Cumberland, and not his marital home in Cambridge, as the place he would wish during his after-life to revisit if this was possible. Hallsteads, on Lake Ullswater, was the scene of his love affair with his cousin's wife. His poems and other writings all make it clear that above all things he desired communication with the dead woman. Whether this desire sprang solely from the deep feeling she had aroused in him, which possibly went beyond mere sensuality, or whether there was a further ingredient of remorse over her mysterious and quite horrifying death and a desire for forgiveness, we shall probably never know.

What connexion had Myers's longing for the establishment of telepathy with the proof of survival? Sir Oliver Lodge, writing in his memoirs of the formation and early aims of the S.P.R., said:

> "Its object was to investigate obscure human faculties; and telepathy was the one faculty which it had, so to speak, experimentally established. Myers, indeed, went further, and held that, if mind could act on mind without the use of the bodily organs, the possibility of human survival likewise, without those organs, became increasingly probable. If mind could act without the use of the body, it might be able to survive without the use of the body too."[1]

The motives, then, of Barrett and Myers, the two other members of the trio who were to work with Gurney on the establishment of thought-transference, we can understand. But why did the unenthusiastic Gurney of 1878, who was so little impressed after four years contact with the so-called physical phenomena of spiritualism that he lost interest, allow himself to be drawn in 1882 into the activities of the S.P.R. in connexion with alleged mental phenomena, to the extent that from the first he became the Society's most active member? He had no personal craving for a future life, according to Myers in his obituary of Gurney.[2]

[1] Sir Oliver Lodge, *Past Years* (London, 1931), pp. 275–6.
[2] *Op. cit.*, pp. 363–4. And see Myers's remarks on p. 112, *Proceedings*, S.P.R., 1900, xv.

The evidence suggests that it was due to Myers's influence, just as it was Myers who had persuaded Gurney in 1874 to experiment with the alleged physical phenomena of occultism, for there can be no doubt regarding the newly founded S.P.R.'s acute need of someone like Gurney in 1882. As Myers said in the obituary, with reference to the inception of Gurney's work for the Society:

> "But there was urgent need of someone to give the *coup de collier* to the new enterprise;—of an Honorary Secretary— as far removed as possible from fool or fanatic—who should devote his whole time and energy gratuitously to the task."[1]

From the Society's point of view, Gurney could hardly have been more suitable to undertake the lion's share of the work. It has to be remembered that Myers, for example, was an Inspector of Schools and like Henry Sidgwick, who was professor of moral philosophy at the University, lived in Cambridge. William Barrett was professor of physics at the Royal College of Science in Dublin, whilst Frank Podmore, who admittedly lived in London, was employed in the Secretary's Department of the General Post Office. Almost alone amongst his colleagues, who were necessarily preoccupied with academic or professional work, Gurney had the whole of his time available, and lived in London where the head-quarters of the Society was situated. Of almost equal importance to the new organization was the fact that Gurney required no salary for his services. Myers recorded that Gurney possessed "a competence"[2] but this was an understatement, for on his death he left a considerable fortune, as we know.

I do not think that Myers, supported by Barrett, would have any insuperable difficulty in persuading Gurney that experimenting with the Creery girls and the "willing game" in an endeavour to prove thought-transference, was more "respectable" (or less ridiculous) than investigating patently fraudulent mediums. But the compelling reason for Gurney's vulnerability to the suggestion, of which Myers would be fully aware, was Gurney's mental indisposition and the cruel milestone in his life which he had reached in 1882. At the age of 35, he was without an occupation. Yet his personality, during phases of consuming energy which

[1] *Op. cit.*, p. 365.
[2] *Op. cit.*, p. 361.

alternated with lassitude and depression, urgently needed intellectually demanding labour in which he could wholly immerse
himself if life was to be bearable. That necessity existed more
urgently in 1882 than in any preceding years.

The evidence points to Gurney's having simply turned in desperation, under the pressure of Myers's persuasion, from law to
psychical research as he had turned from medicine to law and, in
earlier years, from music to medicine. And once he became
interested in it, as Myers well knew, no further encouragement
would be needed. Once persuaded, it is clear from what we know
about him that his psychological structure was such that he would
pursue his new interest and activity with unremitting and almost
desperate diligence and skill. He became, as we have seen in
earlier chapters, the mainspring of the Society, pouring out his
immense energy upon its experimental work, writing at times as
many as fifty to sixty autograph letters in a day and being
responsible both as Editor for the Society's publications, and as
Hon. Secretary for its administration.

What reward and satisfaction Gurney obtained from his new
field of endeavour it is now our task to ascertain. His first work,
as the reader will have gathered, was in connexion with a rather
curious clergyman, the Rev. A. M. Creery, and his thought-
reading daughters, to whom we now turn.

CHAPTER FIVE

THE CREERY SISTERS

A CCORDING to *Crockford's Clerical Directory*, Andrew Macreight Creery obtained his B.A. and passed the Divinity Test at Trinity College, Dublin, in 1849. He became a deacon in 1850, and a year later was ordained as a priest by the Bishop of Down. Two curacies followed in Moira in County Down and in Ingatestone in Essex.

When the eldest of his mind-reading daughters, Mary, was born on 18 May, 1864, in Clarendon Avenue, Altrincham, Cheshire, Creery described himself as a "Unitarian Minister". He used the same description and address three years later when his child Alice was born on 4 March, 1867. On the occasion of the birth of Maud, however, on 19 June, 1868, also at Clarendon Avenue, Creery then styled himself a "Presbyterian Minister". These vicissitudes seem to have ended some time before Barrett first visited Creery at Buxton at Easter, 1881, for the S.P.R. leaders, in their preliminary report on the mind-reading abilities of the Creery girls, referred to Creery's original approach to Barrett in the following terms:

> "Our informant was Mr. Creery, a clergyman of un-blemished character, and whose integrity indeed has, it so happens, been exceptionally tested."[1]

What the S.P.R. leaders evidently regarded as complete proof of Creery's integrity seems to have been his penitent return to the Church of England, about which he wrote a booklet, *Reasons for giving up the Unitarian Ministry*, published in 1883.

Creery, despite his decision by 1881 to return to his original faith and calling, did not obtain an appointment as a Church of England curate for at least two years. On the assumption that he was about twenty-one when he graduated in 1849 he would be in his middle fifties when, in 1883, he was appointed curate of

[1] "First Report on Thought-Reading", *Proceedings*, S.P.R., 1882, i, p. 20.

Heaton Moor, Stockport. His subsequent career appears to have been wandering, dissatisfied and undistinguished. In 1884, after a year at Heaton Moor, he spent the remainder of his life in a series of curacies, first at Broughton, Manchester, from where he moved in 1889 to Harwood, Bolton, in Lancashire. In 1891 we find him at Davyhulme, Lancashire, which he left in 1893 for Carnforth in the same county. In 1896, nearing the age of seventy, he finally became curate of Wadsley, Sheffield, in Yorkshire, which he relinquished two years later.

The evidence points to the fact that when Creery had ceased to be a Unitarian or Presbyterian Minister in Altrincham and was living in Buxton in Derbyshire in 1881 developing his daughters' alleged powers of thought-reading, he was without an appointment. This would seem to be confirmed by the fact that the *List of Clergy*, 1882 (compiled in 1881), shows no entry for A. M. Creery.

In July 1882 Creery, who had been elected an Associate of the S.P.R., read a paper about the history of his daughters' powers to the newly formed Society which was afterwards published in *Proceedings*.[1] He said that his interest, like Barrett's, had been aroused in the "willing game", and that he had experimented for many months with four of his daughters and a twenty-year-old servant girl named Jane Dean. Names of towns, people and playing cards were chosen by the company in the absence of the selected "mind-reader", who divined the choice with almost unerring accuracy on her return to the room. On one occasion seventeen playing cards, according to Creery, had been named correctly in succession, a feat which would cause a sensation today if it could be approached by those modern psychical researchers who still devote themselves to "thought-transference" or, as it is now termed, "extra-sensory perception".

It would seem that before he established contact with Barrett and the Society, Creery was giving lectures upon the remarkable abilities of his daughters and Jane Dean. Whether he charged fees for his services I do not know. However that may be, he said in his paper that a lecture by him to a philosophical society in Derby was reported in a local newspaper and that he sent the cutting to Barrett, who he knew was interested in proving the existence of

---

[1] "Note on Thought-Reading", *Proceedings*, S.P.R., 1882, i, pp. 43–6.

thought-transference.[1] Barrett paid his first visit to Buxton at Easter, 1881, and a demonstration was given for his benefit. Mary, Alice and Maud Creery, aged respectively about seventeen, fourteen and thirteen, assisted by the servant girl Jane, were the performers. Barrett was much impressed, and seems to have regarded thought-transference as virtually proved.

As the Creery girls were later caught in trickery, and confessed to having used a code, it would be tedious for the reader to study the experiments in any great detail. However, an independent account is available, and it may be of interest to refer to it briefly. Professor Balfour Stewart and Professor Alfred Hopkinson, both of Owens College, Manchester, and both members of the S.P.R., visited Buxton, which was fairly near at hand, to see these wonders for themselves, presumably at the suggestion of Barrett. Balfour Stewart's account of their two visits to Derbyshire on 12 November, 1881, and 18 February, 1882, was published in *Proceedings*, and is of value in disclosing the entirely loose conditions which prevailed and which absolutely invited trickery.

Balfour Stewart said that on the occasion of their first visit the daughter chosen as the "thought-reader" was placed outside the door. The object thought of was written down on a piece of paper and handed round to all the company in the room, which included Mr. Creery and the rest of the girls. The "thought-reader" returned to the room and stood facing the others. After an interval the object or card was named, but not with the almost invariable success claimed by Mr. Creery as having been achieved during the earlier private trials. During this visit eleven first correct guesses were registered in twenty-nine appropriate tests. Professor Hopkinson, whose critical faculties had evidently not been rendered entirely dormant by his interest in psychical research, suggested that on the occasion of the proposed second visit it might be advisable if the thought-reader turned her face to the wall after she had returned to the room. The results did not differ much from those on the first occasion, seventeen correct first guesses being obtained during fifty-seven trials. Professor Balfour Stewart remarked, moreover, with understandable caution:

[1] It is instructive to compare this circumstance with the later baiting of the trap for the credulous S.P.R. leaders by George Albert Smith and Douglas Blackburn, through the tantalizing letter to the spiritualist paper *Light* describing the wonders allegedly taking place in Brighton.

"I ought to state that the object thought of was marked on paper by one of the company, and handed round silently, so that all present might be aware of it. I ought also to mention that the thought-reader was aware of the general character of the things thought of; for instance, that it was definite objects in the first place; cards in the second, and so on."[1]

Myers and Gurney seem first to have visited Buxton on 12 April, 1882, and with Barrett published an article in a magazine in June of that year describing with enthusiasm the results of tests both in the Creerys' house and in the lodgings of the S.P.R. leaders.[2] In their article the authors said, somewhat recklessly, that the miracles of thought-transference which they had observed were "unlike any which had been brought within the sphere of recognized science" and that "the possibility must not be overlooked that further advances along the lines of research here indicated may necessitate a modification of that general view of the relation of mind to matter to which modern science has long been gravitating".

In the following issue of *The Nineteenth Century* the pontifications of the S.P.R. experimenters were subjected to a somewhat devastating criticism by Dr. Horatio Donkin.[3] Dr. Donkin pointed out that the naïve belief of the S.P.R. leaders that persons of "unblemished character" were quite incapable of deception in a subject like psychical research was without any basis in fact, adding that in scientific inquiries the alleged good faith of the individuals concerned should form no part of the data on which

[1] *Proceedings*, S.P.R., 1882, i, p. 40. The "thought readers" were perhaps wise in insisting on the second precaution that they should know the classification of the object which they were supposed to divine. As the reader will learn later, when Douglas Blackburn and G. A. Smith were deceiving the S.P.R. by means of a code in their demonstrations of "thought-transference" they came to grief on this very point. The experimenters evidently decided to change from the "transmission" of groups of numbers by Blackburn to Smith to drawings, and for some reason Blackburn omitted to code to Smith the fact that a change was being made. After concentrating upon the drawing of a cat placed before him, Blackburn coded the numbers 3, 1 and 20 to indicate to Smith that the drawing was that of a "CAT", i.e. the third, first and twentieth letters of the alphabet. Because Smith thought that he was still supposed to be divining numbers, his "mental impression" of his confederate's visualization of the drawing was the number "3120". According to Sir Oliver Lodge, even the S.P.R. experimenters realized from this that they were being deceived.
[2] "Thought-Reading", *The Nineteenth Century*, June 1882, pp. 890–900.
[3] "A Note on 'Thought-Reading'", *The Nineteenth Century*, July 1882, pp. 131–3.

the conclusion is to rest. He said that much of the evidence which had propped up the spiritualistic craze was based on the alleged results obtained from mediums in private families whose virtuous reputation had been largely sustained by the suggestion that they did not take money for their trouble, no regard being paid to other motives and tendencies to deception. Dr. Donkin said that the feats of the Creery sisters differed in no way from the ordinary platform performances of child clairvoyants who amused the public in the name of "second sight", and in the more honest one of conjuring. He said that such performers, using a very simple code of signals, could produce results much more startling than those about which the S.P.R. leaders were so enthusiastic.

Dr. Donkin pointed out that the children were not blindfolded, and that in most of the experiments no mention was made as to silence being preserved and that indeed the contrary could be assumed, as the children must have been corrected when their first guesses were wrong, as they very often were. He noticed, as had Professor Balfour Stewart, that in order to reduce the work of coding the child was previously informed of the nature of the object, e.g. a playing card or a name. Donkin said that the theory of trickery was strongly supported by the mediums being children who were always ready mischievously to join in any game of deception and of the association with them of the young servant girl. The abilities of Jane, said Dr. Donkin, put out of court any question of inherited special quality peculiar to the family as an explanation of the alleged marvels which might be plausible to some minds. Donkin said that the experiments made in the presence of the family were obviously scientifically untrustworthy and that it was curious that, in the words of the authors, the presence of the father "seemed decidedly to increase the percentage of success".

The Creery story ended in disaster so far as Gurney was concerned. In 1886 *Phantasms of the Living* was published in two volumes over the names of Gurney, Myers and Podmore. Myers wrote the Introduction and Podmore assisted in the collection of cases, but Gurney was stated to be solely responsible for the writing of the remainder of this enormous book. Its significance will be discussed later, but it is sufficient to say here that it was an attempt to show that telepathy accounted for spontaneous phantasms of persons undergoing some crisis, especially death, being perceived by their friends and relatives with a frequency which chance could not explain. Gurney said that experiments had proved that telepathy was a fact in nature, whilst the collection of testimony proved that ordinary persons had the experience of perceiving the apparitions and that these two established facts supported one another. He said:

> "These phantasms then, whatever else they may be, are instances of the supersensory action of one mind on another. The second thesis therefore confirms, and is confirmed by, the first. For if telepathy exists, we should anticipate that it would exhibit some *spontaneous* manifestations, on a scale more striking than our *experimental* ones. And, on the other hand, apparitions are rendered more credible and comprehensible by an analogy which for the first time links them with the results of actual experiment."[1]

Gurney went on to endeavour to persuade his readers of the experimental proof of thought-transference by an account of the tests of the "willing game", making the following fatal statement:

> "I have dwelt at some length on our series of trials with the members of the Creery family, as it is to those trials that we owe our own conviction of the possibility of genuine thought-transference between persons in a normal state."[2]

It was grievously unfortunate for Gurney that during some later sittings in Cambridge at which Professor and Mrs. Sidgwick and Gurney himself were present, the sisters were detected in their use of both auditory and visual codes. It was confessed that signalling had taken place during the earlier experiments. W. H. Salter, writing of these events in a paper on Gurney's work, remarked how unfortunate it was that the discovery of the code was made after *Phantasms of the Living* had been published, and what a serious tactical error it had been to put so much stress on this series of experiments, all of which must be regarded as suspect. He added "The authors were perhaps influenced by Barrett, who

---

[1] *Phantasms of the Living* (London, 1886), i, p. lxvi.
[2] *Ibid.*, p. 29.

had conducted the first experiments with the sisters, and always strongly upheld the genuineness of their paranormal powers".[1]

The last contribution by Edmund Gurney to S.P.R. *Proceedings*, made shortly before his death in June 1888, was a published account of this discovery.[2] It seems to me significant that despite the fact that the earlier favourable and enthusiastic reports of the Creery trials had been signed jointly by Barrett, Myers and Gurney it was over Gurney's initials alone that the retraction appeared, involving an implied admittance that most of the case for the proof of telepathy by experiment set forth in *Phantasms of the Living* had collapsed. As the complementary part of the thesis, the enormous collection of ghost stories, had already been the subject of devastating criticism, as we shall see, the blow must have been a bitter one for Gurney.

Gurney's article was not dated, but as it was subsequent to his two papers published after 13 April, 1888, and was immediately followed on p. 271 by a report of the twenty-eighth general meeting of the Society held on 16 July, 1888, it is reasonable to suppose that it was prepared in May or early June. In his report of the Creery confession Gurney gave no date of the occurrence and merely said "It is necessary, therefore, to state that in a series of experiments with cards, recently made at Cambridge, two of the sisters, acting as 'agent' and 'percipient', were detected in the use of a code of signals; and a third has confessed to a certain amount of signalling in the earlier series to which reference has been made". (p. 269). When the sisters were in sight of each other the signals used were an upward look for Hearts, downwards for Diamonds, to the right for Spades and to the left for Clubs. Various movements of the hands indicated the value of the card. The experimenters decided that on the matter of values the tricksters used codes only for the court cards, the ace and the ten to give a sufficient degree of success to impress the experimenters, without the inconvenience and risk of too much coding.

In experiments in which a screen was placed between the sisters auditory signs such as scraping the feet on the carpet, sighing, coughing, sneezing and yawning were used. Gurney wrote (pp. 269–70):

[1] "Our Pioneers. V. Edmund Gurney." *Journal*, S.P.R., June 1959, p. 51.
[2] E. Gurney, "Note Relating to Some of the Published Experiments in Thought-Transference", *Proceedings*, S.P.R., 1888, v, pp. 269–70.

"The sisters are naturally very restless, which made the movements above described less obvious than they would otherwise have been. As soon as some clue to the code used had been obtained, Mr. Gurney and Mrs. Sidgwick, and sometimes Professor Sidgwick, set themselves to guess the card (which they took care should be unknown to them) from the signals, secretly recording their guesses. Their success afforded a complete proof of the use of the signals."

With what anguish of mind Gurney wrote these last lines for the *Proceedings* of which he had been Editor for so long we can only imagine, by comparing them with his published statement two years earlier in *Phantasms of the Living* that the authors owed their conviction of the existence of thought-transference to their experiments with these young persons. As always, it fell to Gurney to publish the correction alone, and what his collaborators' views were at the time I do not know. The later attitude of Barrett, at any rate, seems to have been one of insistent published belief in the face of any evidence of fraud. Incredible as it may seem, he still considered the Creery sisters to possess genuine powers, despite their confession of trickery.[1] This is not perhaps surprising when it is realized that in his book *Psychical Research*, published in 1911, Barrett described the work of George Albert Smith with unqualified approval, and entirely omitted to reveal to his readers that Smith's partner, Douglas Blackburn, had publicly stated in 1908 and 1911 that he and Smith had completely hoaxed the S.P.R. experimenters.

Mr. Creery, who had been elected an Associate of the S.P.R. during its first year of existence, resigned either voluntarily or under pressure, when the trickery was discovered. In a letter to the Society's *Journal* dated 18 October, 1887,[2] he denied that a code of signals had ever been used during the experiments with which he had been concerned, or that if signals had been employed he was not aware of it. He said that the fact that his daughters had unquestionably been caught using a code in Cambridge did not mean that they had used a code on other occasions. In support of his argument Mr. Creery referred to the many performances

[1] "Some Reminiscences of Fifty Years' Psychical Research", *Proceedings*, S.P.R., 1924, xxxiv, pp. 275ff.
[2] *Journal*, S.P.R., November 1887, pp. 175–6.

that his mind-reading children had given without detection in trickery, and rather oddly revealed the fact that in the early days in Buxton his daughters had given their entertainment in "numerous drawing-rooms as an evening amusement". One wonders upon what terms Mr. Creery's lectures and the drawing-room demonstrations were available. Mr. Creery ended his letter by observing somewhat acidly that if the self-styled scientific investigators of the S.P.R. had indeed been deceived by a few children using a code of signals, then their powers of observation and their abilities as experimenters were less than he could have imagined.

The sensible reader, looking back on these events of long ago, may well wonder how men like Myers, Barrett and Gurney could possibly have been taken in for a moment by such nonsense as the "phenomena" of the Creery girls. The answer is, I fancy, threefold. First, the leaders of the S.P.R. seem to have been rendered credulous to a degree almost impossible to understand by their overwhelming desire to believe in the marvels about which they wrote with such enthusiasm in the *Proceedings* of the Society. Secondly, they seem to have been entirely ignorant of the elementary principles of conjuring. Thirdly, they held the curious idea that any story, however improbable, told by a person of "unblemished character" such as a clergyman, a judge, a man of academic standing or a member of one of the professions, must necessarily be factual and could be accepted and published virtually without examination, a naïve belief which is still fostered by some parapsychologists today. The first and the third of these tendencies are jointly well exemplified by three amusing cases of the period; the remarkable affair of the Theobald family, the story of Sir Edmund Hornby's apparition, and the fantastic business of "Mr. X.Z.'s" haunted house.

CHAPTER SIX

PHANTASMS OF THE S.P.R.

THE Theobald case, as Dr. Eric J. Dingwall has said, is of importance because it demonstrates how blind, unquestioning belief in the occult powers thought to be about them could reduce the attitude of a private educated family of the England of the 1880's towards their own lives to a condition where it becomes difficult to believe that they were of sane mind. Morell Theobald was a well-known chartered accountant, a member of the first Council of the Society for Psychical Research and its first Hon. Treasurer. Over a period of some years the most extraordinary phenomena were alleged to have occurred in Mr. Theobald's house, in which the whole family ultimately became involved. Dr. Dingwall wrote:

> "In 1882 Mr. Theobald had engaged a new cook who turned out to be a powerful physical medium. Since she found it very difficult to get up in the morning and to get breakfast at 8 a.m. so that Mr. Theobald could catch his train, the spirits intervened. Fires were lit in the kitchen: the table laid: kettles put on to boil: the tea made, and occasionally the boiling water transported at a distance from one kettle to another. Hundreds of spirit-writings were found on ceilings and walls and other astonishing phenomena went on from year to year. Not only did the spirits help in the domestic work of the house: they helped to move the baggage when the family was away: and on one occasion the cook and Miss Theobald passed a bath, laden with various objects, going down the stairs by itself just as they were going up."[1]

Theobald described these wonders in a series of letters to the

[1] *Mediums of the 19th Century* (New York, 1963), i, p. xii. For a discussion of the overwhelming evidence of trickery in this case, largely by the cook, Mary, and Theobald's daughter Nellie, *see* Frank Podmore's *Modern Spiritualism* (of which the book cited above is a modern reprint with an introduction by Dr. Dingwall), ii, pp. 91–4.

spiritualist magazine *Light* in 1884, and in his book *Spirit Workers in the Home Circle* published in 1887. Other incredible events included the unpacking of a picnic hamper by the spirits, and the supernatural cooking of puddings for the Sunday evening meal whilst the family were holding séances. Whether the spirits assisted Theobald in his auditing of the accounts of the S.P.R., a duty which he carried out for ten years, I do not know. His attitude to those who expressed scepticism in regard to his stories, in which he appears to have believed implicitly, is stated on p. 291 of his remarkable book:

> "Such phenomena can never be received until faith in accredited narrators and reliance on the commonplace integrity of ordinary reputable people is admitted as one of the canons of scientific attestation."

The account by Barrett, C. C. Massey, W. Stainton Moses, Podmore, Gurney and Myers of the famous case of Sir Edmund Hornby first appeared in *Proceedings* in May 1884.[1] In order to give such an apparently outstanding proof of their theory of telepathic hallucinations maximum publicity, the S.P.R. leaders published the story two months later in the magazine *The Nineteenth Century*.[2] Their informant was Sir Edmund Hornby, formerly Chief Judge of the Supreme Consular Court of China. Judge Hornby said that it had been his habit when he was in Shanghai to allow certain journalists to come to his house in the evening to report upon his written judgments for the next day's paper. After dinner one evening Sir Edmund had written out his adjudication of the case he had been trying that day, and had given it to the butler to be called for by a particular reporter known to the Judge.

At twenty minutes past one in the morning a phantasm of the reporter, so life-like that it was thought to be the real man, appeared at the foot of the bed occupied by Sir Edmund and Lady Hornby asking for the judgment. Sir Edmund was justifiably annoyed at this unwarranted invasion of his privacy, but after some conversation, during which the wraith of the reporter said sombrely that this was the last occasion upon which he and the

---

[1] "Fourth Report of the Literary Committee. A Theory of Apparitions. Part II", *Proceedings*, S.P.R., 1884, pp. 157–86. The Hornby case was described on pp. 180–2.
[2] "Visible Apparitions", *The Nineteenth Century*, July 1884, pp. 68–95.

Judge would meet, Sir Edmund gave the intruder the judgment verbally and briefly in order to get rid of him. Lady Hornby was awakened by the conversation, and her husband told her what had happened and repeated the astounding story whilst dressing next morning.

On arriving at court that day Sir Edmund was informed that the reporter had been found dead in his own house at half-past one in the morning. At midnight he had been still alive, working in his room, for his wife had asked him when he would be ready for bed. His answer was that he had only to prepare his account of Sir Edmund Hornby's judgment for his paper and his work would be finished. The doctor, said Judge Hornby, had placed the time of death between one o'clock and half-past, i.e. coinciding exactly with the appearance of the apparition in the Hornby's bedroom, a mile and a quarter away. The Judge said that when he went home to lunch he asked Lady Hornby to repeat what he had said during the night, and that he had made brief notes of her replies and of the facts.

In Sir Edmund's story, as published by the S.P.R., he said:

> "As I said then, so I say now—I was not asleep, but wide awake. After a lapse of nine years my memory is quite clear on the subject. I have not the least doubt I saw the man— have not the least doubt that the conversation took place between us."[1]

The authors added that Lady Hornby had kindly confirmed the facts to them so far as she was cognizant of them. They were so proud of the case because of what they called the "high authority" of its provenance, and because it so amply demonstrated their theory of spontaneous telepathic hallucinations, that they could not resist the temptation to report it in *The Nineteenth Century* as well as in *Proceedings*.

Unfortunately, a copy of the July issue of *The Nineteenth Century* found its way to Shanghai, where it was read by Mr. Frederick H. Balfour, the editor of the *North China Daily News & North China Herald* and of the *Supreme Court and Consular Gazette*, who had known well both Sir Edmund Hornby and the gentleman whose apparition was supposed to have paid the Judge the noc-

[1] *Op. cit.*, p. 182.

turnal visit, a Mr. Hugh Lang of the *Shanghai Courier*. Mr. Balfour was also well acquainted with the facts of the remarkable story which Sir Edmund was apparently in the habit of telling. He wrote to the editor of *The Nineteenth Century*, Mr. James Knowles, on 13 August, 1884, pointing out that the whole tale was a tissue of errors and imagination, which bore little relation to the facts. Among other absurdities, Sir Edmund Hornby was not even married at the time, whilst Mr. Lang had died not in the small hours, but between eight and nine o'clock in the morning three months before the date given by Sir Edmund. Mr. Balfour's letter was published on p. 851 of the issue of *The Nineteenth Century* of November 1884.[1]

As in the case of the Creerys, it was Gurney alone who published the withdrawal of the case, although it was over the joint signatures of five others besides himself that the original enthusiastic account had appeared. Gurney wrote in an article "Retractations and Alterations of View":

"The first instance is that of Sir E. Hornby, who told us of a certain death as having occurred coincidentally with a vision of his own; whereas the death was afterwards asserted, by a person apparently acquainted with the facts, to have occurred at least three months previously. Sir E. Hornby at once admitted—with complete candour—that if this assertion turned out to be true, his memory must have played him the most extraordinary trick. We then did what I take blame to myself for not thinking of before the case was published—searched the files of Chinese newspapers at the British Museum; we found that the critic's assertion was correct, and that the man did die three months before Sir E. Hornby supposed. And the case, as recorded, thus completely breaks down."[2]

[1] On 29 November, 1884, Henry Sidgwick wrote in his "Journal" that psychical research was growing dark and difficult, and that his opinion of the evidence for telepathy was shaken by the breakdown of Judge Hornby's narrative. He said sadly that it was difficult to believe now that any of this elaborate story could possibly be true, despite the apparent corroboration of Lady Hornby (*A Memoir*, p. 392). J. A. Symonds, Sidgwick's close friend to whom he was in the habit of sending his "Journal", said in reply on 5 December, 1884, that he was sorry to hear "that the S.P.R. evidence is so untrustworthy". Symonds said that he had made up his mind that quite excellent persons gave unsatisfactory evidence in the case of miracles, and that he was not surprised to find such evidence breaking down under scrutiny. (H. F. Brown, *Letters and Papers of John Addington Symonds*, London, 1923, p. 172.)

[2] *Journal*, S.P.R., August 1885, p. 3.

Fearful, no doubt, that public confidence in their ghost stories would be rudely shaken by the Hornby fiasco, the S.P.R. took the drastic step of withdrawing Part VI of the second volume of *Proceedings* and issuing a reprint, with another case substituted for that of Judge Hornby. Copies of the "first edition" of Part VI containing the discredited story are now collectors' items.

Gurney took the opportunity in his article of withdrawing another case which had also turned out to be a fiasco, that of Mr. X.Z. In *Proceedings* in 1882 had appeared an extraordinary and thrilling tale of a haunted house occupied by Mr. X.Z.,[1] alleged by the S.P.R. leaders to be "a gentleman of considerable intellectual distinction", who had provided his account of his experiences to Mr. Frank Podmore.

The house, the location of which was not revealed, was alleged to have been haunted by the ghost of an old man in a dressing gown. So hideous and evil was the face of the apparition that Mr. X.Z. could never forget it, and had to take a dose of physic the morning after he saw it although, as he hastened to add, he was not at all frightened. Diligent inquiries by Mr. X.Z. were stated to have elicited the information that the grandfather of the existing owner of the house had strangled his wife, and then cut his own throat on the very spot where Mr. X.Z. had seen the figure. Most wonderful of all, it was stated, when Mr. X.Z. consulted the parish registers, he discovered that the date of 22 September, when Mr. X.Z. saw the ghost, was found to coincide exactly with the day and month of the two tragic deaths in earlier years.

Finally, on the fatal date of 22 September in the year following the experience of Mr. X.Z. a friend, staying in the haunted house and knowing nothing of the story, departed abruptly in the traditional fashion on the following morning, after being kept awake all night by the sounds of groans, blasphemous oaths and harrowing cries of despair. It was stated that the door of the bedroom he was occupying opened on to the spot where the murderer had cut his own throat, whilst it was in the bedroom that the wife had been strangled. This cheerful story was rounded off by Mr. X.Z.'s account of how some years later he visited his

[1] W. F. Barrett, A. P. P. Keep, C. C. Massey, H. Wedgwood, F. Podmore and E. R. Pease, "First Report of the Committee on Haunted Houses", *Proceedings*, S.P.R., 1882, i, pp. 106–8.

landlord in London, and to his complete surprise saw on the mantelpiece a portrait of the figure he had seen. He was told that it was that of the wretched grandfather, both a murderer and a suicide and, according to the mild comment of his grandson, "no credit to the family".

The house, according to the story told in *Proceedings*, not unlike Borley Rectory, had an accompaniment of mysterious noises and other "phenomena" as well as the hideous apparition:

> "Doors also opened and shut in the house without apparent cause; bells were rung in the middle of the night, causing all the household to turn out and search for burglars; and the inmates of the house declared that unseen footsteps had followed them down the whole length of the passage already mentioned."

The authors said that in this instance they had evidence for the occurrence, in a house where a murder had been committed, of an apparition observed on the scene of the murder on its anniversary and subsequently recognized from a portrait of the murderer, together with articulate sounds of appropriate significance heard also on the scene of the murder on a later anniversary of the tragedy by a second witness, who was entirely ignorant of the facts.

Just as in the Hornby case, in which the S.P.R. leaders had relied upon the "high authority" of the provenance of the story, so the tale of Mr. X.Z., despite his "considerable intellectual distinction", proved to be nonsense when it was examined. It was Gurney alone, who had played no part in obtaining the story from Mr. X.Z. or in writing it up for *Proceedings*, who conceded in print that it was valueless:

> "The account of his examining the parish register, and finding there the record of the two deaths—the murder and the suicide—as having occurred in 179–, is entirely wrong. We have now done what we ought to have done before—had the register searched; and we find no record of the sort at all. We have ascertained otherwise that a former owner of the house did commit suicide, but not in this house, and, moreover, not till 1809, and in May instead of September. Mr. X.Z. further told us that he went with a friend to call on the

landlord in London, on which occasion the portrait of the apparition was recognized; but he proves to have been wrong as to the friend with whom he went; and the friend who, as he now tells us, accompanied him, is dead."[1]

Whilst it could be urged that these not unamusing revelations demonstrate that this kind of error, this anxiety to publish without proper investigation the stories sent to the Society, was wholly responsible for the embarrassments for Gurney which followed the publication of *Phantasms of the Living* in 1886, I do not think that the explanation is as simple as that. In the first place, as I have shown, Gurney's attitude to the subject differed from that of some of the S.P.R. leaders and in no way resembled, for example, the absurd and extravagant credulity of men like Morell Theobald, Russel Wallace and Stainton Moses. He was in no doubt, as we have seen, as to the "inherent rottenness" of the evidence for the phenomena of spiritualism. He had no personal motive, as had Barrett and Myers, for seeking to prove at all costs the existence of thought-transference and other psychic phenomena. He was not committed, as was Barrett, to any published belief in mind-reading, and, unlike Myers, he had no personal craving for the proof of survival, to which the establishment of thought-transference was to be the essential and immediate preliminary.

In my view, Gurney's first motive in working so devotedly upon the affairs of the Society was, in essence, merely the unconscious seeking of an outlet and a relief for his immense intellectual energy during his manic phases, preceded and followed as these were by periods of acute depression of both body and mind. On the other hand, I have not the least doubt that Gurney did become intensely interested in the work itself, as Myers knew would be the case when he persuaded Gurney to take it up. Nor have I any doubt that Gurney brought to bear upon his inquiries all the mental acuity and extreme diligence with which we know he was so richly gifted.

Gurney knew, moreover, how this kind of work should be done. He was fully aware, as we have seen, that in historical investigation newspapers and other sources of information of the period

---

[1] E. Gurney, "Retractations and Alterations of View", *Journal*, S.P.R., August 1885, p. 3.

should be consulted at the British Museum, and that the dates of deaths and other alleged events could be confirmed or otherwise from public records which are available. In 1884, two years before the collection of ghost stories in *Phantasms of the Living* was published, he wrote with wisdom and common sense upon the assessment of the evidential value of stories of alleged psychic occurrences:

> "And the due estimation of these depends, in the broadest sense, on the due estimation of testimony; on what may be called historical, as opposed to experimental, methods of enquiry; on that sort of many-sided acumen by which the historical student judges the record of actors and witnesses, many of whom had no idea of 'making history'; on the general sagacity by which questions of possibility and credulity, and disputes as to a accident, coincidence, and design are decided in the matters of everyday life."[1]

The suggestion that Gurney, during the periods when his health made it possible for him to apply his considerable gifts of penetration and exactitude to the work before him, was probably more critical and competent than many of his colleagues (and unlike some of them, patently honest, as I hope to show) is I think supported by an entry in the "Journal" of Henry Sidgwick made three weeks before Gurney's death.

> "June 1 [1888]. S.P.R. meeting and Nora's [Mrs. Sidgwick's] paper on premonitions. Paper difficult to write because she does not believe in them, and yet we fear that too negative an attitude would prevent our getting the full supply of fresh stories which we want to complete our *telepathic* evidence, the simple minds of our audience not distinguishing between telepathy and premonition. I thought she succeeded tolerably well, but Gurney thought she erred on the side of too great indulgence to weak evidence."[2]

It seems obvious that Gurney was a man of complete intellectual integrity, anxious to follow the truth wherever it might lead him,

---

[1] "The Nature of Evidence in Matters Extraordinary", *Tertium Quid*, i, p. 251. The article had previously appeared in *The National Review*, December 1884, iv. pp. 472–91.
[2] *A Memoir*, p. 489.

and willingly publicly to concede in the S.P.R. *Journal* that grievous mistakes had been made. In these corrections he seems to have been ready to attach more blame to himself than the circumstances justified. It would almost seem that Gurney was willing to sacrifice himself for his friends, and that they were content to remain silent and allow him to do so. Indeed, their attitude seems generally to have been dictated by a determination to conceal all criticisms, mistakes and even evidence of fraud (especially, as will be seen, in the case of Blackburn and Smith) that might militate against public acceptance of their stories in *Proceedings*.

How then, the reader may ask, did the grave failure to obtain contemporary corroborative testimony for virtually every one of the seven hundred or so cases cited in *Phantasms of the Living*, to which Mr. A. Taylor Innes and others were to draw attention, come about, in view of the fact that the main burden of the work was ostensibly borne by Gurney, although Myers and Podmore were co-authors? It is fair to point out that such a failure in diligence and exactness was completely out of character so far as Gurney himself was concerned.

The work on *Phantasms of the Living* seems to have started about 1884. In his memoirs Sir Oliver Lodge described how he had lunch with Gurney at his house in Clarges Street, Mayfair. They had a talk in Gurney's study:

> "All the furniture in this study, including the floor, was littered over with an orderly collection of extracts, some of them done up into packets, the nucleus of a book which he was preparing, and which ultimately appeared under the title *Phantasms of the Living*, by Edmund Gurney and others. The book struck me as a meaningless collection of ghost-stories which he was classifying and arranging. . . . Attention to such gruesome tales seemed to me a futile occupation for a cultivated man, but Gurney evidently regarded seriously the narratives he had been collecting, and thought he had a clue whereby some of the stray legends or assorted experiments could be rationalized and brought under a coherent scheme."[1]

Lodge was, however, later "impressed with the energy and

[1] Sir Oliver Lodge, *Past Years* (London, 1931), pp. 270–1.

seriousness Edmund Gurney devoted to his laborious task", which we can well understand. His idea, as we have seen earlier, was first to prove the existence as a fact in nature of thought-transference by reference, in the main, to the experiments with those favourites of W. F. Barrett, the Creery sisters. It was of the Creerys that Gurney was fatally to write that it was to them that "we owe our own conviction of the possibility of genuine thought-transference between persons in a normal state."[1] This alleged experimental proof was to be linked with hundreds of stories of supposed telepathic phantasms of persons undergoing a crisis, being perceived by their friends. These two sections of evidence for telepathy, the experimental and the spontaneous, were to support each other and jointly prove the central theme of the book. The conception of Gurney's idea was brilliant; it was the disastrous vulnerability of the evidence presented which caused its collapse. How, in view of what we now know of Gurney, can we account for this?

The Preface to *Phantasms of the Living* makes it quite clear that apart from Myers's contribution to the Introduction and a "Note on a Suggested Mode of Psychical Interaction", Gurney wrote the whole of the book. As the two large volumes of *Phantasms of the Living* contain over 1,300 pages, a substantial part of them consisting of closely reasoned argument, it might be thought that as a purely literary effort it would consume the whole of Gurney's available time. It has to be remembered that he was heavily and simultaneously engaged in his daily work as the secretary of the Society and the editor of its *Journal* and *Proceedings*, to which he made large contributions himself, and in his extensive and time-consuming experiments in connexion with hypnotism.

Of equal importance is the fact that there can be no doubt that during his two years' work on the book there must have been more than one not inconsiderable period when Gurney was in his depressive phase, and was quite incapable of any intellectual application at all. It will be recalled that his undergraduate course at Trinity had been lengthened to five years by broken residence for exactly this reason, and that Myers wrote of the times when all effort became distasteful to Gurney. Can it really be believed that in all these circumstances Gurney had the time and energy to

[1] *Phantasms of the Living*, i, p. 29.

make the meticulous inquiries that were necessary to check the authenticity of some seven hundred ghost stories, and to satisfy himself that the documentary evidence proving their validity was available? Knowing what we do of Myers, the fact that Gurney's co-author placed this responsibility in retrospect entirely upon his dead friend, *after* the criticisms had appeared, need not be taken seriously.[1]

In my opinion Gurney made the fatal mistake, which would be entirely typical of his warmly sympathetic personality, of placing implicit trust in the care and diligence of those who assisted him in the gathering and checking of the material on which the book was based. In the Preface it was stated:

> "But the most difficult and important part of the under-taking—the collection, examination, and appraisal of evidence—has been throughout a joint labour; of which Mr. Podmore has borne so large a share that his name could not possibly have been omitted from the title-page."[2]

It seems natural that Podmore should have been the principal assistant, for the work was done in London, where he lived and worked at the Post Office, whereas Myers and Sidgwick were permanently in Cambridge and Barrett in Dublin. If this situation is accepted by the reader, he will no doubt recall that it was Frank Podmore who was entirely to blame for the fiasco of the story of Mr. X.Z.'s haunted house, where the tale told to him by Mr. X.Z. was evidently swallowed whole and no attempt of any kind was made to check anything. He will perhaps consider it significant that it was exactly this kind of weakness that made *Phantasms of the Living* so vulnerable to criticism, and that in both cases it was Gurney alone who bore the blame.[3]

It would seem very probable that Gurney had another assistant

---

[1] It is noteworthy also that by 1894 Gurney's other co-author, Frank Podmore, was describing *Phantasms of the Living* as "Edmund Gurney's book" on the first page of the Preface of his *Apparitions and Thought-Transference* in which, incidentally, no mention of the Smith–Blackburn experiments or those with the Creery sisters was made.

[2] *Phantasms of the Living*, i, p. v.

[3] It is of great interest in this connexion to notice that in a penetrating summary of the criticism of Mr. A. T. Innes and of Gurney's reply, to the great advantage of the former, the author of the article "Where the Letters are Not" in *The Saturday Review* of 8 October, 1887, remarked upon the curious fact that Gurney shouldered the whole responsibility of the defence himself without any support from his collaborators.

in the routine work. Myers said in his remarks about *Phantasms of the Living* in his obituary of Gurney, that George Albert Smith's "competent help as secretary was of essential service". Smith, of whom the reader will hear a great deal later, was an energetic, good-looking young man of considerable personal charm.

If Myers was right, and Smith was indeed entrusted with any part of the task of collecting, checking and writing up the ghost stories, we may be fairly certain that there would be serious deficiencies. It can scarcely be believed that Smith, aged twenty in 1884 and a former seaside entertainer, could possess the training and the experience for successfully carrying out the meticulous historical inquiries demanded by such a task. The reader may think, moreover, in view of Smith's history and background (when he left the employment of the S.P.R. in 1892 he reverted to type and became the proprietor of a pleasure ground in Brighton) that he was at heart a professional showman. It is quite probable that he genuinely considered that part of his duty to his employers at the S.P.R. was to give them what they evidently wanted, whether it was fraudulent thought-transference and hypnotic demonstrations, or the embellishment (or when appropriate the suppression) of the details of stories of alleged psychic experiences to make them more convincing.[1]

The reader has now before him the suggested background against which *Phantasms of the Living* was written and published as the initial major accomplishment of the S.P.R. after its first four years of existence.[2] Its reception by the critics of the periodical press of this country was not encouraging, and Sidgwick's comment in his "Journal" on 22 August, 1885, when the book seems to have been partly in galley-proof, that he could hardly imagine

---

[1] For an example of Smith's proclivities in this direction the reader is referred to his over-egging of the pudding in his report to the S.P.R. in favour of the genuineness of one of the slate-writing tricks of the notorious medium William Eglinton, described on pp. 213–15 of the second volume of Podmore's *Modern Spiritualism*. It is significant that Podmore actually thought it necessary to say that he thought no less of Smith on account of this incident (p. 215, n. 2).

[2] The reader may think that the assumptions I have made are probably confirmed by a letter from Miss Helen Gurney to me, spontaneously commenting upon *Phantasms of the Living*, which I had not previously mentioned in our correspondence. Miss Gurney referred to a remark made by her father, which could perhaps be regarded as a sad epitaph upon the book. Gurney said, in retrospect, that the narrators of the ghost-stories always claimed "to have made notes and done the right thing *before* they knew whether the dream (or apparition) came right or not. Nobody ever did this really! And my father did *not* find it so with those he examined *himself*!!"

THE STRANGE CASE OF EDMUND GURNEY

anybody reading it, "and the reviewers will doubtless only select the weak stories to make fun of", was curiously prophetic.

Serious and informed attacks, however, began to develop. Soon after the book appeared, Professor W. Preyer opened the campaign.[1] Gurney, as always alone, published a courteous reply in booklet form in the following year.[2] Another attack came from Professor C. S. Peirce in the United States, against which Gurney defended himself with his customary skill and good manners, and as always, without the support of his co-authors.[3] But, as has been foreshadowed in these pages, the most fatally damaging criticism came from Mr. A. Taylor Innes in 1887 in a widely-read magazine of the period.[4] Innes pin-pointed with deadly effect the inherent weakness of the structure of the whole edifice of the hundreds of cases cited of alleged telepathic phantasms being perceived at a distance by friends or relatives at a moment of crisis for the original of the apparition, the existence of the crisis being unknown to the percipients at the time of the experience. In a large number of cases Gurney had stated that according to the percipients' narratives the truth of their testimony was proved by corroboration from contemporary documents. They had, they said, immediately written letters giving accounts of the phantasms and posted them, before they heard the confirmation of the events of the crisis, unknown to them until then by any natural means. Gurney himself had mentioned in his book the desirability of obtaining written records, dated and signed, regarding the alleged experiences.

What was required, Innes said, and what was lacking, was any statement in *Phantasms of the Living* that relevant documents, such as post-marked letters which had passed out of the hands of the percipients before the confirmatory news was received, had been examined by the authors. He said that in the large number of cases where the existence of such letters was alleged, there was *not one* which had been proved, and not one which had not failed

---

[1] "Telepathie und Geisterseherei in England", *Deutsche Rundschau* (Berlin, January 1886), pp. 30–51.

[2] *Telepathie: ein Erwiderung auf die Kritik des Herrn Prof. W. Preyer* (Leipzig, 1887).

[3] C. S. Peirce, "Criticism on *Phantasms of the Living*", E. Gurney, "Remarks on Professor Peirce's Paper", C. S. Peirce, "Mr. Peirce's Rejoinder". *Proceedings*, American Society for Psychical Research, 1885–89, i, pp. 150ff.

[4] "Where are the Letters? A cross-examination of certain Phantasms", *The Nineteenth Century* (London, August 1887), pp. 174–94.

in this easy documentary demonstration. He said, "How many are there of the seven hundred cases of psychical research—how many even of these three hundred and fifty first-hand narrations of our letter-writing age—in which the indefatigable editors have 'seen or ascertained' a letter or document issued at the time by the narrator, so as to prove his story to be true? *The answer must be, not one.*" Innes critically examined case after case where letters were said to have existed, and others where the documents were supposed to have been lost, destroyed, or were not to be found. He wrote in conclusion, "I am not aware of anything that can account for this, unless it be that this whole class of stories is without real foundation. But any other solution will be welcome— to those especially who have for many years kept open to themselves a possibility which these records of psychical research unexpectedly threaten to close."

Gurney alone replied to this challenge in the same magazine with his customary courtesy,[1] although the last paragraph of Innes' criticism suggested rather unkindly that *Phantasms of the Living* had actually destroyed rather than proved the possibility of tele- pathic hallucinations. Gurney was, unhappily, able to point only to three cases which satisfied the requirements demanded by Innes in his challenge, and of these one was admitted later to have been a hoax. After Gurney's death Innes returned to the attack in *The Nineteenth Century*[2] but the leaders of the S.P.R. showed little desire to continue the discussion and the matter was allowed to drop. As has been said, a contributor to *The Saturday Review* in October 1887 summed up the controversy entirely in favour of Innes, concluding with a sardonic paragraph saying that it was perhaps as well that the documents which might have proved the existence of the phantasms had been shown to be non-existent. If the existence of apparitions had been proved, said the author of the article, everybody would acknowledge it and there would be no more interest in believing in such phenomena than there would be in believing in rain. This would mean that the S.P.R. would no longer serve any useful purpose, and that its members would have little choice but to dispose of their offices and devote themselves to more useful occupations.

[1] "Letters on Phantasms", *op. cit.*, October 1887, pp. 522–33.
[2] "The Psychical Society's Ghosts: A Challenge Renewed", *op. cit.*, November 1891, pp. 764–76.

It does not seem too much to say that Gurney's situation in regard to his five-and-a-half years' devotion to the work of the Society for Psychical Research was a near tragic one in the autumn of 1887. So far as *Phantasms of the Living* was concerned, the only section of the result of his monumental labours remaining unchallenged was that dealing with the so-called experimental proof of telepathy in which Gurney had publicly placed his principal faith in the Creery sisters. Although he did not know it until those last sad, darkening months of 1887, this too was to end in disaster before long. However, he bravely and diligently continued the experiments with the boys in Brighton, assisted by his youthful secretary and hypnotic operator G. A. Smith. This, the reader may think, was virtually all that was left to him.

Gurney's final contribution to *Proceedings*, in the spring of 1888, was his short account of the discovery in trickery of the Creery sisters and their confession. After this further catastrophe Gurney continued, no doubt in desperation and certainly, as Professor Croom Robertson recorded, in "nervous exhaustion that went on ever increasing", his work on hypnosis and his administration of the Society's affairs during the spring and early summer of 1888. At his side in all this activity, as had been the case throughout Gurney's years of devoted work for the S.P.R., was his secretary, G. A. Smith. It is to the career of that unusual young man that we must now direct our attention, and to that of his friend Douglas Blackburn. As we look back through the years, we return full circle to where our story started; to Brighton, where in my opinion the principal tragedy of Gurney's life began and ended.

CHAPTER SEVEN

THE CONJURERS

O<small>N</small> 6 August, 1857, Mrs. Elizabeth Blackburn gave birth to a son, Douglas, at 13 Lombard Street in the registration district of Southwark in London. His father was a journeyman leather dresser. I have been unable to discover any details of Douglas Blackburn's boyhood. One of the mysteries about him is that at a fairly early age he demonstrated such marked ability as a writer that it seems reasonable to suppose that he had the advantage of some formal education. A statement by him in later years that his childhood was spent with a medical family (he did not claim that he was a doctor's son) suggests that he may possibly have been adopted. However this may be, by the time he was twenty-three Douglas Blackburn was already the Editor of a small journal published in Brighton. In his middle twenties two operettas, *Disenchantment* and *Angelo; or, an Ideal Love*, for which he wrote the librettos, were produced with success at the Brighton Aquarium in 1882 and 1883. When he died of lobar pneumonia in the Victoria Cottage Hospital at Tonbridge, Kent, on 28 March, 1929, at the age of seventy-one, he had established himself, as Stanley Portal Hyatt said in his two-page review of Blackburn's *Secret Service in South Africa*, as "the founder of the modern school of South African novelists."[1] Forty-five friends attended his funeral, and his obituary and the published appreciations of his work covered several pages of print.[2] He died, as he had lived, unmarried.

The first stage of our study of Douglas Blackburn's life is concerned with his activities as a young man. The weekly journal of which he was the part-time Editor, *The Brightonian*, combining

---

[1] *The Bookman* (London, October 1911), p. 53. The reviewer said that Douglas Blackburn knew more about the Kruger administration than any other British writer, whilst Andrew Lang stated that with Olive Schreiner's *Story of a South African Farm*, Blackburn's *Prinsloo of Prinsloosdorp* was the South African classic, "outstanding, unsurpassed in the copious literature of the Sub-Continent".
[2] *Tonbridge Free Press*, 5 April, 1929.

this with his existing duties as a reporter on the staff of the *Sussex Daily Post*, commenced publication from its offices at 24, Duke Street, Brighton, on 22 October, 1880. The proprietor was Mr. R. J. Railton, who played his part in the curious drama which was to unfold in Brighton in the next year or two. Mr. Railton seems to have placed sufficient confidence in his young Editor to give him a fairly free hand in the policies he followed.

It seems clear that the twenty-three-year-old Blackburn was enthusiastic and efficient in his new duties. When *The Brightonian* made its appearance, the Editor of another Brighton journal, *The Dolphin*, wrote of it:

> "The Brightonian came out last Friday, and as I antici-
> pated, took the popular fancy at once. It is clearly the
> smartest attempt at an independent journal that has yet been
> run in Brighton, and the only question is whether it can keep
> so and pay. I sincerely hope so."

Blackburn's writings in *The Brightonian* make it clear from the beginning that he was greatly interested in the world of entertainment, especially in conjuring performances and in the public exposure of spiritualism. He much admired the skill of Washington Irving Bishop, a professional conjurer, as a "muscle reader", but his opinion of two-person "second sight" acts seems to have been that not only were they very simple conjuring feats, but that generally speaking the public had seen too many of them to be particularly impressed by this form of entertainment. It is possible that Blackburn's view may have been influenced, and his knowledge of the subject increased, by two long articles which appeared in *The Dolphin* commencing with the issue of 16 October, 1880. These were entitled "Second Sight Exposed—by ex-Medium" and were anti-spiritualist in tone, explaining codes and providing detailed instruction as to how information was conveyed from the agent to the "medium" in a second-sight act. However that may be, less than two months later Blackburn wrote:

> " 'Little Louie', the marvel of second sight as the advertise-
> ment has it, is at the Aquarium this week, this being her third
> appearance there. Little Louie is now a big girl but her

extraordinary skill has in no way deteriorated with advancing age. The thing does not draw, however, for the general public understands that sort of thing too well now."[1]

Little Louie's impresario and partner was "Professor" Heriot. It is curious to reflect that due to a remarkable and unforeseen series of circumstances, Blackburn himself was later to be a partner in a paid second-sight act at the Aquarium.

This published view of Blackburn's is important. If it be assumed for the moment that he and George Albert Smith (who Blackburn was not to meet until 1882) were later to prepare and practice a second-sight act during July and August 1882, then the reason for the tempting of Gurney and Myers to Brighton by means of the tantalizing accounts of miracles in *Light* and *The Brightonian*, to be discussed in detail later, is not difficult to understand. If Blackburn and Smith believed that for the act to be successful (a not unworthy ambition for a youthful seaside entertainer like Smith) it would have to differ significantly from the run-of-the-mill performance with which Blackburn thought the public was too familiar, is not the reason for their actions reasonably obvious? The lay mind must be persuaded at least to dally with the idea, as in the case of the temporarily highly successful Piddingtons[2] sixty-five years later, that the alleged thought-transference *might* be genuine. To this end, what could be more impressive and financially rewarding than the ability to claim that the feats had been declared inexplicable and genuine by the supposedly scientific investigators from the Society for Psychical Research?

It is of great interest to find that in July 1881 Washington Irving Bishop was appearing at the Brighton Pavilion and that *The Brightonian* carried a prominent advertisement of his show, which consisted of "muscle-reading" and of spiritualistic tricks which Bishop undertook to expose in full view of the audience.[3] Bishop's show was evidently successful, for he was still at the Pavilion in August, when Blackburn devoted much space to praise

---

[1] *The Brightonian*, 3 December, 1880, p. 5.
[2] When the Piddingtons' B.B.C. contract was over and they were embarking upon a tour of the music-halls, they discussed the whole mechanics of their excellent act with the late Dr. H. Park Shackleton, O.B.E., an Hon. Vice-President of the Magic Circle, and the present writer.
[3] *The Brightonian*, 23 July, 1881, p. 2.

of his performances. He wrote that these "were most entertaining, and particularly the last one, at which he let the cat out of the bag, and the public into the secret". He added that his *"exposé* of the tricks of the mediums was excellent; and we have heard of one emulative individual who has disjointed his fingers in endeavouring to produce the table rapping phenomenon".[1]

In the same issue of the magazine Blackburn gave a detailed account of how Bishop by a psychological trick of misdirection, persuaded first Dr. Taaffe, the Medical Officer of Health for Brighton, and then a Mr. Gibson that an iron ring had appeared inexplicably on their arm without their grasp of Bishop's hand being released for an instant. Blackburn said that "The principle involved in it undoubtedly underlies the whole of the deception of spiritualism. . . . The secret of this trick evidently lies in the power Mr. Bishop has of deceiving the sensitive powers, and we can easily imagine how conclusive such an experiment would have appeared to an ignorant person, prepared to accept all that a spirit medium poured down his throat."[2]

On 2 December, 1881, Blackburn gave a dinner at the offices of *The Brightonian* attended by the Mayor of Brighton, six aldermen, six councillors and the town clerk, the ostensible purpose of the affair being to honour Mr. Bishop, after which the conjurer evidently gave an impressive demonstration of "muscle-reading" and escapology.[3] No doubt Blackburn thought that the publicity which the gathering would attract might not be unhelpful in regard to the circulation of the magazine. This social occasion seems to have been a cheerful affair in which there was a good deal of chaffing of the City Fathers of Brighton by Mr. Bishop. The Town Clerk, for example, on being asked what particular trick he would like to see, said that he had been much impressed by the ease with which Mr. Bishop had extricated himself from securely tied knots and he would like to know if Mr. Bishop could show him some easy way of "getting out of a mess—a metaphorical one, of course—without injury to himself or reputation". Mr. Bishop said that the best advice he could give to the Town Clerk was to keep out of the mess in the first instance.

[1] *The Brightonian*, 6 August, 1881, p. 6.
[2] *The Brightonian*, 6 August, 1881, p. 10.
[3] *The Brightonian*, 3 December, 1881, p. 2.

Douglas Blackburn's sceptical views upon occultism and his enthusiastic regard for the art of the conjurer are left in no doubt by his writings at this time. His knowledgeable admiration for Bishop's skill as a "muscle-reader" is also perfectly clear. He said, for example, that Bishop's performances were "sufficient to convince the most incredulous that he actually possesses the powers he claims".[1] That Blackburn thoroughly understood that Bishop's "powers" relied entirely upon the simple mechanics of "muscle-reading" is demonstrated not only by Blackburn's own later experiments but by his very shrewd comment on Bishop's performance. He said that thought-reading was "a very comprehensive title, and whilst it actually describes Mr. Bishop's strange acquirement, it is likely to give the general public an erroneous and exaggerated idea of his capabilities."[2] He anticipated almost precisely what later writers were to say about "muscle-reading" when he added that "Mr. Bishop does not profess to discover thoughts on an abstract subject. This latter notion seemed to have possessed many who went to see him, and they were consequently disappointed."

Any doubts that Bishop's performances of "thought-reading" at Brighton consisted simply of the location of hidden objects by "muscle-reading", are dissipated by a very interesting account by Blackburn of a private party he attended when the company tried some experiments of their own endeavouring to emulate Bishop's feats. The hidden article used in these tests was a small pair of scissors. Blackburn was frank to say that whilst a journalistic friend of his was successful in finding the concealed object twice, naming the precise spot within a few minutes of entering the room, he himself was not so adept. Blackburn said that his own first attempt was a failure but that the second was sufficiently successful to satisfy him that there was something in it.[3]

For the benefit of the reader who is not familiar with the possibilities of pseudo-mind-reading by conjuring methods, a brief account of two entirely different accomplishments of the professional magician which were extremely popular in the 1880's, "muscle-reading" and the "second-sight act", may not be out of

[1] *The Brightonian*, 6 August, 1881, p. 6.
[2] *The Brightonian*, 3 December, 1881, p. 7.
[3] *The Brightonian*, 10 December, 1881, p. 10.

place. In the case of the former, no partner or "medium" was necessary, and the quite astonishing results were obtained by the performer working with a volunteer member of the audience. Dr. E. J. Dingwall, an Hon. Vice-President of the Magic Circle, wrote:

> "The second fact to be taken into account is the rise [in the second half of the nineteenth century] of what was called muscle-reading. In demonstrations of this kind by such performers as Randall Brown, Stuart Cumberland, Washington Irving Bishop and Alfred Capper, many simple people found it difficult to believe that the successes of the performers were due solely to the unconscious indications given by the voluntary assistant and by the spectators, at least by some of them."[1]

John Mulholland, the American book collector, writer and magician, said of the "muscle-reading" of Washington Irving Bishop:

> "He was the originator of the 'pin-test', and caused a sensation with his 'blind fold drive' and other performances which seem to transcend the natural. The pin test consisted simply of hiding a common glass-headed pin somewhere in the theater. Bishop would seize the wrist of the man who had done the hiding, and would race about the theater, eventually leading the man straight to the pin, which he would find. . . . The fact of Bishop's performances is that he may have been peculiarly skilful in them, thanks to long practice and some degree of 'hyperesthesia', but in general anyone not too unobservant and horny-handed can do the same sort of thing. The performer seems to lead the assistant to the pin, but in truth the assistant, by involuntary hesitations and other signs, leads the performer."[2]

The reader may suspect that the reason why Smith, when questioned in later years by Miss Alice Johnson of the S.P.R., as the reader will learn, asserted that the paid performances in Brighton had been limited to "muscle-reading" in private houses,

---

[1] E. J. Dingwall, "The Simulation of Telepathy", *Ciba Foundation Symposium on Extrasensory Perception* (London, 1956), p. 143. A rare offprint of this article exists, bound in soft red boards.
[2] John Mulholland, *Beware Familiar Spirits* (New York, 1938), pp. 202–5.

was that he wished to avoid any discussion of the subject of codes and confederates, which form no part of this kind of exhibition, but which were dangerously relevant so far as his stage shows with Blackburn were concerned.

Whilst "muscle-reading" first became popular as late as the second half of the nineteenth century, the "second-sight act" in which the performer supposedly transmitted to the blindfolded "medium" on the stage the identity and frequently quite complex description of objects offered to him by members of the audience, is much older in origin. Dr. Dingwall wrote:[1]

> "At the end of the eighteenth century, the famous magician Pinetti and his wife were giving a second-sight act, and by the middle of the nineteenth century books began to be issued explaining the codes used by the thought-readers in their performances. At first, audible codes were used, and such performers as Robert-Houdin and Heller were famous in their day, to be followed by mind-readers like Donato and his pupil Pickman, who combined a thought-reading show with a hypnotic demonstration, which gave an air of pseudo-science to their performances.
>
> As the development of new and subtle codes proceeded, so did these simulations of telepathy become more puzzling. The Zancigs, the Zomahs and the Piddingtons will long be remembered for their performances, but the demand for even more convincing tests had to be met and thus the development of silent acts showed marked improvement."

Washington Irving Bishop published a small book in 1880 for sale at his performances which described in detail the methods used in the older two-person second-sight acts. In the introductory chapter he wrote:

> "The many inquiries made of me as to the process of mesmeric exhibitors and Clairvoyants proves how widespread is the curiosity on the subject. The absence of any explanation gives rise to the belief among weak people that there is something supernatural in the matter, and that, in fact, the supposed professor of the power of second-sight is working

[1] *Op. cit.*, p. 145.

85

under the influence of some occult force. In the following pages I propose to show exactly how Clairvoyance, or Second Sight, is managed."[1]

Neither Bishop, Cumberland, nor their many imitators claimed spirit aid in their performances although many spiritualists and psychical researchers attributed it to them. Bishop, indeed, actually combined exposures of spiritualism with his performances of "muscle-reading".

As early as 1880 Bishop said in his book that any two persons with moderate practice could demonstrate alleged second sight, with the percipient blindfolded, a shawl over his head and his back to the audience; a position, incidentally, exactly assumed by Smith during the performances with Blackburn two years later. It is useful to record the extent and quality of the results which were possible in these conditions by normal conjuring methods, as described by Bishop.

> "Objects presented to the controller, or simply shown him by people in the audience, are, at his request, correctly described by the Clairvoyant; and, in some cases, the audience is furnished with a description more detailed than even the possessors of the articles themselves could give of them. Strange coins with ancient dates, railway tickets with numbers, bank notes with numbers and dates, curious instruments, mathematical and technical, outlandish charms, eccentric heirlooms, are all produced in rapid succession; and each and all are described with an accuracy and clearness by the blindfold Clairvoyant that is inexplicable and astounding. Then figures are written down by persons in the audience, and the Clairvoyant, with unfailing accuracy, states what these figures are; and even if a question is asked by a person in the audience instead of by the Conjurer, the Clairvoyant's answer will be correct. Only one condition is insisted on throughout the proceedings, and that is, that the controller of the Clairvoyant should be made acquainted with the thing shown or the figures written, on the principle that the sight of the Clairvoyant is second sight, and that what her kindred spirit

---

[1] *Second Sight Explained. A Complete Exposition of Clairvoyance and Second Sight* (Edinburgh, 1880), p. 8.

sees, she can see; for she, in fact, sees through the medium of the controlling personality instead of her own physical eye, and that she can do so by communion of spirit, the operation of which is superior to space and defies natural laws.

These being the characteristics of a Clairvoyant exhibition, I have now to describe how the process is brought about by simple natural arrangements."[1]

Bishop's chapter headings are of revealing interest, examples being "Preparing the Way", "A Code for Figures", "A Code for Words", "General Principle of Coding", "A Code for Cards", etc.

It is of great interest to discover that Bishop was appearing professionally in Brighton continuously from July 1881 for a period of some six months, giving "muscle-reading" demonstrations and public exposures of spiritualism, during which time he became friendly with Blackburn who reported his shows in his magazine, was intensely interested in Bishop's work, and even gave a dinner in Bishop's honour at the offices of *The Brightonian*. By the spring of 1882 at latest Smith, who was a professional entertainer in a small way, had met Blackburn. It is for the reader to decide whether it is conceivable that Bishop's little book on pseudo "second-sight" acts, of which hundreds of copies must have been sold during the conjurer's long stay in Brighton, could have escaped the notice of Blackburn and Smith. Is it reasonable to suppose that Blackburn, as the Editor of *The Brightonian*, could have missed seeing the important articles in *The Dolphin* exposing the codes, and secrets of "second sight"? If the reader is of the opinion that neither of these possibilities are believable then he will conclude that the statement by Smith in later years to Miss Alice Johnson of the S.P.R., that he and Blackburn knew nothing whatever of codes until these were explained by Myers and Gurney during the S.P.R. experiments, was clearly a deliberate lie.

We have before us in the preceding pages the background of Douglas Blackburn's considerable and knowledgeable interest in the field of professional conjuring. It is now our task to examine the circumstances in which the youthful Editor of *The Brightonian* elected to embark, for a short period, upon a career as a showman himself in partnership with George Albert Smith.

[1] *Second Sight Explained*, pp. 9–10.

CHAPTER EIGHT

THE SECOND-SIGHT ACT

IN the early 1880's a retired barrister named Henry Munster was living in Brighton. He was wealthy and egocentric, and seems to have been generally detested in the seaside town. He was addicted to litigation and young women, his "adopted daughters" being evidently notorious in Brighton. He was a man of violent disposition with an unsavoury past, who had served one prison sentence and was to go to prison again during the series of remarkable events now to be described, which were ultimately to end the life of *The Brightonian*, and be the indirect cause of Blackburn becoming a partner in a professional second-sight act.

In March 1881 Munster brought charges against a William Hill and his wife Ellen, who were accused of burgling Munster's house. A firm of Brighton solicitors, Evett and Lamb, vigorously defended the Hills at the hearing, at which William was convicted but Ellen acquitted. Munster was incensed at the result and the way in which Mr. Charles Lamb had fought the case on behalf of Mrs. Hill, and approached both the *Sussex Daily News* and the *Sussex Daily Post* with the curious request that both should print a libellous statement (for which Munster offered to pay!) implying that Mr. Lamb had shared in the proceeds of the burglary. Both papers naturally refused to have anything to do with this fantastic suggestion.

The employee of the *Sussex Daily Post* whom Munster saw at the office of that newspaper was Douglas Blackburn, the part-time Editor of *The Brightonian*. In the face of the flat refusal to print the libellous statement he had prepared, Munster became angry, and violently abused Blackburn, the *Sussex Daily Post* and its owner, Mr. Curtis. Foiled in his original project, Munster then printed his attack on Mr. Lamb in the form of a circular, one of which he signed and sent through the post to Mr. Curtis, addressed to "the low blackguardly proprietor of the Sussex Daily Post". The circular openly referred to "unsupported statements made by thieves or their lawyers, hired with part of their booty, to throw mud about in the hope that some will stick". Both the owner of *The Sussex Daily Post* and the solicitor, Charles Lamb, naturally issued writs for libel against Munster.

In the meantime, Munster had not been inactive in regard to his fury over the acquittal of Ellen Hill. He brought a further charge against her of administering drugs to Munster's servants to facilitate the burglary. Whether Blackburn thought that it was his duty as the Editor of a local paper to use his pen in defence of the wretched Ellen, or whether he merely disliked Munster and was still smarting under Munster's abuse of him at the *Sussex Daily Post* office, I do not know. It is, however, fair to point out that Blackburn was not alone in his published criticism of Munster. Mr. H. R. Davis, the Editor of another Brighton paper *The Dolphin* (owned by Mr. A. M. Robinson) was evidently equally infuriated by Munster's pursuit of Ellen Hill, and referred to him as "hounding down his prey" in his editorial of 11 June, 1881. This was the same day that Blackburn was sufficiently reckless and indignant to publish the following paragraph in *The Brightonian*:

> "It is generally considered ill-advised, if not absolutely immoral, to comment on a case that is *sub-judice*, but we cannot help remarking on the pertinacity with which Mr. Munster has run to earth the woman Hill, whom he failed to convict on a charge of house-breaking with her husband. He has at length got her safely in the dock after spending no end of money in hunting her down, and he now proposes to get her convicted on a charge of administering noxious drugs with the intent to commit a robbery. Surely this is persecution, not prosecution."

It seems certain, to say the least of it, that Blackburn was not admonished by his employer for this, his first published criticism of Munster, for it was to be by no means the last. Both Blackburn and Mr. Railton may have been encouraged by the fact that a week later, on 18 June, 1881, the Editor of *The Dolphin* vigorously renewed the attack on Munster in regard to the Ellen Hill affair.

On 9 July, 1881, the *Brighton Herald* reported that a Grand Jury had returned a true bill against Munster in regard to his libel of Mr. Charles Lamb, the solicitor, which Lord Justice Bramwell said should go to the next Assizes. This was obstinately opposed by Munster, who alleged, possibly significantly, that he would not receive a fair trial within the boundaries of the county of Sussex. After the hearing, Munster struck Mr. Evett, Mr. Lamb's partner, across the face with a horsewhip. This incident was reported in *The Dolphin* of 9 July, 1881, under the uncomplimentary heading "Munster still on the Job". In the next issue of *The Dolphin* of 16 July a leading article, in terms offensive to Munster, somewhat jubilantly described his appearance before the Lewes Bench on a charge of assaulting Mr. Evett. He was fined £5, and bound over in his own recognizance of £100, with two sureties in sums of £50 in addition. These were not inconsiderable amounts in 1881, and it does not seem to be in doubt that Munster was regarded as a violent and unpleasant character. On the same date of 16 July Blackburn wrote in *The Brightonian* of these occurrences that "Mr. Munster will soon make Brighton too warm to hold him".

The reader may think that this further published criticism of Munster by Blackburn demonstrates that his employer, Mr. Railton, tacitly approved of his young Editor's policy in regard to Munster, for clearly he had been in a position to forbid Blackburn to mention Munster in *The Brightonian* again, had he wished to do so at any time after the article by Blackburn on 11 June. Mr. Railton, indeed, admitted this during the hearing of the later libel action brought by Munster against *The Brightonian*. It may well be that both Blackburn and his employer thought mistakenly that there was safety in numbers, for at one period Munster simultaneously issued writs for libel against the *Brighton Times*, the *Sussex Daily Post*, *The Dolphin* and *The Brightonian*. Be that as it may, after *The Dolphin* had reported at the beginning of November 1881 upon the successful result of the libel action brought by Mr. Lamb, the solicitor, against Munster in regard to the libellous circular, Blackburn was reckless enough to publish the following scurrilous verse in *The Brightonian* on 12 November, a few days after the article had appeared in *The Dolphin*:

> "He began his career at a huckster's stall,
> He eloped with the wife of a neighbour;
> At 20 he made at Old Bailey a call
> And retired for six months hard labour.

Today he's too wealthy and too proud to thieve
And moves on a high social level,
And by aping great piety, makes us believe
He was ever bad friends with the ———."

It is of interest to notice that whilst Blackburn stated during the libel case that there was nothing to show that this regrettable doggerel referred to Henry Munster, the latter furiously claimed that it did, from which it is reasonable to suppose that there had been some unsavoury episode in Munster's life which Blackburn had clearly pin-pointed. There is some support for this suggestion in the fact that when Munster did bring an action for libel against *The Brightonian* and other periodicals, the proceedings came to an end somewhat abruptly when certain letters were produced in court by the defence, to the consternation of Munster. He complained that they had been stolen from him, which may conceivably have been the case as his house had been burgled by Hill. He accepted 40/-d. damages and costs in each case, although he had, for example, claimed no less than £1,000 (an enormous sum in 1882) against *The Brightonian*. Whether, in November 1881, the young Editor and Mr. Railton were under the mistaken impression that the ability to justify what had been written was a defence against an action for criminal libel, I do not know. It was, of course, no defence at all, and Munster may have decided that this was the opportunity for which he had been waiting. On 6 February, 1882, the *Brighton Gazette* reported the preliminary hearing of the case of Munster against the owners of *The Brightonian* and the other periodicals concerned. The case was not actually tried until June 1882, resulting in the formal victory and meagre damages for Munster already described. Blackburn admitted in the witness box that he had written the matter in regard to which the complaints were made, although denying that there was anything to show that the doggerel referred to Munster. Railton did not deny that what had been done was with his consent.

The fact that Munster even technically won his case was a triumph for British justice, for during the proceedings he was as objectionable as ever to everyone and offensive to the judge. When rebuked, he recklessly walked out of court and drove away, as a result of which he was imprisoned for four days for contempt of court.

There can be no doubt that after the first hearing in February 1882 Blackburn's employer would be angry and extremely disturbed, for he would no doubt be advised by his solicitor that the libel would be proved, and that justification would be no defence when the case was tried in June. He would know that Munster was claiming the very considerable sum (in 1882) of £1,000 as damages, and that as he was not a wealthy man *The Brightonian* would be finished if anything like this amount was awarded to Munster. Some of his annoyance and anxiety would no doubt be directed at his young Editor, and human nature being what it is his anger would not be reduced by the fact that he himself had done nothing to prevent the publication of the libel. Blackburn was not dismissed, but it can scarcely be doubted that in the spring of 1882 Blackburn felt that his appointment with *The Brightonian*, and indeed the position of the journal itself, was precarious, and that it would be advisable for him to look around fairly soon for some alternative source of income. He would know, moreover, that his editorial indiscretions would be widely publicized by the coming hearing, and that his chances of obtaining a similar appointment would be small. As matters turned out in the event, he did not relinquish the editorship of *The Brightonian* until the early months of 1884, shortly before it ceased publication, having been working without salary for over a year. He could not, however, foresee that in February 1882. It is for the reader to decide whether the Munster affair and the events of the early months of 1882 were connected with what is to follow.

In the issue of *The Brightonian* of 22 April, 1882 (p. 8) Blackburn began to publish a series of extremely complimentary reports upon the public performances as a stage mesmerist of a local youth named George Albert Smith. Smith, who had been born of fairly humble parents in the Cripplegate district of East London on 4 January, 1864, was eighteen. He was in later years to claim that his father had been Mr. G. Reeves Smith, the well-known manager of the Brighton Aquarium, but this was quite untrue. His father's name was Charles Smith, and on the certificates of Smith's birth and marriage he was described respectively as a "ticket-writer" and an "artist". In 1882 Smith's father was dead, and his mother kept a seaside boarding-house in Brighton. If G. A. Smith followed any gainful occupation at this time other than the precarious one of a local seaside entertainer I can find no mention of it. He was described admiringly by Blackburn as a handsome, curly-headed, short, square-built youth with a wide knowledge of conjuring and considerable ingenuity in the invention of new tricks. Blackburn said, in later years, that he first found Smith giving his hypnotic show in a small Brighton hall, and was intrigued to discover that his own office-boy, Mahoney, was amongst the lads who were going on to the platform to be "put under the influence and made to do ridiculous things". Blackburn added that it was when Mahoney confessed that Smith was paying him a shilling a night that "the bogus character of the business became obvious."[1]

Although at the beginning of Blackburn's accounts of his abilities Smith's modest performances were confined to suburban church halls and the like (during April and May for example his appearances were limited to a hall in New Road, Brighton, and the Ventnor Villas Lecture Hall at Hove), Blackburn henceforth devoted a surprising amount of space in leading articles in *The Brightonian* to the excellence of Smith's work; much more, indeed, than he had given even to his admired Washington Irving Bishop.[2] In his first article he said that Smith was "providing the best entertainment we have had in town for many a day", that other mesmerists were put "very much in the shade", that Smith's control over his subjects was "simply marvellous" and that his powers of personal attraction in persuading subjects to come on to the stage were remarkable. He said that he could "safely predict" fame and fortune for the young hypnotist, although, as we shall see later, in the event Smith sacrificed this prophesied golden future to become successively the salaried private secretary to two members of the Society for Psychical Research before ultimately becoming, perhaps not surprisingly, the proprietor of a Brighton pleasure-ground.

Possibly as a result of this favourable publicity, which continued unabated in *The Brightonian* throughout April and May 1882, Smith secured an engagement at the Town Hall, Brighton, early in June which was duly reported in the issue of Blackburn's

---

[1] *John Bull*, 5 December, 1908, p. 590.

[2] In his article in *John Bull* of 5 December, 1908, Blackburn said that as the editor of a widely-read paper he was in a position to "boom Smith very effectively, I remaining in the background as the impartial journalist investigator who occasionally assisted at an experiment".

paper dated 3 June (p. 4). Blackburn described it as the "most amazing and remarkable entertainment in Brighton this week", with the comment that it was astonishing that anyone after witnessing Smith's performance could doubt his ability. By July Smith was fulfilling engagements at the Brighton Aquarium, with announcements on the front page of *The Brightonian* on 8 July and 15 July, and glowing accounts of his performance by Blackburn on p. 10 of each issue. On p. 7 of *The Brightonian* of 15 July was a report of Smith's show being marred (or deliberately enhanced?) by a dramatic collapse of the performer on the stage, allegedly due to the unbearable mental strain. In the issue of his paper of 22 July (p. 5) Blackburn said with enthusiasm:

> "Mr. G. A. Smith's concluding appearance at the Aquarium on Saturday evening was an event in the history of the institution. The crowd was simply enormous, and the excitement and enthusiasm proportionate. Someone calling himself a doctor seized one of the subjects whilst under control and administered sundry brutal kicks and prickings, and the boy still remaining unconscious the sceptic had the audacity to denounce him as a fraud. This was too much for the audience, so they threw the interrupter out.
>
> The engagement has proved the most successful ever made by the Aquarium management, and throws Crowther, Little Louie and the Midgets far into the shade. Mr. Smith has received an offer for a re-engagement in a fortnight, but he proposes giving a series of select high-class séances for the popularizing of the science."

It seems certain that the twenty-five-year-old Blackburn had some strong motive for his curiously unrestrained eulogies of the eighteen-year-old entertainer, and it is unfortunate that at this distance of time we have no means of knowing the precise relationship between them. Blackburn clearly went much beyond the normal duty of a journalist in describing the no doubt very creditable performances of the youthful Smith. It may have been a warm friendship and admiration for the boy which prompted Blackburn to write as he did. In the alternative, since by September 1882 the two were giving paid public entertainments in pseudo-thought transference in some sort of partnership, it is possible

IIIa. Douglas Blackburn

IIIb. F. W. H. Myers

IV. George Albert Smith. His resemblance in this photograph to
D. D. Home will be observed

that during the spring and summer an understanding had already been reached between Blackburn and Smith, whereby the former received a percentage of Smith's takings from his hypnotic shows in return for affording him a considerable amount of publicity in the pages of *The Brightonian*. On the other hand, there may have been a more complex motive for Blackburn's flattery and support of Smith.[1]

In my view, the reader's scrutiny of the sequence of events now to be described, which occurred during the second half of 1882, is of the greatest possible importance in enabling him to decide whether it was Smith or Blackburn who spoke the truth during the later controversy as to what really happened at this time. Smith was to claim that what he and Blackburn did was genuine telepathy, whilst Blackburn was to say that their performances were simply conjuring. For Smith's explanation to be true, it has to be assumed that Blackburn, despite his quoted writings in *The Brightonian*, was a *bona fide* telepathic agent (if such exists) who discovered that Smith was an equally genuine percipient (if such exists) of vivid mental impressions and diagrams, numbers and so forth which had only to be thought of by Blackburn to be reproduced by Smith. The reader may think it curious, moreover, that when Blackburn retired from the scene, the S.P.R. thought-transference experiments with Smith as the percipient ceased with significant abruptness and were never repeated.

If Blackburn was speaking the truth in later years, and Smith was lying, all these difficulties disappear. He and Smith were public entertainers, and the thought-transference experiments with the S.P.R., accomplished by means of a code, were a trick. The purpose was presumably to ensure the success and earning capacity of the projected Blackburn–Smith second-sight act by being able to claim in future advertisements that scientific investigators could offer no explanation and accepted the feats as genuine. Professional conjurers have obtained excellent publicity for themselves by precisely this kind of suggestion since the days of Blackburn and Smith, and will no doubt continue to do so.

In the case under discussion, the plan of the tricksters did not

---

[1] It is possible that the fact that Blackburn was at the time "walking out" with Smith's sister, a circumstance later to be discussed, may have had its influence upon him.

come to fruition, due to an unexpected circumstance with which Blackburn apparently did not seek to interfere. During the experiments the engaging and youthful Smith was evidently able to ingratiate himself with the S.P.R. investigators, and he was offered employment by the Society. Having decided that his future lay with his new friends in the S.P.R., he abandoned his partnership with Blackburn and his precarious career as a local seaside entertainer, to become Edmund Gurney's secretary and the trusted operator in the Society's hypnotic experiments with a group of Brighton youths of his acquaintance. Blackburn, seeing which way things were going, evidently became tired of wasting his time and withdrew from the thought-transference experiments and from further contact with the S.P.R. without, however, spoiling things for Smith by revealing his secret until twenty-five years had gone by and he believed Smith to be dead. It is for the reader to decide which of the two alternatives is supported by the facts, always bearing in mind that trickery in a two-person mind reading act is indivisible. If Smith was genuine, so was Blackburn. If one was a hoaxer, so was the other. With the philosophy of the matter before him, the reader's first task is to examine the circumstances which led to the contact between Blackburn and Smith and the S.P.R.

After the final published eulogy of Smith's hypnotic show by Blackburn on 22 July, 1882, a curious period of comparative silence followed. The pages of *The Brightonian* suddenly ceased for a period of six weeks lavishly to praise Smith's entertainment. Whether this period was devoted solely to the "select high class séances" mentioned in *The Brightonian* on 22 July, or whether Smith and Blackburn were busy preparing and practising a code for a second-sight act, is a matter of opinion. However that may be, a very curious coincidence occurred at this time which may not be lacking in significance.

On 26 August, 1882, under the heading "Thought-Reading Extraordinary", a letter signed by Blackburn was published in the spiritualist paper *Light*.[1] The ostensible purpose of this communication was to announce to the spiritualist world that he and

---

[1] *Light* was obviously familiar reading for the S.P.R. leaders. It will be recalled that it was to its pages that Mr. Theobald, the Society's Treasurer, contributed the story of his extraordinary experiences.

Smith had discovered that they possessed powers of thought-transference which were "almost without precedent", and that "a strong concentration of will and mental vision" by Blackburn enabled Smith to read his thoughts "with an accuracy that approaches the miraculous". It was claimed that Smith could "read numbers, words, and even whole sentences" which Blackburn alone had seen. It was carefully pointed out in advance, however, that Smith's powers as a mind reader were evidently limited, in that only if Blackburn was the transmitting agent were good results obtained. Blackburn remarked in his letter to *Light* in regard to Smith's alleged trials with other (unnamed) transmitters that "on no occasion has he attained to anything like the power he invariably displays when *en rapport* with myself". The trap, thus baited, was set in the concluding sentence of the letter:

> "We shall be happy to receive a visit from any Spiritualist or scientific enquirer who may be at Brighton during the ensuing month, especially as we are about to inaugurate a series of private seances, at which this most interesting phase of psychic force may be investigated and developed."

The coincidence to which I have referred, and which to my mind provides the clue to the way in which the affair was planned, is partly contained in the opening sentence of Blackburn's letter:

> "The following details of the latest and most remarkable development of that form of Thought-reading popularized by Mr. Irving Bishop may prove of interest to your readers."

It will be obvious to the reader, who may suspect that Blackburn and Smith were fully aware that Bishop was no more capable of genuine thought-transference than they were, that the mention of the conjurer's name must have been put in for some purpose. An examination of the periodical literature of the time makes it reasonably plain what Blackburn's reason for remarking on Bishop was, and above all why the timing of the letter published in *Light* on 26 August, 1882, was so appropriate.

In the issue of *The Nineteenth Century* of June 1882, only one month before Blackburn suddenly ceased to praise Smith's hypnotic shows, had appeared a long paper by Barrett, Gurney and Myers under the title "Thought-Reading".[1] This article was an un-restrained eulogy of the allegedly paranormal powers of the Creery children in thought-transference tests conducted by the S.P.R. leaders and was probably mainly written by Barrett. However that may be, the joint authors were sufficiently credulous to write (p. 899) that the crudities of the Creerys' parlour con-juring constituted "phenomena" which were "unlike any which had been brought within the sphere of recognized science" and (p. 900) "that the possibility must not be overlooked that further advances along the lines of research here indicated may necessitate a modification of that general view of the relation of mind to matter to which modern science has long been gravitating".

It is reasonable to assume that Blackburn and Smith would be much encouraged by these extravagant profundities. Of equal importance is the fact that in the introductory part of their article the S.P.R. leaders said (p. 892) that the results obtained by the professional mind-readers Bishop and Cumberland seemed "in some cases sufficiently unlike mere 'muscle-reading' to warrant further enquiry". No other explanation seems necessary for Blackburn's description of the alleged powers of Smith and himself in the opening paragraph of his letter to *Light* as "the latest and most remarkable development of that form of Thought-reading popularized by Mr. Irving Bishop". If the S.P.R. wanted to dally with the idea that Bishop might be genuine, then Blackburn and Smith were ready to dally with them.[2] But if what the S.P.R. really believed in without qualification was the parlour second-sight act of the Creery girls, and they actually regarded this per-formance as outside the sphere of recognized science, then Black-burn and Smith were ready to produce something much more startling. Gurney and his friends had only to come to Brighton to be convinced.

The first experiments in Brighton did not commence until nearly the end of the year. In Gurney, Myers and Barrett's "Second

[1] Pp. 890–900. As mentioned in an earlier chapter, the paper was subjected to deadly criticism in the next issue by Horatio Donkin. ("Thought-Reading", *The Nineteenth Century*, July 1882, pp. 131–3).
[2] There is no doubt that this simple device was successful in arousing the pre-liminary interest of W. F. Barrett, who quoted Blackburn's letter in his "Appendix to the Report on Thought-Reading" (S.P.R. *Proceedings*, 1882, i, p. 63), with the comment "The following extract from a letter published in *Light* shows that a Mr. Smith, of Brighton, has powers analogous to those claimed by Mr. Bishop".

Report on Thought-Transference" it was stated that after the publication of the letter in *Light* they entered into correspondence with Blackburn, who "took the trouble to send us a paper recording in detail his experiments with Mr. Smith. These statements appeared to be so carefully made that two of our number, Mr. Myers and Mr. Gurney (Mr. Barrett being unable to go at the time), arranged to pay a visit to Brighton personally to investigate the joint experiments of Mr. Blackburn and Mr. Smith".[1] According-ing to a note in Myers's diary (for which I am indebted to Dr. Alan Gauld), he and Gurney first went to Brighton to meet the hoaxers on 15 November, 1882. The next journey to Brighton was made on Saturday, 2 December, and experiments took place in the lodgings of the S.P.R. leaders on the Sunday and Monday.

Why Myers and Gurney waited until November to meet Smith and Blackburn I do not know. It may be that Barrett, who lived in Dublin and whose time in England would obviously be limited, hoped in the first instance to be one of the party. On the other hand, it is possible that the fact that Smith was a seaside enter-tainer may have caused some initial hesitation on the part of the S.P.R. leaders. The one discouraging feature of their paper, so far as the hoaxers were concerned, in the June issue of *The Nineteenth Century* was the comment (p. 893) that the experience of the authors had warned them against "paid or public exhibitions". However this may be, Blackburn and Smith waited until September 1882 before baiting the trap afresh.

In the issue of *The Brightonian* of 2 September (p. 3) Blackburn wrote that Smith and he had given "a private exhibition of thought-reading" at Smith's residence (his mother's boarding house) in Grand Parade. He said that "the experiments were of the most successful description and were witnessed by several scientific gentlemen interested in psychology". Blackburn added that in the near future Smith would be giving his hypnotic entertainment at the Aquarium and that demonstrations of thought-reading would be shown in addition.[2]

---

[1] S.P.R. *Proceedings*, 1882, i, p. 78.

[2] The idea of adding the second-sight act to the hypnotic show confirms Blackburn's account twenty-six years later. He said (*John Bull*, 5 December, 1908) that Smith, who had "a large amount of the enterprising showman spirit" was anxious to in-corporate thought-reading into his mesmeric entertainment, in which interest was beginning to decline.

On 30 September, 1882, *The Brightonian* announced (p. 8) not only that Smith and Blackburn were giving public demonstrations of thought-reading at the Aquarium, but that their performances had "received the attention of the British Society for Psychical Research, and a paper on the subject is to be read by Professor Barrett at the next meeting of the Society". This would appear to indicate that contact by correspondence had already been achieved with the S.P.R. leaders, and it is noteworthy that the hypothesis here advanced of the motives of Smith and Blackburn is supported by this use of the Society's name as an ingredient in the publicity at the first opportunity offered.[1]

The Brightonian of 7 October, 1882, carried an advertisement on its front page announcing the show at the Aquarium in which demonstrations of mesmerism and thought-reading would be given by Smith and Blackburn. Admission was 1/–d. and 6d. It is noteworthy, perhaps, that in every advertisement and press notice at this time Smith's name was placed first, leaving little room for doubt as to who, despite his age, was now the senior partner in the project.[2] The same issue (p. 11) reported with enthusiasm that the shows were most successful and that the thought-reading had interested everyone who had witnessed it.

On 25 November, 1882, *The Brightonian* announced (p. 9) that Smith had taken (presumably on a short tenancy) St. James's Hall, Grand Parade, Brighton, for mesmeric and thought-reading demonstrations, the prices of admission being similar to those being charged at the Aquarium. Blackburn's name did not appear in the advertisements. After 2 December, moreover (the date of the second visit of the S.P.R. leaders to Brighton), Smith's advertisements of his shows never again mentioned mind-reading as part of the entertainment, although he continued to announce his mesmeric demonstrations until 23 December. After that date Smith's name was never mentioned in *The Brightonian* again. His

[1] Smith and Blackburn had the audacity to suggest that a gentleman attended their show as a representative of Professor Barrett, and took part in the demonstration. This person, over the initials "J. W. C.", wrote to the Editor of the *Brighton Herald* on 21 October, 1882, to say that he was present at the performance without Barrett's knowledge and was in no sense his representative.

[2] This is confirmed by the advertisement in *The Brightonian* of 2 December, 1882, after the show had been moved to St. James's Hall in Grand Parade with nightly performances at prices of 2/–d., 1/–d. and 6d., of "Mr. G. A. Smith's Experiments in Mesmerism and Thought Reading". Blackburn was not mentioned, and his role seems by now to have become a subsidiary one.

career as a seaside entertainer was soon to be over, until he resumed it in 1892. By 5 May, 1883, Blackburn was to record in *The Brightonian* (p. 4) that St. James's Hall "after being closed for some time, has been re-opened by Mr. Fred Foley". Smith's curious powers of attraction over those with whom he came into contact, which he had used to such effect in his shows that Blackburn had remarked on them in print,[1] had brought him the offer of a salaried position as Gurney's secretary and full-time employment by the S.P.R.

As has been said, tests of Smith and Blackburn took place on 3 and 4 December, 1882, at Gurney's lodgings in Brighton. Whether the S.P.R. investigators were accommodated at Smith's mother's boarding house in Grand Parade is not stated. Those present were Gurney, Myers, Blackburn and Smith.[2] The first eleven tests, dealing in colours and numbers, were only partially successful despite the almost entire absence of restricting conditions. To quote the S.P.R. leaders:

> "S[mith] was blindfolded at his own wish to aid in concentration, and during the experiment sat with his back turned to the experimenters. B[lackburn] *holds S's hand, and asks him to name a colour,* [my italics] written down by one of us and shown to B. . . . After a rest *numbers* were then tried in the same way.[3]

When Smith and Blackburn ceased to sit side by side holding hands, the thought-transference mysteriously dried up. Gurney and Myers reported:

> "Several trials of colours and numbers were now made with S. and B. in separate rooms, which failed."

The next four experiments were with names, the subjects holding hands in the same room as had been done earlier, and were

---

[1] Blackburn wrote "Mr. Smith's powers of attraction are remarkable. He draws subjects from the audience *nolens volens* with the greatest ease and we have no doubt could successfully draw anything from a cart-load of bricks to a caricature." (*The Brightonian*, 22 April, 1882, p. 8.)

[2] Gurney, Myers and Barrett, "Second Report on Thought-Transference" (S.P.R *Proceedings*, 1882–3, i, pp. 70–97.

[3] See the earlier discussion (pp. 85 ff.) of Bishop's book on pseudo-second sight sold during his performances in Brighton, and the certainty of the hoaxers' familiarity with it. Chapters IV and XII of *Second Sight Explained* deal respectively with the coding of numbers and colours.

partially successful. The temptation to score 100 per cent was no doubt considerable, but as Blackburn was later to observe:

> "The experiments at first took place at the lodgings of Mr. Gurney at Brighton, and were distinctly elementary. Indeed, in some cases the problems set us were so simple that we purposely bungled them so as not to make ourselves too cheap, just as the astute conjurer will make several failures before succeeding in a trick."[1]

For experiments numbers 16 and 17 two names were attempted without contact (it is not stated whether Smith and Blackburn were in separate rooms) and both failed. After this second lack of success, the S.P.R. leaders evidently realized that the "phenomena" were likely to cease if any conditions were imposed. Incredible though it may seem, Smith and Blackburn were actually urged to hold hands for the remainder of the tests. Gurney and Myers reported:

> "Contact between S. and B. was now resumed by our express desire, as the increased effort of concentration, needed when there was no contact, brought on neuralgia in B.

Name Chosen		Answer
Expt. 18	Queen Anne	Queechy, Queen
„ 19	Wissenschaft	Wissie, Wissenaft

> As B. was ignorant of German he mentally represented the word 'Wissenschaft' in English fashion."[2]

The remainder of the tests, consisting of the transmission of the location of parts of Blackburn's body pinched by the experimenters and of simple diagrams, were all accomplished with the subjects in contact and so require no further detailed discussion. To anyone with the smallest knowledge of elementary conjuring principles the

---

[1] *John Bull*, 12 December, 1908, p. 628.

[2] Chapter VI of *Second Sight Explained* deals with "A Code for Words". Blackburn's attack of neuralgia is not without its humorous aspect. He wrote drily twenty-six years later, "It was sometimes necessary for Smith and me to communicate during an experiment, as, for example, when I wished to convey to him that I was ready to begin, or was temporarily out of action from neuralgia—an ailment that often attacked me very conveniently in the midst of an experiment." (*John Bull*, 2 January, 1909, p. 7.)

simplicity of the whole thing is astonishing, and it seems almost beyond belief that the S.P.R. leaders attached no significance to the fact that the alleged thought-transference completely ceased to function unless the two subjects were in sufficiently close proximity to hold hands. Yet Myers and Gurney said of these Brighton tests:

> "The results of these trials give us the most important and valuable insight into the manner of the mental transfer of a picture which we have yet obtained."[1]

If the reader is of the opinion that the hypothesis advanced earlier in this chapter is correct, and that the purpose of Smith and Blackburn in making contact with the S.P.R. was to obtain material for future advertising of their second-sight act, he may regard the following announcement in *The Brightonian* of 16 December, 1882, as of some interest:

> "At a General Meeting of this Society [S.P.R.] held at Chandos Place, London, on Saturday and presided over by Professor Sidgewick [*sic*], Messrs. F. W. H. Myers and Edmond [*sic*] Gurney presented an interesting report on a series of experiments in thought-reading conducted by them on Mr. G. A. Smith, the Brighton Mesmerist, and Mr. Douglas Blackburn. These experiments, with those reported by another Committee of investigation, were regarded as having satisfactorily established the existence of Thought Reading. The London *Daily News* and the *Echo* have called special attention to the proceedings."

[1] *Proceedings*, S.P.R., 1882–3, i, pp. 78–9.

CHAPTER NINE

THE TELEPATHISTS

A T the close of their report on the Brighton experiments the
S.P.R. leaders added a postscript to say that since their
account had been prepared further tests had taken place, and that
"striking and successful results were obtained under conditions still
more stringent than those previously imposed". The critic might
think that they could hardly be less. The authors claimed that no
contact whatever between Blackburn and Smith was found to be
necessary in these improved experiments, and that a full report
would appear in the next issue of the Society's *Proceedings*. Their
account ended with a challenge. "The burden of explaining these
results rests upon those who deny the possibility of thought-
transference."[1]

The promised account was the "Third Report on Thought-
Transference",[2] which was prepared on 24 April, 1883. It described two series of experiments with Smith and Blackburn which
took place at the Society's rooms at 14 Dean's Yard, Westminster.
The tests began on 19 January, 1883, and "were continued for
three or four days in succession". The second series of experiments
took place "in April" on dates which, surprisingly enough, were
not given.

This curious lack of precision in regard to the dating of the
second set of experiments is not the only point upon which the
"Third Report on Thought-Transference" is open to criticism.
The account did not even give the names of the persons who were
present during the experiments. These deficiencies are, however,
insignificant compared with the discovery, from an independent
published source, that impartial scientific critics were present by
invitation on at least one occasion during these experiments and
gave it as their opinion that what they had witnessed was "patent

---

[1] *Proceedings*, S.P.R., 1882–3, i, p. 82.
[2] E. Gurney, F. W. H. Myers, F. Podmore and W. F. Barrett, *ibid.*, pp. 161–215.

imposture". No mention whatever of this incident was made in the "Third Report on Thought-Transference".

Worse still, the S.P.R. account entirely concealed from the reader a fact of crucial significance in regard to the claim that Smith and Blackburn were working without contact. During the experiments when Smith was sitting blindfolded at the table with Blackburn standing behind him at a distance of two feet gazing at the back of his head, a lady friend of the two subjects was sitting on the other side of the table, facing both Smith and Blackburn, in what might be thought was an ideal situation to relay coded information. No mention whatsoever of the presence of this person occurs in the report at all.[1] These deceptions become quite incredible when it is considered that the authors included these words in their report:

> "It is almost needless to point out that in these observations, so foreign to our common experience, it is indispensable to be minutely careful and conscientious in recording the exact conditions of each experiment. This we have striven to be; and the reader will thus be enabled to form an independent judgment by making allowance for whatever mental bias he may discover in our conclusions. He has thus, moreover, the means afforded him of detecting possible errors, or of suggesting precautions which we may have overlooked."[2]

Knowing what he does of Gurney's character from earlier chapters, I think it probable that the reader will share my convinced opinion that he could not conceivably have taken any part in the writing of this evasive and deficient report. We know that he was completely honest, and only too willing (unlike his colleagues) to admit grievous mistakes in order to present the truth of the matter in question. Can we really believe, against the

[1] The reader may regard it as significant that when Miss Alice Johnson, later the Secretary of the Society, prepared a privately printed pamphlet, *Mr. Blackburn's Confession*, in 1909, claiming that the experiments proved telepathy and that Blackburn's published statement that they were conjuring was false, she omitted all reference to these highly relevant matters. Dr. R. H. Thouless, a Past-President of the Society and a member of its Council, did the same thing in his *Experimental Psychical Research* (London, 1963), which I had occasion to review in *The Yorkshire Post* of 29 November, 1963.
[2] *Op. cit.*, p. 162.

background of all that we know of Gurney's work, that he would knowingly put his name to an account of this kind which lacked dates, names and such vital information as that described?

A point in this connexion which the reader will later have to consider in more detail is that there are two pieces of evidence which may lead him to believe that Gurney actually caught Smith and Blackburn in trickery during the experiments, and forgave the youthful Smith for the part he played in the deception. We do not know all the facts, but we can perhaps imagine Gurney being reluctant actually to expose Smith in a published report, in view of his youth and charming persuasiveness, his probable claim that he had been influenced by Blackburn, and his willingness to be of service to the Society and to Gurney in the hypnotic experiments which the latter regarded as of outstanding importance. All this would fit into the pattern of Gurney's decision to omit the Smith–Blackburn experiments from the relevant section of *Phantasms of the Living* in which he sought to prove the existence of experimental thought-transference. What would, however, be at complete variance with such a sequence of events would be the positive writing of a report by Gurney in glowing terms on the dubious and highly suspicious experiments at Dean's Yard.

The fact that Gurney's name appeared with those of Podmore, Myers and Barrett at the head of the report has no significance in itself, for the account was ostensibly prepared by the "Committee on Thought-Transference", of which Gurney was of course a member. Most of the early reports in the S.P.R. literature were the responsibility of one committee or another. What may, however, be of considerable significance is the fact that when the Dean's Yard report was published, the name of Frank Podmore appeared for the first time as a fourth and additional member of the "Committee on Thought Transference", and an ostensible part author. There must have been some reason for this. Unlike Barrett and Myers, Podmore conveniently lived in London, and it seems probable that he was recruited to the Committee for the specific purpose of actively assisting in the preparation of the third report, the initial one to bear his name. If this was necessary, we can readily imagine the reason. Gurney, to the consternation of his colleagues, had entered one of his depressive phases and was quite incapable of any literary work at all at the relevant time.

I find some support for this suggestion in the fact that when Podmore took part in later years in the defence of the report against formidable criticism, he demonstrated a similar evasiveness and willingness to conceal evidence to that shown in the body of the account itself. As the reader now knows, a critic drew attention in print, among other matters, to the presence of a young lady confederate at Dean's Yard, whom he mistakenly thought to be Mrs. Blackburn. Podmore simply said that as Blackburn was not married, his wife could not have been present during the experiments. He neither admitted nor denied that a lady had been there, and that the report had completely concealed the fact of her presence, which was the whole point at issue.

Whether Podmore had any secret personal motive in avoiding giving offence to Smith and Blackburn in 1883 is a matter for the opinion of the reader when he has read Appendix I. Whatever Podmore's relations with the Brighton youths may or may not have been (and I am frank to say that I regard the evidence in this connexion as mainly circumstantial) I am of the opinion that there could have been a simpler explanation for his possible willingness to write a deliberately uncritical report at this time.

He was young (Podmore was twenty-seven in 1883) and was keenly ambitious to make progress in the Society. This ambition was soon to be realized, for by 1884 he was working with enthusiasm on the collection of ghost stories for the projected *Phantasms of the Living*. He would be fully aware of the policies and beliefs of leaders of the Society like Barrett and Myers, whom he may have been anxious to please. It may of course be urged that Podmore later emerged as a highly critical psychical researcher who almost, but not quite, denied the existence of any genuine phenomena of any kind, but I fancy that there are two answers to that. In the first place, there is no reason to suppose that as early as 1883 Podmore had entirely abandoned his earlier faith in spiritualism, which no doubt was an ingredient in his reason for joining the S.P.R. in the first place. Like many sceptics, he had originally been a believer. Two years before he was elected to the Council of the Society for Psychical Research, for example, he had joined the Council of the National Association of Spiritualists. It is of great interest in this connexion to compare Podmore's first view of the Worksop poltergeist case, which he investigated in

1883, with his revised opinion in 1896.[1] Secondly, it is fair to point out that Podmore's extreme scepticism in his more mature years was in any event almost wholly directed at alleged physical phenomena, all of which he regarded as fraudulent or capable of normal explanation. His belief in telepathy does not seem to have wavered thoughout his life. Indeed, in *The Independent Review* of June 1904, he described the trials of thought-transference by Professor and Mrs. Sidgwick and G. A. Smith after Gurney's death as "the classic experiments in telepathy", although the reader may have doubts whether this accolade was fully justified.

With my opinion of the possible authorship of the "Third Report on Thought-Transference" before him, the task of the reader is to consider the criticisms, and the defence offered by the S.P.R. leaders, in regard to the alleged supernormal transmission of drawings from Blackburn to Smith in January and April 1883. The report stated:

"The Percipient, Mr. Smith, is seated blindfolded at a table in our own room; a paper and pencil are within his reach, and a member of the Committee is seated by his side. Another member of the Committee leaves the room, and outside the closed door draws some figure at random. Mr. Blackburn, who, so far, has remained in the room with Mr. Smith, is now called out, and the door closed; the drawing is then held before him for a few seconds, till its impression is stamped upon his mind. Then, closing his eyes, Mr. Blackburn is led back into the room and placed standing or sitting behind Mr. Smith, at a distance of some two feet from him. A brief period of intense mental concentration on Mr. Blackburn's part now follows. Presently, Mr. Smith takes up the pencil amidst the unbroken and absolute silence of all present, and attempts to reproduce on paper the impression he has gained. He is allowed to do as he pleases as regards the bandage round his eyes; sometimes he pulls it down before he begins to draw, but if the figure be not distinctly present to his mind, he prefers to let it remain on, and draws

---

[1] Podmore said (*Proceedings*, S.P.R., 1896, xii, p. 57), "If my verdict on the Worksop disturbances in 1896 differs from that which I gave in 1883, it is because many things have happened since, which have taught us to discount testimony in matters of this kind".

fragments of the figure as they are perceived. During all this time, Mr. Blackburn's eyes are, generally, firmly closed (sometimes he requests us to bandage his eyes tightly as an aid to concentration), and except when it is distinctly recorded, he has not touched Mr. Smith and has not gone in front of him, or in any way within his possible field of vision, since he re-entered the room.

When Mr. Smith has drawn what he can, the original drawing, which has so far remained outside the room, is brought in, and compared with the reproduction. Both are marked by the Committee and put away in a secure place. The drawings and reproductions, given at the end of the Report, are in every case fac-similes of the untouched originals, from which they have been photographed on the wood blocks."[1]

In *The Westminster Gazette* of 26 November, 1907, Dr. H. B. Donkin wrote that there were two occasions during the winter of 1882–3 when outside critics were invited by the S.P.R. leaders to witness the experiments with Smith and Blackburn at Dean's Yard. Dr. Donkin added:

"On one occasion the tests, applied to prevent possible *auditory* communication, put a stop to the phenomena; on the other, similar prevention of *visual* communication had a like effect. In the published Proceedings of the society, which were sent to me for review some few years afterwards by the editor of a well-known weekly, no mention was made in the reports of these meetings of the presence of the critics or of the consequent cessation of the phenomena. I declined to review the Proceedings, on the sole ground of one of the prominent members of the society, now long ago deceased, being an intimate friend of my own. I was aware of the dates of these meetings at the time, for my own name had been suggested, as of one who might be invited as a critic, but was rejected, I believe, on the ground of my having had some controversy on these matters with some of the Psychical Researchers in the *Nineteenth Century* and elsewhere in 1882 and previously. I was well acquainted with both of the gentle-

[1] *Op. cit.*, pp. 162–3.

men mentioned, who were invited as critics, and who personally gave me the details to which I have referred. I urge that the omission of these details from the Proceedings gives rise to more than suspicion of the fallaciousness of the experiments in 'telepathy' carried on by the society, and of the candour of those who were responsible for the publication of those Proceedings."

Mrs. E. M. Sidgwick, the honorary secretary of the Society in 1907, replied to this surprising disclosure in *The Westminster Gazette* of 29 November, saying:

"He complains that certain experiments in telepathy carried on under the auspices of the society failed on two occasions witnessed by two friends of his under conditions suggested by them; and that this fact was suppressed. As the friends are unnamed, the date remote and uncertain, and the agent and percipient concerned, as well as the persons conducting the experiment, also unnamed, I am, of course, unable to identify the experiments in question."

Mrs. Sidgwick's curious lack of knowledge of the dates of experiments recorded in the *Proceedings* of her own Society was taken up by Dr. Donkin in the issue of *The Westminster Gazette* of 18 December, 1907:

"The *experiments* which I alleged were successful until tests were applied by outside critics invited *ad hoc* by the Psychical Research Society, were those relied on as the chief experimental evidence for 'Telepathy as a fact in Nature'. The series of experiments to which I referred took place in the months of December 1882 and January and April 1883. On two occasions, within the times specified, there were present, respectively, Sir James Crichton-Browne and the late Dr. A. Hughes Bennett. The names of the persons experimented on were Smith and Blackburn. The names of those who conducted the experiments until the outside critics excluded by their tests all ordinary channels of communication between Smith and Blackburn, and thus arrested the 'manifestations', could be ascertained by reference to the 'Proceedings', though no mention of the presence of the outside critics

would be found there. There is no 'fallacy, obvious' or concealed, in my inferences that adequate tests had not been
previously applied by the society's members, and that the
omission of all notice of the crucial experiments above mentioned gravely discredits the value of the society's methods
at that time."

The reader may think that the S.P.R. would have been wiser to
refrain from comment upon Dr. Donkin's criticism, for his second
letter precipitated confirmation of what had occurred from Sir
James Crichton-Browne, F.R.S., in *The Westminster Gazette* of 29
January, 1908. As an independent account of the tests it could
scarcely be of greater interest.

"It is an old story, and I have to trust entirely to memory
in recalling it; for no notes were taken, and, indeed, I believe
it was stipulated that the invited guests were not to make
notes, and were to publish no account of the conference until
the official record had appeared. I jot down what I remember
definitely, and omit much about which I am vague and
uncertain.

I was invited to join the conference by George Romanes,
who told me that he had been asked by some members of the
Psychical Research Society to bring together a few friends
interested in such matters to witness a remarkable manifestation of thought-reading by a youth who could without contact
receive and reproduce, not words but figures, diagrams, or
pictures, present to the mind of an operator with whom he
was in some way *en rapport*.

I cannot recall the date of the conference, I am not even
certain about the month or year in which it took place; but I
believe it was in 1882 or 1883. I am sure, however, that it
was held in some rooms—first floor, I believe; a large front
room and a smaller back one—in Dean's-yard, Westminster;
the rooms, I was told, of Dr. Stone.

There must have been present at the conference some
twenty persons. I cannot recall the names of all of them, and
some of them, indeed, I did not know; but the following I am
sure were there:

1. Mr. Henry Sidgwick.   5. Dr. W. Stone.
2. Mr. Frederic Myers.   6. Mr. George Romanes.
3. Mr. Edmund Gurney.   7. Dr. Francis Galton.
4. Dr. G. Wyld.   8. Myself.

The performers, if I may without disrespect use the term, were in the room when I arrived. They consisted of Mr. B. and Mr. S., a young man who had, we were informed, been a professional mesmerist. With them was a lady, the wife of Mr. B.

I believe it was Mr. Henry Sidgwick who, in a few introductory words, indicated the phenomena we were to witness. Mr. B., he said, had discovered that he had the power, by a strong exercise of the will, of transmitting to the mind of Mr. S. any visual image that might be vividly present to his own mind. The peculiarity of the case was that he could not, so far, transmit words or letters, but merely figures or pictures. He had been experimenting with Mr. S. for some time. At first contact was necessary for the communication of the impression, and Mr. B. used to hold Mr. S.'s hand or place his hand on his head; but now no personal contact, which made possible conscious or unconscious signalling, was necessary. There was aerial conduction.

Mr. B. corroborated Mr. Sidgwick's statement, and invited us to put him to the test.

Mr. S. was blindfolded in the usual way, a white handkerchief being drawn over the bridge of his nose and eyes and tied behind his head; and was seated at a table in the middle of the room, facing the windows and with his back to the door leading into the back room, with a pencil in his hand and a large sheet of white paper on the table before him. Facing Mr. S. on the other side of the table was Mrs. B.

A committee was then nominated to prepare and conduct the experiments. The composition of the committee I cannot remember, but I am certain that Romanes and Galton and I and Sidgwick and Myers were on it. We retired into the back room, and there, with closed doors, Romanes, being requested to draw a diagram or figure, made on a sheet of paper a rough sketch of an owl. Mr. B. was then called in, and, again with closed doors, the sheet of paper was handed to him. He held it up before him in a strong light and gazed at it intently for about two minutes, and then, intimating that he was ready, we accompanied him into the front room, the sheet of paper being left lying on the table of the back room.

Mr. B. stood behind Mr. S. at the distance of about a couple of yards, and gazed at the back of his head. I remember distinctly that he had his hands in his trousers pockets and that he contracted his brows from time to time and made faces. This went on for, I suppose, about five minutes, and then Mr. S. drew on the paper before him a crude and clumsy outline of an owl. It was very different from Romanes' sketch, but it was undoubtedly suggestive of an owl.[1]

Some other simple experiment, I believe, followed on the same lines, and with the same approximate result; and then it occurred to me and to Romanes that some kind of code might be in use, and we proceeded to draw a figure without a name, a sort of nondescript arabesque, simple enough, but not easily describable in words. When Mr. B. was brought in to the back room and this drawing was placed in his hand, I noticed, or thought I noticed, that his face fell. He gazed at it in the usual way for a little, and then said, 'This is rather complicated; I have a difficulty in fixing it in my mind'. 'Oh, no!' we replied. 'We can look at it, turn away, and reproduce it without difficulty.' So Mr. B. was constrained to go on. He stood behind Mr. S., as before, a few minutes, and I believe that this time he made some passes in the air with his hands. Ultimately Mr. S. drew a few lines on the paper, but there was not the slightest approach to the figure drawn.

Still further to test the code theory, it seemed desirable to give a little rope; so the next diagram drawn was the shield from the signet-ring, which Dr. Galton was wearing on his finger. After the usual procedure, Mr. S. drew the outline of a shield; but—and this is significant—the shield on Dr. Galton's ring was oval and the one reproduced was triangular;

---

[1] Sir James's memory was, it seems, more acute than that of Mrs. Sidgwick, who could not remember the experiments at all. The drawings of the owl are to be found on p. 207 of S.P.R. *Proceedings*, 1882–3, i.

it may have been vice versa; but of this I am sure—that Mr. S.'s drawing did not correspond in shape with the diagram which Mr. B. was supposed to have imprinted on his mind.

By this time I was quite satisfied that Mr. S. was not effectually blindfolded, and that it was practicable for Mr. B. to communicate with him both by sight and hearing; so Romanes and I asked permission, which was granted, to blindfold him anew. We proceeded to do so *secundum artem*. Cotton-wool was procured, the sockets were packed, the ears were plugged, and a large handkerchief made all secure. After that several experiments were tried as before, but there never was the smallest response on the part of Mr. S. to Mr. B.'s volitional endeavours. There was no more flashing of images into his mind. His pencil was idle. Thought-transference was somehow interrupted.

Now, I can only give the impression on my mind; and I know it was the impression on the minds of Romanes and Galton. It is an impression, and must be taken for what it is worth; and it was that the Morse alphabet was in use. I did not detect any coding, but all the circumstances were highly suggestive of it. It seemed possible that a word might be winked to the lady opposite S., who winked it on to him, who was at first not really blindfolded; or that it might be clicked out on coins in the pockets of Mr. B., or even conveyed by the shadows of passes. The moment that Mr. S.'s senses were thoroughly occluded all transference stopped.

I was invited to be critical and sceptical, and I was so. I dare say more credulously inclined people will think that my suspicions were unjust and that no trick was practised—that was clearly the feeling of some of the Psychical Researchers present.

The last scene of all, or passage-at-arms, I vividly recollect. Mr. Myers, standing in front of the fireplace, said: 'It must be allowed that this demonstration has been a total failure, and I attribute that to the offensive incredulity of Dr. Crichton-Browne.' To which I rejoined: 'I hope I always will show offensive incredulity when I find myself in the presence of patent imposture.'

I understood that minutes of that conference were taken,

and were to be submitted to all who took part in it for correction; but from that day to this I have never heard a word about it. All the drawings and diagrams used in the experiments were signed by all the members of the committee and left at Dean's-yard. Perhaps they are still in existence.

I have no doubt Dr. Francis Galton will be able to confirm or amend my recollections."

This independent account of what went on in the S.P.R. rooms in Dean's Yard eighty years ago, and especially the attitude of the angry Myers, as recalled by Sir James Crichton-Browne, is of great interest. It would almost seem that whilst the S.P.R. leaders liked to be able to describe their experiments as having been held under test conditions, their anxious desire to prove the existence of telepathy at all costs caused them to object strongly to conditions that were sufficiently fraud-proof to stop the "phenomena" occurring. In this connexion it will be recalled that in the Brighton tests, when it seems certain that no confederate was employed, Smith and Blackburn were actually urged by the experimenters to hold hands once more when it was found that separating the two subjects brought on Blackburn's neuralgia and caused the "thought-transference" to cease. In Dean's Yard hands were not held and Smith had his back to Blackburn, but their lady friend was evidently allowed to sit in a position facing both of them, one method of normal communication thus being replaced by another, a fact of which the reader with access only to the report in S.P.R. *Proceedings* would be completely unaware.

It may be desirable at this point briefly to discuss the matter of the blindfolding of Smith. Both the accounts of the S.P.R. leaders and of Sir James Crichton-Browne made it clear, of course, that it was merely a handkerchief or bandage passing over the bridge of Smith's nose and that it was, in the opinion of the impartial critics, a quite inadequate safeguard. The S.P.R. report, moreover, stated that Smith was actually allowed to remove the blindfold before attempting to reproduce the diagram if he so wished.

These considerations apart, it is important to point out that the student of elementary conjuring procedure knows that it is virtually impossible to prevent a person using his eyes by a simple blindfold. "Sightless vision", as professional magicians term it, is a traditional conjuring feat. It forms no part of my responsibility as a Vice-President of the Magic Circle to broadcast the secrets of conjuring, and it will perhaps be sufficient if I quote an extreme example of what can be accomplished by entirely natural means. On 10 July, 1935, Kuda Bux, a professional conjurer who styled himself "the man with the X-ray eyes", before an audience consisting of Professor William McDougall, Dr. C. E. M. Joad, Dr. S. G. Soal and Harry Price, is said to have been blindfolded by the following elaborate procedure. Lumps of dough were squeezed into each eye socket and over the dough were placed pads of cotton-wool. Over the wool were placed strips of adhesive tape, crossing from the supercillary arch to the cheek bone. Round the head and upper part of the face of Kuda Bux was wound a surgical bandage. Over all this was placed a black mask composed of two thicknesses of heavy black cloth, between which was sandwiched a layer of cotton-wool. I may mention that Kuda Bux's nostrils and mouth were free. In these conditions the conjurer read quickly and easily chosen paragraphs from books picked at random whilst messages written on pieces of paper and placed before him were read at once. He was able immediately and infallibly to duplicate shorthand outlines drawn on a blackboard.[1]

It may be urged that the published recollections of the impartial observers at Dean's Yard, based on unaided memory after an interval of twenty-four years, should be ignored. I fancy that such a defence would only carry weight if too much importance is attached to details. It would, I think, be reckless to suggest that the accounts published in *The Westminster Gazette* were pure invention, and that Sir James Crichton-Browne and his friends did not attend some of the experiments. It should be recalled, too, in this connexion, that in defending their position the S.P.R. leaders made no attempt to say this. If this is accepted, then the principal criticism that the S.P.R. report concealed the entire incident, whilst at the same time claiming that pains were being taken to give the reader the minutest details of the experiments, is clearly valid and extremely damaging.

I do not think, moreover, that Sir James Crichton-Browne's memory could possibly have been at fault in recalling the con-

[1] H. Price, *Confessions of a Ghost Hunter* (London, 1936), pp. 314–17.

trasting presence of one woman at Dean's Yard in an otherwise exclusively male gathering. This, again, was not denied by the S.P.R. leaders when Sir James's statement was published. Capital was merely made, the reader may think, from the fact that Sir James was mistaken in assuming that the lady was Blackburn's wife. Podmore's answer, in *The Westminster Gazette* of 3 February, 1908, was limited to a single evasive sentence. "Mr. B., at the time in question, was not married, so that his wife could not, as stated by Sir James, have been present at the experiments." Podmore did not deny that there was a lady there. At this stage it would be premature to present the argument in regard to her identity, but I may say now that her shadowy presence dominated more significant aspects of this Victorian drama than the trickery at Dean's Yard.

The last mention of Blackburn in S.P.R. *Proceedings* occurs on the penultimate page of the "Third Report on Thought-Transference" (p. 166) in the description of the final phase of the second series of tests at Dean's Yard in April 1883. The experimenters had prepared a drawing of an arrow on a sheet of paper, and Blackburn had to transmit to Smith in which of the four possible simple directions (up, down, left or right) the arrow was pointing. Forty-two tests were made and according to the S.P.R. report, Smith guessed correctly twenty-seven times.

The report says "After the 37th trial, Mr. Blackburn was obliged to leave", and so far as I am aware, this was the end of his connexion with the S.P.R. The available evidence points to Blackburn having become increasingly unenthusiastic about the experiments for a reason which now seems fairly obvious, and to a decision on his part to disengage himself in April 1883. The S.P.R. leaders, indeed, in the introduction to their report, provided some confirmation of this:

> "At the invitation of the Committee, Mr. Blackburn and Mr. Smith came from Brighton in January last, and met us at the rooms of the Society in Dean's Yard, where all the experiments about to be described were conducted. As Mr. Blackburn came only in answer to the urgent request of the Committee, and at considerable inconvenience to himself, we feel it our duty to mention this fact, and, at the same time,

to express our hearty obligations to him for the unrecompensed trouble which we have so frequently imposed upon him."[1]

The flavour of these remarks, coupled with the fact that Blackburn excused himself from the last five tests[2] (possibly to catch his train to Brighton) makes it reasonably clear that according to the S.P.R. account Blackburn received no payment for his services, that towards the end he was a reluctant participant in the experiment and only came to Dean's Yard for the second series of trials at "the urgent request" of the S.P.R. leaders, and that it was he who severed his relationship with the Society. It is of great interest to read Miss Alice Johnson's later contrasting story of the cessation of Blackburn's contact with the S.P.R. in her privately printed pamphlet:

> "I was already aware that, for reasons unconnected with the experiments, but which Mr. Myers and Mr. Gurney considered sufficient, they had made no more experiments with Mr. Blackburn after the series published in *Proceedings*, Vol. I."[3]

It will be seen that the S.P.R. report at the material time does not offer any evidence for this insinuation.

Why did Blackburn withdraw in April 1883? If the hypothesis here advanced is right, that the original object of the planned entanglement with the S.P.R. was to ensure the continued success of the professional second-sight act of Smith and Blackburn by

---

[1] *Proceedings*, S.P.R., 1882–3, i, pp. 161–2. On p. 163 it was added that the second series of Smith–Blackburn tests at Dean's Yard was made "in April".

[2] The S.P.R. report (p. 166) stated that after Blackburn left "we continued the experiments, one or two of the Committee taking Mr. Blackburn's place, and with fair success". In fact, in the last five trials with Blackburn as the transmitter, Smith scored correctly four times out of five. During the last five tests without Blackburn, the "fair success" amounted to one correct guess in five (which is in fact slightly below probability), according to my copy of S.P.R. *Proceedings*, in which Smith is shown to have failed in experiments 38 to 41 inclusive, and succeeded in No. 42 only. Inexplicably, in the similar volume of *Proceedings* in the Leeds Library, he is shown as having succeeded in both Nos. 41 and 42, giving a result slightly *above* probability. Why two variants of Part III of *Proceedings* should exist showing different results of the same experiment is a matter for conjecture, against the background of the obliteration of the Hornby story in Volume 2 of *Proceedings*. The details of this very odd business are discussed in Appendix II.

[3] Alice Johnson, *Mr. Blackburn's Confession*, privately printed, London, 1909, p. 3. Miss Johnson was the secretary of the S.P.R. in 1909.

material for future advertisements, the sequence of events becomes immediately comprehensible. The date of the "Third Report on Thought-Transference" was 24 April, 1883. The same date was appended to the "First Report of the Committee on Mesmerism".[1] It was in this second report that it was recorded that mesmeric phenomena "were observed, for the most part, in a willing and intelligent young man of 20, Fred Wells by name—the son of a baker in Brighton. Other youths have also been tried, and some are now under experiment. The operator in every case has been Mr. G. A. Smith of Dulwich, S.E., and lately of Brighton."[2] This makes it clear that by 24 April, 1883, Smith had left his mother's boarding house in Brighton, had moved to London and was already acting as the S.P.R. hypnotist. His decision to throw in his lot with the S.P.R. leaders had been taken and there were to be no more second-sight performances at the Aquarium or St. James's Hall. As the reader knows, on 5 May, 1883, Blackburn reported that the latter building which had been taken by Smith for his entertainments in November 1882, had been re-opened by Mr. Fred Foley "after being closed for some time".

It seems probable that it was also in April 1883 that Smith, the former seaside entertainer, became the paid private secretary of Edmund Gurney.[3] F. W. H. Myers, in his obituary of Gurney, said that when Gurney was assembling the material for *Phantasms of the Living*, "Mr. G. A. Smith's competent help as secretary was of essential service".[4] Smith himself, on the occasion of his marriage in 1888, described himself as a private secretary, and in a later published interview, moreover, said that he had been secretary in turn to both Gurney and Myers.[5] By the time of his marriage Smith had moved to 54 Beauchamp Place, S.W.3,[6] across the Brompton Road and virtually within a stone's throw from Gurney's house in Montpelier Square.

[1] W. F. Barrett, E. Gurney, F. W. H. Myers, H. N. Ridley, W. H. Stone, G. Wyld and F. Podmore, *Proceedings*, S.P.R., 1882–3, i, pp. 217–29.
[2] *Ibid.*, p. 221.
[3] Mrs. E. M. Sidgwick wrote of Smith's appointment with the S.P.R., "He took part not only in experiments, but in inquiries, investigations, and clerical work, and acted for some considerable time as Mr. Gurney's valued private secretary and assistant." *Journal*, S.P.R., October 1911, p. 130.
[4] *Proceedings*, S.P.R., 1888–9, v, p. 371.
[5] *Daily News*, 4 September, 1911.
[6] This was described in the directories of the period as a lodging house run by Mr. Thomas Williams.

One would have thought that a less suitable person as a secretary, as regards both background and training, then the youthful Smith could scarcely have been selected. It is, however, probable that it was Smith's alleged abilities as a hypnotist that were attractive to Gurney, and there is no doubt that Smith's services in this connexion were extensively used by Gurney between 1883 and 1888. The reader will have observed that according to the report of 24 April, 1883, Smith was already acting as the hypnotizer in experiments with Fred Wells of Brighton as the subject, together with other youths. Whether Smith's salary was paid from the Society's funds or by Gurney personally I do not know, nor do the Society's published accounts throw any light on the matter. Gurney was a fairly wealthy man and it would probably have been within his means to pay Smith a modest salary.

One solution of the problem posed by the ending of the Blackburn–Smith experiments in thought-transference in the normal state (as opposed to the hypnotic) is that trickery was detected by Gurney at Dean's Yard, although no mention of this possibility appears anywhere in the published literature. It is, however, supported by the very curious fact that no reference whatever to these trials was made by the authors of *Phantasms of the Living* in the section of the book claiming that experimental proof of telepathy was established. The oddity of this omission is increased by the fact that the transmission of pictures and diagrams by Blackburn to Smith was ostensibly much more impressive than the guessing of cards and names by the Creery sisters, upon whose "phenomena" the authors chose to rely. The S.P.R. leaders, indeed, claimed as much in their reports in *Proceedings*. On the other hand, one is faced by the indisputable fact that trickery in a "second-sight act" is indivisible, and that if coding was detected then Smith, who was thenceforth to be employed by the S.P.R. for nine years, had been discovered to be just as much a fraud as Blackburn.

The point is one of some importance in an understanding of the relationship between Smith and Gurney, and I fancy that the answer may well be contained in a letter from Sir Oliver Lodge to Mr. J. G. Piddington, both of whom occupied the Presidential chair of the S.P.R. When Blackburn published a statement in 1908, which he repeated in 1911, that all the experiments had relied on trickery, Piddington evidently invited Lodge's view as to whether the later hypnotic work with the boys in Brighton was also made worthless. Lodge said on 5 December, 1908, that his recollection was that "the 'code' or deception practised by Smith and Blackburn" had been detected by Gurney. Lodge recalled a ludicrous incident when Blackburn had evidently failed clearly to indicate to Smith that what had been a series of tests with numbers had ceased, and that pictures were instead being "transmitted". A picture of a cat was divined by Smith as "3120", and the experimenters noticed the damning fact that the third, first and twentieth letters of the alphabet are "C", "A" and "T".

Lodge's memory can hardly be supposed to have been at fault in regard to the occurrence of such an incident, and his comment upon the problem of Smith's subsequent work as a hypnotic operator is enlightening.

"I suppose the question in your mind is whether these also [the later experiments with the Brighton boys] are rendered valueless. I do not see how some of them could be, because they depended upon nothing but getting the boys hypnotized, and Smith could do that however fraudulent he might be."

My own view is that Gurney forgave Smith for his part in the deception in the face of Smith's persuasive charm and youth, and that he accepted Smith's probable assurance that he had been led unsuspectingly into what he first thought was a harmless trick by the older Blackburn. Smith may well have insisted that but for this single slip he had never deceived anyone in his life and would never do so again. In this connexion it is important to remember that Gurney's view of his fellow-men was an intensely sympathetic one, and that he was violently interested in hypnotism and urgently needed Smith's services, being unable himself to hypnotize. It is also fair to point out that if the other S.P.R. leaders knew of Gurney's discovery at the time (and Gurney may even have agreed not to discuss the matter with his friends in exchange for Smith's guarantee of future integrity)[1] they would not be in a strong position to object to any course Gurney had decided to

[1] This possibility would seem to be supported by the fact that as late as December 1896 Henry Sidgwick was still referring to the Smith–Blackburn experiments as genuine. (*Proceedings*, S.P.R., 1896, xii, p. 311.)

follow. He was the unpaid secretary and Editor and the indispensable mainspring of the Society.

I am of the opinion that obviously both Smith and Blackburn were equally guilty of deception, and in this connexion I think it is of some interest to record a comment made by Sir James Crichton-Browne in his book. He followed quite closely his earlier account from *The Westminster Gazette,* but added the following impression, in which it will be noted that no differentiation was made between Blackburn and Smith:

> "I tried to keep an open and an even mind, but I admit that at the first glance I was not prepossessed in favour of the performers. They did not seem to me to be the sort of persons from whom we might expect scientific accuracy or any new revelation."[1]

It follows from what I have said that I believe that when Blackburn said in later years that the experiments had depended upon trickery he was speaking the truth, although I believe that he was inaccurate in many of the details. He was an author and a journalist, and he may well have tried to increase the dramatic effect of his article by describing incidents which were partly apocryphal, or attempted to fill in details which he had forgotten. I have no brief at all for Blackburn, who in his youth was a deceiver and an adulterer. But he wrote much in later life that is of great interest, as the reader will see later, and which can be confirmed from other sources. My belief that what Blackburn wrote in 1908 was true in essence seems to me to be strongly supported by his writings in *The Brightonian* before he came into contact with either Smith or the S.P.R., when his keen interest in conjuring and the entertainment world, his knowledge of all forms of pseudo-thought-reading and his complete scepticism as regards telepathy and the claims of spiritualists were amply demonstrated.

Equally, I am of the opinion that Smith was deliberately lying when he claimed, after the death of both Gurney and Myers, in the face of Blackburn's published statement, that he and Blackburn had been genuine telepathists and that no trickery had taken place. In this connexion I think it helpful to refer to the published

---

[1] Sir James Crichton-Browne, M.D., LL.D., F.R.S., *The Doctor's Second Thoughts* (London, 1931), p. 60.

comment made by Dr. Ivor Tuckett in his *Evidence for the Super-natural* (London, 1911, p. 397), because this expresses the view of a contemporary writer who was not a member of the Society for Psychical Research. It is also of great interest that Dr. Tuckett brought out the significant points that Smith had profited financially from his connexion with the S.P.R. (whilst Blackburn had not) and had therefore a strong reason for denying the assertions of Blackburn, that the later Sidgwick experiments entirely depended upon his *bona fides* (as of course did all the early work with Gurney) and, putting the matter at its best, that either Smith or Blackburn was clearly a liar.

"This assertion[1] was flatly contradicted by Mr. Smith three days later; but, whether Mr. Blackburn's statement was true or false, Mr. Smith had a very strong motive for denial, as he had acted as secretary to both Mr. Gurney and Mr. Myers. At any rate, Mr. Blackburn, while apologising for having put Mr. Smith (whom he thought was dead[2]) into such an awkward position, adhered to his story, and amplified it with details as to how certain tricks, including the one when Mr. Smith's head was enveloped in a blanket, were carried out (*The Daily News*, September 5th, 1911). To these statements also Mr. Smith gave a categorical denial (*The Daily News*, September 6th, 1911).

Now, the important point about this controversy is that there can be no doubt that either Mr. Blackburn's or Mr. Smith's regard for truth is not of the strongest. And as both were employed in these experiments, this fact alone vitiates to some extent their value. Also Mr. Smith does not deny that he had been engaged with Mr. Blackburn as his partner in giving thought-transference exhibitions, the description of which in *Light* (August 26th, 1882) led—after some corre-

[1] Dr. Tuckett was referring to Blackburn's article "Confessions of a 'Telepathist'. Mr. Douglas Blackburn & the Scientists. 30-Year Hoax Exposed. How the Deception was Planned and Worked", which appeared in the *Daily News* of 1 September, 1911. It was an epitome of a series of articles in *John Bull* some three years earlier.

[2] This seems entirely possible for a reason which is sufficiently obvious and which has created difficulties in the present inquiry. During a search for Smith's marriage at Somerset House, for example, it was found that during the April–June quarter of 1888 no less than three George Albert Smiths had married, in the registration districts of Ellesmere, Thanet and Pancras.

spondence with the S.P.R.—to their investigation by Messrs. Myers and Gurney.

Whatever be the truth in the matter the moral is plain: how beset with difficulties is the path of the investigator working with more or less irresponsible agents, who claim, or are supposed to possess, telepathic sensitiveness, especially if they have given public entertainments in thought-transference or mesmerism.

I should be very sorry to assert that Mr. Smith's honesty cannot be relied upon; but, nevertheless, it is unfortunate that, in the more famous and important experiments carried out at Brighton in 1889–1891, Prof. Sidgwick so largely made use of his agency and hypnotic powers, instead of calling in the assistance of a scientifically trained and medically qualified hypnotist such as Dr. Bramwell."[1]

As I have indicated, Dr. Tuckett made it plain that in his opinion either Smith or Blackburn was dishonest, whilst at the same time attributing a motive only to Smith. I do not think that there can be much doubt that his book was defamatory of Smith, and if this is so it is interesting to speculate why Smith brought no action for damages against the author and the publisher in 1911.

[1] It seems possible, from this reference, that Dr. J. M. Bramwell and Dr. Tuckett may have discussed the whole matter. However that may be, it is noteworthy that in 1896, when Dr. Bramwell contributed two papers to S.P.R. *Proceedings*, "Personally Observed Hypnotic Phenomena" and "What is Hypnotism?" he declined even to discuss the alleged marvels produced by G. A. Smith under the observation of F. W. H. Myers, Professor and Mrs. Sidgwick and Miss Alice Johnson. Nor, in his extensive experiments with his patients, did Dr. Bramwell seem to have encountered any trace whatever of the thought-reading, clairvoyance, community of sensation and other "higher phenomena" of the hypnotic state with which G. A. Smith had delighted the S.P.R. leaders.

CHAPTER TEN

THE CONFESSION

I N April 1883, after Smith had left Brighton to attach himself to the S.P.R. and Blackburn had withdrawn from the experiments, the latter seems to have resumed his ordinary activities. In the early summer of 1883 his operetta, *Angelo: or, an Ideal Love*, written in collaboration with Jacques Grube, the conductor of the Brighton Aquarium Orchestra, was evidently produced with some success by Madame Cave-Ashton's company in Brighton. However, in the meantime, other and more sinister events were developing in which Blackburn and *The Brightonian* were to be publicly and discreditably involved.

It will be recalled that in the libel case brought by Henry Munster against Blackburn's employer, Mr. R. J. Railton, costs were awarded against the latter. These amounted to the substantial sum (in the 1880's) of approximately £500. Railton seems to have sought for some means of evading this liability and finally committed a criminal offence in order to do so. When Munster ultimately tried to levy execution at Railton's office on 20 August, 1882, he discovered that on the previous day Railton had transferred by means of a bill of sale his business and goods to a friend, Mr. R. C. Cox, a Brighton chemist, thus deliberately leaving himself without any assets to meet the debt. Munster claimed that the bill of sale was fraudulent and that Railton and Cox were guilty of conspiracy to defraud him of his taxed costs in the libel case, which was unquestionably true. The matter was complex, however, and it was not until April 1883 that the courts agreed that Cox should be included in the charge, whilst the case itself was not heard until the spring of 1884.

This long delay arose in part because Railton and Cox had sought the advice of a solicitor named Goodman in regard to the legal aspects of the documents concerned in the fraud. Goodman naturally denied having advised his clients to commit a criminal offence, but his evidence was of value to the prosecution as it demonstrated independently that the proposed conspiracy had been discussed. Goodman appeared as a witness for the prosecution under subpoena, after prolonged legal argument as to whether a solicitor could give evidence in regard to confidential professional advice offered to his clients.

Blackburn was called, with Goodman, as a principal witness by the Public Prosecutor. Apparently Railton had also disclosed to Blackburn his plan to evade paying the heavy costs awarded to Munster, and this was the evidence the prosecution required of Blackburn. He was under subpoena and under oath, but despite this pressure he certainly did not do his best for the Public Prosecutor who had forced him into the witness box to give evidence against his employer.

It is almost unnecessary to say that the defending counsel, Mr. Edward Clarke, Q.C., M.P.,[1] subjected Blackburn to severe cross-examination in an endeavour to discredit his reluctant but fatal evidence. Blackburn had refrained repeatedly from making any plain statement in regard to the alleged conversations between himself and Railton about the fraudulent plan of the latter to evade paying Munster's costs, which had annoyed the Public Prosecutor and drawn a rebuke from the Recorder. Clarke referred to "shifty and evasive answers" which Blackburn had given, and to his certainty that the jury would not convict Railton and Cox upon the evidence of Blackburn who had "failed to give a direct answer to any one question". In his cross-examination Clarke endeavoured to press Blackburn repeatedly into making a statement on oath which could be rebutted, which Blackburn avoided time after time, even audaciously telling his formidable opponent that he was fully aware of the trap which had been set for him, and into which he had no intention of falling. Clarke was furious with Blackburn, presumably because he was a spirited and skilful witness and defeated Clarke in his object. The famous and formidable Q.C. was probably not accustomed to passages like the following being reported as part of his cross-examination of a young man of twenty-five years of age:

Blackburn: "You will not fluster me, Sir."
Clarke: "I am not trying to."

[1] Who later defended Oscar Wilde.

Va. G. A. Smith's home in Grand Parade, Brighton

Vb. Smith and Blackburn's advertisement in the *Brighton Herald* of their "thought-reading" performances at The Aquarium, Brighton, in 1882
By kind permission of the Director of Brighton Public Library

VI*a*. The Aquarium, Brighton, *c.* 1880

VI*b*. Smith's advertisement in the *Brighton Herald* of the "Demon of the Air" at St. Ann's Well, Brighton, in 1894

By kind permission of the Director of Brighton Public Library

ENTERTAINMENTS.

"ONE OF THE MOST CHARMING RETREATS IN BRIGHTON."

ST. ANN'S WELL AND PLEASURE GARDENS.

A delightful spot within four minutes' walk of the Western-road 'bus route. The place for Afternoon Teas, Ices, &c., under the trees. Monkeys, Baboons, Birds, Free. Lawn Tennis, plenty of Swings, Free. Reading Room. The famous Iron Water, Free. The Gipsy in the Caravan.

OPEN DAILY.

Admission: Week-days, THREEPENCE; Sundays, SIXPENCE.

Sole Lessee and Manager, G. ALBERT SMITH.

SPECIAL ANNOUNCEMENT.

Owing to the brilliant success attending Mr NEIL CAMPBELL'S skilful and daring ascent, Mr G. A. Smith has arranged for another

BALLOON ASCENT & PARACHUTE DESCENT

TO TAKE PLACE AT

ST. ANN'S WELL AND PLEASURE GARDENS, BRIGHTON,

THIS DAY (SATURDAY), JUNE 16th,

At about Six or Seven o'clock in the Evening. Everybody perfectly charmed with the interesting process of inflating the hot-air Balloon, and with Mr Campbell's graceful flight from the Lawn. Come early to get a good place. Band all the Afternoon and Evening.

Admission on this special occasion, SIXPENCE.

Blackburn: "Yes, you are! If you won't listen to what I say, what is the use of asking me questions? I shall certainly answer questions in my own way. You are trying to tie me down. I repudiate it."

It is noteworthy that Clarke admitted defeat and grimly congratulated Blackburn on his performance in the witness box.

There can be no doubt, however, from the reports that there was strong feeling in the court against Blackburn, which in my opinion was understandable in view of the surrounding circumstances. Munster, although unquestionably the injured party in the case, was held in general detestation in Brighton. The resultant sympathy for Railton was increased by the fact that his wife, due to anxiety over her husband's plight, became insane. The fact remains that Railton and Cox were convicted and sent to prison and that Blackburn was regarded with some scorn as the originator of his employer's troubles (although the libels were admitted by Railton to have been written with his knowledge and consent) and who had testified against Railton, albeit admittedly under subpoena and under oath. A month or two later Blackburn was cited as the co-respondent in undefended divorce proceedings brought by a Brighton auctioneer named Parsons against his wife in regard to her association with Blackburn, with whom she had stayed in London hotels in August and September 1883. His reputation was thoroughly tarnished, concurrently with the closing down of *The Brightonian*, and it was at this time that he started a new life in South Africa.

I do not think that it can be suggested, if the dates of these events in Blackburn's life are kept clearly in mind, that the S.P.R. leaders dismissed Blackburn from the experiments (as was later to be insinuated by the Society) because of any foreknowledge of these widely publicized occurrences. In the first place, Blackburn had acquitted himself well in the witness-box in the libel case in 1882, which had in any event been heard and reported before he and Smith made contact with the S.P.R. Secondly, the experiments were over and Blackburn had severed his connexion with the Society as early as April 1883, a year before the conspiracy and divorce cases came to trial in 1884. Finally, in their account in *Proceedings* in 1883 the S.P.R. leaders made it clear, as I have shown, that it was only at their "urgent request" that Blackburn, against his own inclination and without financial reward, had joined in the last series of experiments at Dean's Yard. The reason for his lack of enthusiasm was obvious; he realized that Smith was throwing in his lot with the Society and that the project of the profitable professional "second-sight" act with Smith would now never materialize. Indeed, if what they wrote in their *Proceedings* in 1883 can be believed, the S.P.R. leaders felt it right to express in print to Blackburn their "hearty obligations to him for the unrecompensed trouble which we have so frequently imposed upon him", and for the time he had spent on the experiments "at considerable inconvenience to himself".

Blackburn's attitude towards psychical research and spiritualism seems at this later period to have been consistent with his earlier published writings. In early 1884, shortly before the ill-fated *Brightonian* ceased publication forever, he referred to a lecture by Henry Sidgwick, the President of the S.P.R., reported in an unnamed contemporary newspaper which I have not been able to trace. Blackburn wrote:

> "We have heard of these matters in Brighton before, and to some extent take an interest in them, but there is an expression in our contemporary's notice which is unfortunate. It speaks of a few 'instances of movement' in which 'no contact occurred' or 'by a slack cord only'. The 'slack cord' certainly suggests that the audience is *being had on a string*."[1]

Early in 1884 Blackburn's first book *Thought Reading: or, Modern Mysteries Explained* was published in London by Field and Tuer. It was a small paperbacked volume priced at a shilling and was probably written to make a few pounds, possibly because Blackburn, if we can believe him, was editing *The Brightonian* without salary at this period. Blackburn in his book admitted the possibility of spontaneous telepathy whilst at the same time referring critically and specifically to the invariable use of codes in public second-sight acts, and to the exposure of fraud.

What must have been more disconcerting to the S.P.R. leaders in 1884, however, was Blackburn's description of certain experiments in the transmission of a mental picture from one person to

[1] *The Brightonian*, 2 February, 1884.

another, the blindfolded percipient being able to reproduce the drawing. He did not disclose in his book that this referred to the performances of Smith and himself, but significantly added a foot-note to guide the inquiring reader to the report of the Dean's Yard trials in S.P.R. *Proceedings*. The reference to *Proceedings* was precise, and the reader had only to look it up. He then specifically stated that these trials had failed to establish the existence of thought-reading, without giving a reason, and added that "satisfactory evidence has yet to be produced in support of the assumption that it is within the power of one man to tell in effect the nature of an abstract idea or intention occupying the mind of another" (pp. 29-30). These remarks by Blackburn in 1884 seem to me to be of the highest significance in relation to the later controversy over his "confession" in 1908 and 1911.

What is remarkable is that nowhere in the book is the name of Blackburn or Smith mentioned, even in the chapters on mesmerism, nor did Blackburn disclose that he himself had ever taken part in any demonstration of alleged thought-transference, in public or in private, in partnership with Smith or anyone else. Blackburn was a journalist, presumably anxious to sell his book. This entire omission to mention Smith or himself seems to me to suggest strongly that not only were the experiments at Brighton and Dean's Yard accomplished by trickery but that it was known that this was so by Gurney at least, as was later to be revealed by Sir Oliver Lodge. Had the experiments been genuine, or even fraudulent but unchallenged, then Blackburn could have obtained considerable publicity and additional interest for his book by claiming that they were and describing himself as a genuine and successful telepathist. How else can we explain the contrast between his article in *The Brightonian* in December 1882 *before* the Dean's Yard tests, claiming that the S.P.R. leaders accepted the performances of Smith and himself at Brighton as proving telepathy, and his attitude in his book in 1884?

The reader may think that if Blackburn knew that he and Smith had been caught in trickery by Gurney, and the matter secretly covered up, discretion on his part was the only course left open to him if he wanted to write a popular booklet on mind-reading. Blackburn had sufficient personal experience of libel actions to know that for him to declare in print that the S.P.R. leaders had been tricked, and to reveal that Smith directly or indirectly had utilized the opportunity brought about by the deception to obtain a salaried appointment, could have had very serious results for Blackburn. It is instructive to compare Blackburn's silence in 1884 with his detailed published statement in 1908 when he believed Smith to be dead.

There are two other small mysteries connected with Blackburn's book. In view of his connexion with the S.P.R. and the title and subject matter of *Thought Reading: or Modern Mysteries Explained*, which included an account of the foundation of the Society, it seems very curious that no copy was contained in the Society's extensive library, which was supposed to include every available book dealing, however remotely, with any aspect of psychical research. Yet its title was not included in the *Library Catalogue* of the S.P.R. compiled by Theodore Besterman and issued as Part 104 of *Proceedings* in 1927, nor in any of the four *Supplements* issued between 1927 and 1933. It seems possible that the leaders of the S.P.R., by keeping the book out of their library, were demonstrating their anxiety not to assist in broadcasting Blackburn's guarded remarks in 1884, to what Sidgwick was to describe four years later as the "simple minds" of the Society's ordinary members. Simple they might be, but they would at least have been able to look up the reference to their *Proceedings* given in the footnote on p. 29 of Blackburn's book, and to discover the identity of the experiments which he stated did *not* establish the existence of thought-transference.

Another point about Blackburn's book is its extreme scarcity today.[1] Copies exist in the British Museum and in the libraries of Cambridge and London University and the Magic Circle. I am familiar with the catalogues of most private collections in both England and America of books on conjuring and psychical research, and I do not know of one apart from my own that contains a copy.[2] It is not listed in any bibliography of either subject with which I

[1] So far as I am aware, no copy has been advertised for sale since 1924, when the late Arthur Margery of Brompton included it in a list of scarce books. My friend Mr. H. E. Pratt, the Hon. Librarian of the Magic Circle, thinks it probable that this is the copy now under his care, it having passed through the libraries of the late Dr. Milton Bridges and the late C. H. Charlton. The latter's collection was purchased *en bloc* by the Magic Circle some years ago.

[2] My copy came from the library of an old friend, the late George Johnson of Okehampton, an Hon. Vice-President of the Magic Circle.

am familiar. Yet another book produced by the same publishers in the previous year, *Christmas Entertainments* (1883), in the same series of popular handbooks and of identical format and price, is of fairly common occurrence. Why in these circumstances virtually all copies of Blackburn's book seem to have disappeared is a matter for conjecture.

I have tried to put the reader fairly in possession of the principal facts of Blackburn's life during the relevant years up to 1884, so far as these are ascertainable, for a reason which is reasonably obvious. The reader has to decide, on the basis of Blackburn's activities and writings during this period, coupled with the information about his later years which follows, whether he was likely to have spoken the truth about the experiments with Smith when he made his public statements in 1908 and 1911. The S.P.R. leaders of the day considered that Blackburn was lying when he said that the "thought-transference" demonstrated by Smith and himself was accomplished by trickery and issued a privately printed leaflet to say so.[1] This was a curious position to take up, when it is remembered that what Blackburn stated openly in 1908 was in a sense merely an amplification of what he had said guardedly in 1884. It was not, moreover, revealed to the reader of the circular in 1909 that Blackburn's story was confirmed by the earlier letters of Dr. H. B. Donkin and Sir James Crichton-Browne published in *The Westminster Gazette* during the winter of 1907–8. The unfortunate impression gained is that the Society's leaders were not anxious to show Blackburn in anything but a completely unfavourable light, and that in order to present an uncomplicated picture they were willing to conceal evidence that might have afforded to the student of the affair a better opportunity of considering all the possibilities for himself.

Whether anything was gained by this deception is a matter of opinion. If, as Miss Johnson, the Secretary of the Society in 1909, implied in her pamphlet, Blackburn was capable of making a false confession in 1908 that trickery was used in the demonstrations by Smith and himself a quarter of a century earlier, would the reader's confidence in the genuineness of the demonstrations and the honesty of the performers be increased? If Blackburn was to be regarded as a liar in 1908, was that a good reason for regarding

[1] Alice Johnson, *Mr. Blackburn's Confession*, privately printed, London, 1909.

his work as trustworthy in 1882 and 1883? What, moreover, was the motive for a false confession in 1908? Miss Johnson said that it was done "merely in the hope of creating a journalistic sensation", although no evidence was offered in support of this suggestion. Blackburn by this time was a serious and highly regarded author who would hardly seek this type of publicity to advertise himself. His earlier career in Brighton had been associated with the follies of youth; the libels of Munster, the misconduct with Mrs. Parsons, and the hoaxing of the S.P.R. But in South Africa he had clearly matured, and later in life was obviously held in high regard.

As the reader knows, Blackburn died at Tonbridge, Kent, where he spent the last thirteen years of his life, in 1929. The published appreciations of his career and work covered several pages of print.[1] It is from this material that we know that this was indeed the Douglas Blackburn who had been involved in early life with "the Psychical Research Society" and that he had been an amateur conjurer.[2]

Blackburn spent much of his working life in South Africa, and in all probability went there about 1884 after the divorce and conspiracy cases. Of his career in that country it was said in one of the appreciations after his death:

> "When the South African war broke out he answered the call to arms, and was wounded at the battle of Colenso. He held a number of important posts under the Southern Cross being in turn expert[3] to the Natal Criminal Investigation Department and the Transvaal Republic, editor of the *Standard and Diggers' News* (now the *Johannesburg Daily Mail*) and the short-lived *Johannesburg Daily Express* and an author of note in the sub-continent. As an author he was credited with having a unique knowledge of the Boer mentality. Of his many novels, his best known is *Prinsloo of Prinsloosdorp*, and there is practically no library in South

---

[1] *Tonbridge Free Press*, 5 April, 1929.

[2] I need not weary the reader with the evidence on this point, which is complete. It is sufficient to say, apart from other information, that Mr. A. S. Jarman discovered a cartoon, annotated by Blackburn, among the pages of *The Brightonian*, the handwriting being clearly identical with a long signed note by the author on the fly-leaf of my copy of Blackburn's *The Martyr Nurse*.

[3] On cyphers and the detection of forgery.

Africa that has not got a copy of it on its shelves. . . . Not many Englishmen can have honourably filled so many different positions in life."

One friend who had known Blackburn for twenty-five years wrote of him:

"As all who knew him will agree, he was a man of exceptionally broad viewpoint, and willing to hear and even to test all men's opinions, and tolerant of other people's convictions, whether they coincided with his own or were directly in opposition. . . . I respected and loved the man, and when I recall his large hearted personality, his humour, his flashes of wit and many evidences of broad, sound wisdom, I experience the keenest regret that he has gone, but this I feel sure will be shared by all who had the privilege to know him."

The reader may think that the last sentence of the following appreciation is not without significance in relation to the matter at issue:

"Yet who shall judge of what the reward of such a man could be? Certainly, by gold and silver he set no store. Title and estate likewise, to him were non-scintillating: prizes, and even reputation, which for many count for much, rang with but a muffled tongue upon his ears. To one who knew him well it seems that the fact of living—the right to live, to write, to read, to talk, to eat, to drink—afforded all he asked for what he did. His wants were few, his tastes were simple and emblematic of a well ordered mentality; he had cultivated a philosophic sense which enabled him to seek and find within himself the solace requisite for his rest and conscience. He was a man whose outlook was only narrowed by the horizon. He wrote as he thought and talked, without fear or favour, without flattery or pose."[1]

It is impracticable to quote here more than a few paragraphs from the impressions of Blackburn published after his death. The regard in which he was evidently held in Tonbridge was confirmed

[1] *Tonbridge Free Press*, 5 April, 1929.

by the notes attached to the score or so of wreaths at the funeral, one of which was from no less than eighteen old friends. Perhaps the most enviable tribute of all was an anonymous wreath accompanied by the words "To a man, from a neighbour and friend".

Douglas Blackburn was the successful author[1] of six outstanding and widely reviewed novels about South Africa, where, as the reader now knows, the middle years of his life were spent. Of the first of these, *Prinsloo of Prinsloosdorp* (London, 1899) Andrew Lang (who oddly enough was President of the S.P.R. in 1911, the year of Blackburn's statement in the *Daily News*) said that with Olive Schreiner's *Story of a South African Farm* it was one of the two South African classics, "outstanding, unsurpassed in the copious literature of the Sub-Continent". *The Spectator* said that it was "as brilliant and sustained an essay in political irony as we can remember to have appeared in the last thirty years". A second edition of the highly successful *Prinsloo* appeared in London in 1908.

In 1903 *A Burgher Quixote* was published by Blackwood's, to be followed in 1905 by *Richard Hartley, Prospector*, which was serialized in *Blackwood's Magazine*. In 1908, the year of the first S.P.R. controversy, two further novels by Blackburn were published, *I Came, I Saw*, and *Leaven: A Black and White Story*, as well as the new edition of *Prinsloo of Prinsloosdorp*. Of the second the *Academy* said: "Mr. Douglas Blackburn is in the happy position of realizing that he has given us the very best novel of South Africa that has yet appeared. 'Leaven' is a magnificent story, written with a sense of humour combined with a sense of honour."

Sir W. Robertson Nicoll, in a page review of *Leaven* in *The Bookman* wrote of it (and the last words of the first quoted sentence may be significant to anyone seeking to ascertain the character of Blackburn in his later years):

"There is a spirit of almost inhuman impartiality and calmness, but one feels all the while that the author knows what

---

[1] Blackburn's novels reveal, if further confirmation is needed, his wide knowledge of the technique and psychology of conjuring. In *A Burgher Quixote*, for example, the mental trick with a book, "doctored" to fall open at a page already known to the performer, is described, as is the secret exchanging of envelopes. In the same volume is explained the basic rule that "A clever conjurer never repeats the same trick before the same audience". An excellent and detailed description of the pea and walnut trick covers several pages of *Secret Service in South Africa*.

he is writing about, and that he is telling the truth as he sees it unfalteringly and unshrinkingly. Further, he is dealing with the great problem of the future, the problem of the white and coloured races. . . . Mr. Blackburn is so assured, and gives one such an impression of competence and fairness that whoever reads this book will be impressed by it."

It was in 1908, when these books and reviews appeared, that the leaders of the S.P.R. were denigrating Blackburn in a privately circulated pamphlet, and suggesting that his published admission in regard to the "experiments" of twenty-six years ago was a lie motivated by a desire to create a sensation and to see his name in print. In 1915 Blackburn published his last novel, *Love Muti*, and a biography of Edith Cavell, *The Martyr Nurse*.

Whilst in Africa Blackburn met Captain W. Waithman Caddell, one of the Commissioners for the Repatriation of the Boers and a Magistrate for the Western Transvaal. The two men became life-long friends, and after they returned to England wrote three non-fiction works in collaboration on forgery,[1] on which Blackburn was an expert, the African secret service[2] and an original system of shorthand.[3] The second of these books, published by Cassell, attracted a two-page review in *The Bookman* of October 1911 with a photograph of Blackburn. Stanley Portal Hyatt wrote:

"It is no easy task to review this book, because, as everyone who has studied the literature of the sub-continent is aware, Douglas Blackburn is not only the founder of the modern school of South African novelists, but he also knows more about the inner history of the Kruger administration than any other British writer. Moreover, it is difficult to do full justice to Mr. Blackburn's co-author, Captain Caddell; he is inevitably over-shadowed by the figure of the grim, kindly satirist who created *Prinsloo of Prinsloosdorp*. . . . *Secret Service* is a book to be read—I want to emphasize that fact; and yet, at the same time, I want to protest against the man who wrote *Prinsloo* and *A Burgher Quixote* working on a mere cut and dried narrative, a plain recital of things that

[1] *The Detection of Forgery* (London, 1909).
[2] *Secret Service in South Africa* (London, 1911).
[3] *Blackdell's Print Shorthand* (London, 1912).

happened, instead of using his greater gifts. Other South African novelists—or novelists of South Africa I should say—attempt to follow in his footsteps, often with a fair amount of success; but the biggest man of all, the Master, deliberately keeps out of the public view. Therefore I feel annoyed with him, although I have enjoyed immensely the book which he and Captain Caddell have produced."

These opinions of Blackburn's character, the reviews of his books and especially the fact that he was in his heyday as a widely read and highly regarded author in the early years of the twentieth century, lead one to the conclusion that the motive which the S.P.R. leaders attributed to the publication of his articles in 1908 and 1911 can be disregarded. My own opinion is that the youthful trickery of 1882–3, which had contributed to the foolish self-deception of the founders of the S.P.R., was something which Blackburn felt it was proper to admit when the time came that he believed, as he said himself, that there was nobody left alive to whom distress would be caused. Gurney and Myers had passed away, and believing Smith to be dead he said that he was now the sole survivor of the group of people involved, and that no harm could be done to anyone, whilst the cause of truth might well benefit.[1] When Smith, who had remained silent in 1908, replied in 1911, Blackburn wrote:

> "Whilst pleased to learn that the bright, amusing, and ingenious confrère of thirty years ago is in the prime of life, I am sorry that I should have unintentionally forced him into having to defend a position he has occupied so long. I have been reproached for postponing my article until after the death of the principals. I am satisfied that in doing this I showed my regard for those gentlemen—Mr. Smith included—and my desire to avoid giving them pain."[2]

Most of the evidence assembled in the foregoing pages has never before been published in the literature of psychical research, or even assembled and examined, so far as I know. If the reader finds it convincing, and reaches the conclusion that Douglas

[1] *Daily News*, 1 September, 1911.
[2] *Ibid.*, 5 September, 1911.

Blackburn's version of the curious events of eighty years ago is the true one, he will naturally consider how far Blackburn's published statement confirms the details of what we already know.

Blackburn published his first account in the weekly magazine *John Bull* during the winter of 1908–9.[1] He said that all the experiments in "thought-transference" conducted by the S.P.R. in 1882 and 1883 with G. A. Smith and himself were a hoax so far as the two subjects were concerned and had been accomplished by wholly natural means. He said that the results of the experiments "were produced by an ingenious and elaborate system of code signals, assisted by tricks, coincidences, and fortuitous accidents, and were in no instance genuine", adding that "the mental bias of both Messrs. Myers and Gurney was towards spiritualism, it being the almost invariable rule of the former to give the experiment the benefit of the doubt". Blackburn's comment upon the advantage taken of coincidental successes is significant to anyone acquainted with the mental feats of the conjurer, in which the principle of "lucky breaks" is a planned and practical ingredient.[2] Blackburn's view that Myers was more eagerly wishful to believe than Gurney is of great interest, and was repeated by implication when he used the name of the former only in remarking that "the results were often wide of the mark, and only the pronounced friendly prejudice of a Myers would have credited them as successes. It was their almost guileless enthusiasm which satisfied S. and myself that we had to deal with delightfully simple souls. The 'precautions' they took to guard against deception were of the feeblest." Remembering, for example, the insistence by the investigators at Brighton that Smith and Blackburn should resume their hand-holding because the "phenomena" ceased without it, the reader may think that Blackburn was not exaggerating.

The reader will recall the account by Sir James Crichton-Browne of the success of the hoaxers in coding the picture of an owl, the partial success in coding a shield (of the wrong shape) on Dr. Galton's ring and the complete failure to transmit the "non-

---

[1] *John Bull*, 5 December, 1908, p. 590; 12 December, 1908, p. 628; 19 December, 1908, p. 671; 26 December, 1908, pp. 706–7; 2 January, 1909, p. 7; 9 January, 1909, p. 39.

[2] See, for example, "Name-O-Card", a trick entirely dependent upon this principle, in my *The Testament of Ralph W. Hull* (London, 1945).

descript arabesque" which could not be described in words. In this connexion he may think the following comment by Blackburn to be highly significant, especially in view of Sir Oliver Lodge's recollection of the "CAT/3120" incident:

> "It is fairly obvious that, given a means of signalling words, it is easy to spell out the description of an article which has a name. But when the design is, as some of those given us were, a splotch of ink pressed between two pieces of paper, it would require a good descriptive writer to convey what it was like in ordinary words. . . . If such a person can convey by genuine Telepathy to another a regular figure, which he visualizes, why can he not with equal success visualize and transfer to the brain the picture of an irregular figure like that splotchy blotch? And is it not strange that while he can accurately describe a regular triangle, he should fail when one side of it is curved or wobbly?"

Blackburn recalled the visit to Dean's Yard of Sir James Crichton-Browne, whom he regarded as a scientific observer who refused to be taken in by the "experiments". Smith, on the other hand, as the reader will learn, had little recollection of the incident.

It is, I think, important to record a remark by Blackburn in his statement in 1908 which confirms something I believe myself, that G. A. Smith had some genuine ability as a hypnotist.

> "The hypnotic business of S. was so unquestionably genuine, and my telepathic flukes so obviously not to be explained by fraud, that these trusting souls were quite prepared to accept all we offered subsequently without question, which may be very complimentary and flattering, but it is not strictly scientific."

The situation in which the S.P.R. found itself in 1908 when Blackburn published his statement was exceedingly embarrassing. His connexion with the Society had ceased in 1883, but G. A. Smith's had not. Smith had been elected an Associate of the Society in 1888 (afterwards a Life Associate) and had been employed by the Society from 1883 to 1892, successively as private secretary to both Gurney and Myers, before becoming first a theatrical agent and then the proprietor of a showground in Brighton. More importantly, perhaps, during the period of his employment by the S.P.R. he had been the central and essential figure, as the sole hypnotic operator, in all the Society's published experiments in this subject. The majority of these experiments, especially the ones in later years, were concerned with the so-called "higher phenomena" of the hypnotic state, i.e. telepathy, clairvoyance and community of sensation between the hypnotist and the subject. Much of this immense labour, the voluminous accounts of which had occupied a great part of the early volumes of S.P.R. *Proceedings*, had been done by Edmund Gurney during the six years of his connexion with the Society from its foundation in 1882 to his tragic death in 1888. After Gurney had died, the experiments in thought-transference in the hypnotic state had been continued by Professor Henry Sidgwick and Mrs. Sidgwick in conjunction with G. A. Smith, without whose services as the hypnotist and the provider of the Brighton boys nothing could of course be done, and Miss Alice Johnson, the Secretary of the Society. Papers describing these experiments were published in 1889[1] and 1892,[2] and Smith's name was actually added to those of the Sidgwicks as a collaborating investigator and author, responsible with them for the former of these accounts. Frank Podmore, a member of Council of the Society and a former Honorary Secretary, had included an approving account of the two series of Sidgwick experiments in his *Studies in Psychical Research* (London, 1897).[3]

It will be seen why the leaders of the S.P.R. were so perturbed in December 1908. If Smith, the trusted Associate of the Society upon whose *bona fides* such a mass of the S.P.R.'s early published work depended, had in fact deliberately tricked Gurney and Myers in 1882 in collaboration with Blackburn, and had nevertheless ingratiated himself into a comfortable paid appointment with the Society by means of this introduction, then the whole of his

---

[1] Professor and Mrs. H. Sidgwick and Mr. G. A. Smith, "Experiments in Thought-Transference", *Proceedings*, S.P.R., 1889, vi, pp. 128ff.

[2] Mrs. H. Sidgwick and Miss Alice Johnson, "Experiments in Thought-Transference", *Proceedings*, S.P.R., 1892, viii, pp. 536ff.

[3] Pp. 214–18. Podmore's attitude to G. A. Smith was very difficult to understand. Thus, whilst reporting with unqualified approval upon the Sidgwick experiments, he said earlier in the same chapter "Experimental Thought-Transference" (p. 196) that the thought-reading of the platform could not be regarded as genuine thought-transference at all, although he obviously knew that Smith had been a professional entertainer.

later activities would immediately become suspect. Such a result, so far as the Society's attempts to establish itself as a scientific body was concerned, would be nothing less than catastrophic. It seems hardly too much to say that little would be left of the experimental work in the first five volumes of the *Proceedings*, in which Gurney had written so lengthily on the work with Smith.[1] On the other hand, the position which the Society must try at all costs to maintain, if disaster was to be avoided, might well have seemed impossible. It must be not only that Smith was a genuine percipient of telepathic impressions to a degree that has never been remotely approached in any controlled experiments, but that Blackburn was a genuine transmitting agent of similar calibre, in the face of a detailed published statement from him that the results had relied wholly upon trickery.

In trying to understand the position in which the Society found itself in 1908, the reader will remember that since its formation the S.P.R. had experienced a series of disasters reflecting adversely upon its standards of evidence and critical acumen in its published material. I have described in earlier chapters the melancholy examples of Judge Edmund Hornby's apparition and Mr. X.Z.'s haunted house. The deadly criticisms of *Phantasms of the Living* by A. T. Innes and others, and the confession of trickery by the mischievous Creery sisters, had not been helpful to the Society's reputation. It will suffice to mention one further embarrassing example, the case of the alleged haunting of Ballechin House in Perthshire, with which the name of the Society became associated at the turn of the century. I quote a published comment by Dr. E. J. Dingwall and myself:

> "It is doubtful if in the history of the Society for Psychical Research condemnation of its methods was ever more loudly voiced than over the Ballechin affair. It must be remembered that the Ballechin controversy arose only a few years after

[1] "Second Report on Thought-Transference", "First Report of the Committee on Mesmerism", "Second Report of the Committee on Mesmerism" (*Proceedings*, S.P.R., 1882–3, i, pp. 70 ff., 217 ff., and 251 ff.). "Third Report of the Committee on Mesmerism", "The Stages of Hypnotism", "An Account of Some Experiments in Mesmerism" (*Ibid.*, 1883–4, ii, pp. 12 ff., 61 ff., and 201 ff.). "Local Anaesthesia induced in the Normal State by Mesmeric Passes" (*Ibid.*, 1885, iii, pp. 453 ff.). "Peculiarities of Certain Post-Hypnotic States", "Stages of Hypnotic Memory" (*Ibid.*, 1886–7, iv, pp. 268 ff. and 515 ff.), "Recent Experiments in Hypnotism", "Hypnotism and Telepathy" (*Ibid.*, 1888–9, v, pp. 3 ff. and 216 ff.).

the attack on the Society's work on hallucinations and phantasms of the living. Led by Mr. A. T. Innes, the attack had been centred on the inability of the Society to produce contemporary documents supporting their collection of ghost stories, and the defence, ably led by Mr. Edmund Gurney, did little to foster feelings of confidence in the Society's methods. *The Times* printed a series of letters from persons connected with the Ballechin case, together with some from others who severely censured the conduct of the inquiry. One wrote of the suspicion and disgust which close contact with the Society for Psychical Research always tended to excite and added that what the Society called investigation would 'provide contempt in Bedlam itself'. One of the visitors during the Freer tenancy declared that no real attempt was made in experimentation or research, since the company were simply 'agape for wonders'. Another writer stated that the Society could not have the remotest idea of the legal or scientific meaning and value of evidence, whilst still another urged the Society to eliminate root and branch its childish methods.

The defence led by Mr. Myers and Professor Sidgwick did but little to stem the flood of criticism which grew in volume and intensity. Lord Onslow declared that the methods by which the house was rented savoured of deceit, although it was pointed out that the Society itself as a corporate body had had no actual transactions with the owner. With regard to the noises heard by Mr. Myers and Professor (later Sir) Oliver Lodge, the former declared that it would have been 'pedantic' to apply tests for seismic disturbance to them, an evasive reply which still further damaged the Society's reputation. It was, however, pointed out that in Comrie there were constant rumblings and other seismic sounds, and the suggestion was put forward that simple apparatus might well be employed by the Society in what was termed its 'bogey-hunting expeditions'."[1]

The reader may think that the position of the S.P.R. in 1908 was sufficiently precarious to cause the leaders of the Society to be

[1] E. J. Dingwall and T. H. Hall, *Four Modern Ghosts* (London, 1958), pp. 17–18.

acutely perturbed by Blackburn's published statement. Yet experience had shown, especially in the case of Dr. H. B. Donkin and A. T. Innes, that attempts publicly to defend the Society's position had merely precipitated even more devastating onslaughts. In the circumstances, therefore, it is perhaps not surprising that after some revealing correspondence and discussion, to which I shall refer in subsequent paragraphs, the Council of the S.P.R. decided against any public comment upon Blackburn's statement. A pamphlet was, however, prepared by Miss Alice Johnson[1] (who had, of course, been involved in the later experiments with Smith) for private circulation amongst members of the Society and interested inquirers. This leaflet stated that G. A. Smith had emphatically repudiated Blackburn's allegations, that no code or other trickery had been employed and that the experiments had been entirely genuine.

Unpublished opinion amongst some members of the Society does not seem to have been quite so confident of Smith's *bona fides* and Blackburn's villainy as the downright statements in Miss Johnson's pamphlet implied. Mrs. Margaret de G. Verrall, for example, who discussed Smith with Miss Johnson on 7 December, 1908, disclosed that she was of the opinion that Smith had indulged in trickery with the Brighton boys during the Sidgwicks' experiments in 1889.[2] Sir Oliver Lodge, in a letter to Miss Johnson on 4 January, 1909, said that he was beginning to think rather better of Blackburn, and that his statement "hardly reads like a mere lie". This would seem to confirm Sir Oliver's letter written a month previously to J. G. Piddington saying that his recollection was that Gurney had caught Blackburn and Smith in deception, but that the point about Smith was that he could at least hypnotize, "however fraudulent he might be."

Confidence in the pamphlet cannot have been increased by Miss Johnson's entire omission to mention in it the testimony of Sir James Crichton-Browne and Dr. H. B. Donkin, which had been published a year before Blackburn's statement and which it supported. It must have seemed curious to many in 1908 that Smith,

---

[1] Johnson, Alice. *Mr. Blackburn's Confession*, privately printed, London, 1909. The purpose of this pamphlet was presumably to deny the charges and denigrate Blackburn without incurring the risk of a damaging reply, which a *published* statement might have precipitated.

[2] Miss Johnson's unpublished notes.

who had been publicly accused of fraud (and by implication, as Dr. Ivor Tuckett was later to point out, fraud for the purpose of gain) made no attempt to seek redress or even to defend his reputation.

If this was not the silence of guilt, what was it? *John Bull* was widely read, and Smith's name had been besmirched. A successful lawsuit, in which Smith would obviously have received backing from some S.P.R. members, would have cleared Smith's name and brought him useful damages, but fear of the consequences of perjury would have deterred him. Smith's only safety lay in suffering in silence the charges against him, and in trusting that they would not be repeated. This assumption proved vain, as we shall later see, but even when forced by the press in 1911 into making a statement, it is noticeable that Smith sought no relief from the courts. His name was tarnished, but he still refrained from seeking redress from a jury. He knew that he would be under oath, and that cross-examination would be sharp and merciless. An innocent man would have claimed protection under the laws of libel; a guilty man would have shunned the two-edged sword of justice. Smith chose the latter course.

In this connexion it is valuable to record, probably for the first time in print, that on 3 December, 1908, when the leaders of the S.P.R. were evidently already acquainted with the contents of at least the first of the forthcoming articles in *John Bull* and had possibly been invited to comment upon Blackburn's article in the same issue, Mrs. Sidgwick wrote to Miss Alice Johnson[1] to say that if Smith was innocent then Blackburn's statement was clearly a libel. Five days later, Mrs. Sidgwick wrote, somewhat surprisingly, that it was possible that there was a conspiracy between Smith and Blackburn at their public performances (thus demonstrating that she was fully aware of the paid shows in Brighton) but that she did not think that this could have been the case in the Society's published experiments.[2]

[1] An unpublished letter.
[2] An unpublished letter. As has already been shown by the example of Podmore (p. 139) the subject of G. A. Smith seemed to precipitate confusion of thought amongst the S.P.R. leaders. Thus it was stated by Gurney and Myers on p. 893 of *The Nineteenth Century*, June 1882, that experience extending over several years had warned them against any belief in the genuineness of "paid or public exhibitions" of thought-reading, an assertion that was repeated by Barrett, Gurney and Myers on p. 9 of S.P.R. *Proceedings*, 1883, ii, when it was stated that public exhibitions had "no claim

It is possible that a contributory reason which prompted the S.P.R. not to take up the cudgels publicly with Blackburn in 1908, was that the interview with Smith by Miss Alice Johnson on 11 December (she travelled to Brighton to see him) was not so entirely satisfactory, according to her copious but unpublished notes, as her privately printed leaflet would lead one to suppose. Asked, for example, about the damaging recollection by Lodge of the "CAT/3120" incident, Smith's first reaction was that he had never heard of it before. The following morning, however, he told Miss Johnson that after thinking the matter over (possibly in view of its formidable provenance) he imagined that the explanation might be that some other person present had signalled unconsciously or for fun.

When questioned by Miss Johnson about the published account by Sir James Crichton-Browne a year earlier, Smith's story was that he did remember that two strangers had once attended an experiment but had said nothing, although he had later heard a discussion going on in another room. He did not seem to recollect the name of Sir James Crichton-Browne, or that Mr. George Romanes and Dr. Francis Galton and other eminent Victorians had also been present, or that quite striking tests had been applied, although by comparison Blackburn's memory of the incident seemed clear enough. Be that as it may, Miss Johnson decided for some reason it would be advisable to draw a veil over the whole incident in her pamphlet, although it is clear from the notes of her talk with Smith that it was at the forefront of her mind at the time.

Smith told Miss Johnson that his performances with Blackburn in Brighton before their contact with the S.P.R. had consisted of "muscle-reading" in private houses, and that neither he nor Blackburn knew anything about codes until they were told about them by Myers and Gurney. This was a patent untruth, and as I have shown in earlier chapters, Miss Johnson was in a position to know that it was from readily available published sources.

to be considered 'Thought-reading' at all". As Blackburn and Smith had been giving exhibitions in Brighton that were both public and paid, these remarks lead one to assume that the S.P.R. leaders held the extraordinary view that the Blackburn–Smith second sight act alone was genuine whilst all others were based on trickery. Mrs. Sidgwick, however, seemed to be of the equally curious opinion that Blackburn and Smith could have been tricksters at Brighton and genuine mental mediums during the S.P.R. experiments.

Possibly in order to present an uncomplicated picture in her pamphlet, Miss Johnson decided that it was better to omit any reference at all to the early association and professional performances of Smith and Blackburn in Brighton, despite their overwhelming importance in any informed scrutiny of the affair.

The hope by the Society that if Blackburn's articles were ignored the matter might die a natural death was shattered nearly three years later by a further published statement by the latter gentleman entitled "Confessions of a 'Telepathist'. Mr. Douglas Blackburn & the Scientists. 30-Year Hoax Exposed. How the Deception was Planned and Worked." This article appeared in the *Daily News* of 1 September, 1911, and was an epitome of the series which had appeared in *John Bull*. Blackburn's summary of the situation was contained in the following words:

> "Messrs. Myers and Gurney were too anxious to get corroboration of their theories to hold the balance impartially. Again and again they gave the benefit of the doubt to experiments that were failures. They allowed us to impose our own conditions, accepted without demur our explanations of failure, and, in short, exhibited a complacence and confidence which, however complimentary to us, was scarcely consonant with a strict investigation on behalf of the public. . . . Smith and I by constant practice, became so sympathetic that we frequently brought off startling hits, which were nothing but flukes. The part that fortuitous accident plays in this business can only be believed by those who have become expert in the art of watching for and seizing an opportunity. When these hits were made, the delight of the investigators caused them to throw off their caution and accept practically anything we offered. . . . I shall doubtless raise a storm of protest when I assert that the principal cause of belief in psychic phenomena is the inability of the average man to observe accurately and estimate the value of evidence, plus a bias in favour of the phenomena being real. . . . The reports of those trained and conscientious observers, Messrs. Myers and Gurney, contain many absolute inaccuracies. For example, in describing one of my 'experiments', they say emphatically, 'In no case did B. touch S., even in the slightest manner'. I touched him

145

eight times, that being the only way in which our code was then worked."

The calibre and wide circulation of the *Daily News* meant that the S.P.R. Council could now no longer avoid taking some public action, the repercussions of Blackburn's second statement having travelled as far afield as America where the New York *Evening Sun* published a leading article about the whole affair.[1] On 4 September, 1911, the *Daily News* published an interview with Smith, in which he declared that Blackburn's statement was "a tissue of errors from beginning to end". One wonders what else he could have said in the circumstances. He said that he emphatically denied that he had "ever in any degree, in any way, working thirty years ago with Mr. Blackburn, attempted to bamboozle Messrs. Myers, Gurney and Podmore". He stated that he had no knowledge of trickery and was "the worst conjurer in the world", although, perhaps a little oddly in the circumstances, he claimed two paragraphs later in the published account of the interview that the conditions of the experiments were "too simple and too stringent to admit of conjuring", an opinion which one would have thought it would not be easy for him to form without some knowledge of the subject.[2]

It is natural, perhaps, in view of his doubts about Smith, that Sir Oliver Lodge did not choose to defend him during the *Daily News* controversy in 1911. William F. Barrett, a founder and former President of the Society, however, was interviewed, and his remarks were published in the issue of the *Daily News* of 6 September, where it was reported that he gave "an emphatic verdict for Mr. Smith". This is perhaps not surprising when it is remembered that Barrett's book *Psychical Research* had been published in 1911, in which Smith's work was described with approval and Blackburn's confession, quite incredibly, was not mentioned. Barrett's unqualified insistence upon the reality of telepathy in the

---

[1] Earlier informed American comment had not been favourable. Nineteen years before Blackburn's first confession, for example, Professor C. S. Minot said that "the explanation of the success of Mr. Smith in the reproduction of drawings is more probably fraud than supersensuous thought-transference". *Proceedings*, American Society for Psychical Research, March 1889, pp. 316–17.

[2] For proof from his own hand of G. A. Smith's technical knowledge of conjuring and especially pseudo-mindreading, in S.P.R. literature, the interested reader should refer to his account of the Baldwins' performance in Brighton in S.P.R. *Proceedings*, 1895, xi, pp. 225 ff.

face of evidence of fraud is perhaps exemplified by the fact that he evidently still believed the Creery sisters to be genuine as late as 1924 despite those young ladies' confession of trickery in 1888.

Mrs. Margaret de G. Verrall, another member of the Council, refused to champion Smith, however. This is not surprising, perhaps, in view of her expressed suspicion to Miss Johnson that Smith, in collaboration with the Brighton boys, was deceiving the Sidgwicks in thought-transference experiments in the hypnotic state in 1889 or 1890. Invited by the *Daily News* for her comment she said in that issue of the paper of 6 September, 1911, "I have no first-hand knowledge of the experiments in question, and no opinion to give on the article by Mr. Blackburn".

In a friendly and courteous reply to Smith in the *Daily News* Blackburn re-asserted the position he had taken up, expressing regret, however, that he had placed Smith in a difficult position due to his belief that his colleague of former days was dead, an opinion no doubt strengthened by the fact that Smith had remained entirely silent in 1908. He said:

> "I was informed of his death when I was in Africa, which since my return two persons who claimed to know him corroborated independently, while a letter I addressed to him was returned 'not known'. Had I been aware of his existence I should not have opened up on the subject, for I am aware that Mr. Smith, as he confirms in today's interview, spent many of the years that have elapsed since our acquaintance in close association with leading members of the Society for Psychical Research in a fiduciary capacity. I am also aware that the position was the legitimate reward for his services in connection with our telepathic 'experiments' and his undoubted power as a remarkable hypnotist."

Blackburn, in his penultimate paragraph, invited Smith to repeat the Dean's Yard tests, but the challenge was not accepted. He ended his letter to the *Daily News* in the following words:

> "In conclusion, I wish to convey to Mr. Smith my sincere regret for having unintentionally forced him into his present position. I have always retained a pleasant recollection of our short association, and during a very variegated life have been

more than once able to amuse and bewilder friends by practising some of the feats of legerdemain he taught me, but
which he now so modestly repudiates."

The matter of the Blackburn–Smith controversy has never before
been investigated, but since 1911 the leaders of the S.P.R. have
continued to insist, as opportunities have presented themselves,
upon the integrity of G. A. Smith and the villainy of Blackburn.
Thus as late as 1961, when a belated obituary of Smith was published in the *Journal*,[1] Mr. W. H. Salter wrote somewhat acidly
of the action of the *Daily News*:

> "The newspaper did not take the trouble to ascertain
> whether it was true that all the experimentalists were dead.
> In point of fact not only was G. A. Smith very much alive
> but William Barrett was also still alive, and both of them
> retorted in the same paper, contradicting the whole of Black-
> burn's statement. In this they were supported by Mrs.
> Sidgwick,[2] who, although not a member of the Committee,
> had, of course, been kept very fully informed as to its
> researches.
>
> In any subject other than psychical research it would be a
> matter of surprise that a periodical of standing should print
> a long article imputing fraud to a man who happened still to
> be living, and incompetence in their special subject to persons
> of the distinction of Myers and Gurney, on the uncorroborated
> word of a man who, according to his own statement, had been
> a party to the fraud."

The reader will no doubt wonder whether Mr. Salter was right
in saying that Blackburn's account was uncorroborated, when the
earlier published statement by Sir James Crichton-Browne, the
history of Blackburn and Smith's partnership in Brighton and the
rest of the evidence is considered. He may think it significant that
Smith took no legal redress against Blackburn in regard to the
latter's published statement in the *Daily News* that Smith had

[1] *Journal*, S.P.R., December 1961, pp. 219–21. Smith died on 17 May, 1959, at
Brighton General Hospital.
[2] In considering Mrs. Sidgwick's support of Smith it should be remembered that
she had published two long and detailed papers in S.P.R. *Proceedings*, which would
have been reduced to nonsense if Smith's integrity was not beyond reproach.

obtained his salaried employment with the S.P.R. partly as a result of his participation in fraudulent demonstrations of thought-transference. In addition, so far as Smith's integrity is concerned, he may well be curious about the long association with the S.P.R., both before and after Gurney's death, of Smith and the Brighton boys, to which we now turn.

CHAPTER ELEVEN

THE HYPNOTIST

W E have already learnt that before his contact with the Society for Psychical Research in 1882 G. A. Smith was living in Brighton at his mother's boarding house. We also know that early in 1883, presumably on becoming employed by the S.P.R. (or Gurney) as a hypnotist and private secretary, he left Brighton to live for some time in the Dulwich district of London,[1] probably in lodgings. Smith was nineteen years old in 1883. The dates of the events which followed are important because it was in January and April 1883, as the reader will remember, that the fraudulent experiments in thought-transference with Blackburn at Dean's Yard were taking place. Is it likely in these circumstances that the concurrent experiments now to be described could possibly have been genuine?

On 2 January, 1883, Smith introduced to the S.P.R. leaders the first of what seems to have been his surprisingly large circle of young male acquaintances, "a lad, Fred Wells, who had been a 'subject' of his mesmeric experiments",[2] and who was the son of a baker in Brighton.[3] It seems clear from these observations in S.P.R. *Proceedings* that, in fact, the boy Wells was one of the Brighton youths who, like Blackburn's office-boy, had been in the habit of receiving 1/- for "volunteering" to go on to the stage to be hypnotized by Smith during his public shows in Brighton in 1882. We learn from the "First Report of the Committee on Mesmerism"[4] that experiments by the S.P.R. leaders with various boys aged from twelve to twenty years, had previously been tried without success,[5] and that it was only when Wells was brought from Brighton by Smith that the hoped-for positive results began to be obtained.

[1] *Proceedings*, S.P.R., 1882-3, i, p. 221.
[2] *Ibid.*, p. 232.
[3] *Ibid.*, p. 221.
[4] W. F. Barrett, E. Gurney, F. W. H. Myers, H. N. Ridley, W. H. Stone, G. Wyld, and F. Podmore, *ibid.*, pp. 217–29.
[5] *Ibid.*, p. 220.

This first report of the Committee on Mesmerism makes it clear that even at this early stage it was the "higher phenomena" of the mesmeric state that so deeply interested the S.P.R. leaders. Smith and Wells gave what was evidently accepted as a genuine demonstration of community of sensation. The hypnotized and blindfolded Wells was placed in a chair and Smith stood behind him. Whether the blindfold was adequate and whether any person was present other than Smith, Wells and the experimenters we cannot, of course, be certain. Some part of Smith's body was pinched or pricked, and Wells was invited to say whether he felt anything. According to the S.P.R. report, it was necessary for the questions to be asked by Smith, as Wells conveniently "appeared not to hear any other speaker."[1] In the first sixteen of the twenty-four tests Smith held Wells's hand, but in the last eight trials no contact, so it was said, was made between the operator and the subject.

On twenty occasions out of twenty-four Wells was able correctly to indicate on his own body the spot pinched or pricked on Smith's. The experiments seem to have been concluded on this occasion because Wells evidently became sulky, and refused to answer further questions. He is reported as having said to Smith, "I ain't going to tell you, for if I don't tell you, you won't go on pinching me."[2]

The authors of the report conceded that the impressions might have been conveyed from Smith to Wells by means of a code, but contented themselves by saying that no circumstance occurred during the experiments that threw any doubt upon the "perfect integrity" of Smith. The reader may doubt this, for it seems highly suspicious that success was only achieved in this first work of the Committee when Smith was allowed to bring one of his young cronies from Brighton to be used as the hypnotic subject. He may well think it a curious coincidence that Wells, like Blackburn, had been previously associated with Smith in paid public shows in Brighton, and that in both cases the holding of hands seems to have been essential in the earlier tests.

On the same date that Fred Wells was first working for the S.P.R., 2 January, 1883, another "subject", Sidney Beard, briefly

[1] *Op. cit.*, p. 225.
[2] *Op. cit.*, p. 226.

made his debut in a joint experiment with Smith and Wells. They were referred to as the "three sensitives". No information whatever was given in regard to Beard's age or occupation, however, and so whether he was previously acquainted with Smith we do not know. When the "Second Report of the Committee on Mesmerism" was published on 18 July, 1883,[1] Beard featured rather prominently in it, and was described by the authors of the report as "our friend, Mr. Sidney Beard", but without a single detail about him. In the first List of Members of the Society published in December 1883 he appeared as an Associate living in the Bayswater district of London, but he evidently quickly severd his brief connexion with the Society for some reason, for in the second membership list prepared a year later his name was absent.

It is possible that Beard was used in some of the experiments described in the Second Report because even the authors realized that collusion between the operator and the subject was one obvious explanation of the "phenomena", and that possibly this might partially be countered by "an accumulation of experiments with different 'subjects'."[2] As Beard was an Associate of the Society, moreover, it is possible that he did not require payment for his services, as Wells and the other "Brighton boys" who were ultimately employed on Smith's recommendation undoubtedly did. However that may be, the lad Wells was again the subject in the first series of experiments described in the Second Report, i.e. tests of his sensitivity to whispering by Smith. The second phase of the work covered by the report utilized the services of Beard, who was the subject in trials made of responses by him to the "silent willing" of the operator, G. A. Smith, who conveyed to him the words "Yes" or "No" according to an arbitrary list prepared by the experimenters. Twelve tests of this simple alternative were made, and all were completely successful. Whether Beard and Smith were holding hands all the time is not precisely stated, but there is no doubt that they were doing so during some of the trials. The authors remarked that when Smith was holding Beard's hand "extreme adherents of the theory of 'muscle-reading' might maintain that 'yes' and 'no' indications

[1] *Proceedings*, S.P.R., 1882–3, i, pp. 251–62.
[2] *Ibid.*, p. 254.

were given by unconscious variations of pressure", but added that Beard was completely unaware of any such guidance.[1]

In the "Second Report of the Committee on Mesmerism" was also included the first brief mention of the finger experiments, which were later regarded as of great importance. The subject, blindfolded, was seated at a table on which his fingers were spread. It was stated that a paper screen placed in front of him made it impossible for him to see his fingers. Two of his fingers were chosen by the Committee and silently pointed out to the mesmerist, who made passes over them. After a minute or so the chosen fingers became stiff and insensible. G. A. Smith was named in the report as the operator in these experiments, but without any indication of the identity of the subject. As, however, there are references to "the boy's fingers" and "the youth" it seems very likely that it was Wells unless a further recruit from Brighton had already been introduced.[2]

The final phase of the experimental work described in the Second Report dealt with some surprising effects produced by the alleged influence of the operator, who was unidentified but was presumably G. A. Smith, over inanimate objects. He was taken to a room by the committee and invited to mesmerize small articles chosen by the investigators, such as a cardboard box and a pocket-book, from groups of ten small objects including items like a piece of wax, a paper-knife and a pen-wiper. The subject, who was not named, was able to pick out the appropriate object successfully after handling each of the possible choices. It is perhaps unnecessary to say that if in this supposed demonstration of the "higher phenomena" of mesmerism Smith was the operator, and he was in collusion with the subject, no further discussion is worth while.

I do not intend to weary the reader by taking him through the experiments in hypnotism conducted by Gurney in any detail, for they are not our primary concern, except in so far as they are enlightening on the question of the integrity of Smith, his relationship with Gurney and the other S.P.R. leaders, and the activities of the Brighton youths. By November 1883, when the third of the reports by the Committee on Mesmerism was published, it was

[1] *Op. cit.*, p. 256.
[2] For later evidence that Wells was the subject, see pp. 232–3.

clear that further experiments in community of sensation had been conducted by Gurney at his lodgings in Brighton in September, the operator being G. A. Smith and the subject a young cabinet-maker named Conway.[1] When Gurney published his paper "The Stages of Hypnotism" in January 1884[2] he did not say who the subjects of the experiments had been, but a variety of references to youths and subjects[3] makes it clear that more than one boy was employed.

Sometime between June and November 1884 (the paper is not dated in *Proceedings*, but those preceding and following it are) Gurney published his "An Account of Some Experiments in Mesmerism."[4] This paper described further finger experiments and a continuation of the trials in community of sensation, which had taken place in Brighton in April 1884. From the account of the finger experiments and the identification of the subject on this occasion as Fred Wells, "with whom most of the previous experiments had been made",[5] it is reasonable to assume that the unnamed subject in the Second Report of the Committee on Mesmerism was the same boy. The tests in community of sensation, i.e. pinching and tasting, were carried out with the youth Conway. The operator in all cases was G. A. Smith. It is of some interest to learn that Gurney's fellow investigator in this work was Dr. A. T. Myers, who accompanied Gurney and Smith to Brighton.

In December 1884 Gurney published his long paper "The Problems of Hypnotism."[6] It was a brilliant exposition of the elements in hypnosis which, on the basis of the experiments he had carried out, seemed to Gurney so mysterious and inexplicable. The reader may think that it was in the very excellence of Gurney's many long essays on the subject of mesmerism, which interested him so deeply, and on the so-called "higher phenomena", in which he so earnestly believed, that his tragedy partly lay. For on what kind of foundation did this five years of immense and exacting intellectual labour rest? As one reads the beautiful phraseology of Gurney's many long papers in *Proceedings*, and

[1] *Proceedings*, S.P.R., 1884, ii, p. 17.
[2] *Ibid.*, pp. 61–72.
[3] *Ibid.*, p. 72.
[4] *Ibid.*, pp. 201–6.
[5] *Ibid.*, p. 202.
[6] *Ibid.*, pp. 265–92.

follows the lucid and closely-reasoned arguments in favour of the existence of thought-transference and clairvoyance in the mesmeric state, one's mind cannot help reverting to the doubtful evidence upon which Gurney relied. Did Smith and his boys ever produce a single genuine phenomenon in those Brighton lodgings in those far-off days? It is a question we are entitled to ask, since by the close of the nineteenth century, when Smith had become interested in more profitable matters and the Brighton boys had gone their way, there does not seem to have been a single subject in England who was able to exhibit any of the "higher phenomena" of mesmerism under satisfactory conditions.

In 1885 Gurney and F. W. H. Myers (who from the beginning had been an active member of the Committee on Mesmerism) collaborated in the writing of a long paper "Some Higher Aspects of Mesmerism".[1] No experiments were described, and the authors dealt with the treatment of disease and the phenomena of silent willing by the operator. In March and July 1885, however, further series of finger experiments had taken place in Brighton, utilizing, as always, G. A. Smith as the operator. These were described by Gurney (possibly in conjunction with Dr. A. T. Myers, who collaborated in the experiments with Gurney and the Sidgwicks) in his paper "Local Anaesthesia Induced in the Normal State by Mesmeric Passes".[2] It seems very curious in view of the earlier opinion expressed by the S.P.R. leaders that it was desirable to use a multiplicity of subjects to avoid the possibility of collusion, that Fred Wells was again employed on the grounds that he had "been frequently mesmerized by Mr. Smith, and falls very easily into the sleep-waking state under his influence".[3] In the report a highly significant remark was made which makes it clear that these experiments relied entirely upon the integrity of Smith. It was admitted that the proximity of the operator and the subject was such that it would have been possible for Smith to have indicated to Wells the identity of the selected finger, had he wished to do so. "We have, however" (said the author or authors of the report) "every reason to believe Mr. Smith to be as much interested in carrying out a genuine experiment as the other

[1] *Proceedings*, S.P.R., 1885, iii, pp. 401–23.
[2] *Ibid.*, pp. 453–9.
[3] *Ibid.*, p. 453.

persons present."[1] The only other point of interest for us in this report is that again Dr. A. T. Myers seems to have been Gurney's principal co-investigator, and that for the first time Professor and Mrs. Sidgwick were present.

A paper by F. W. H. Myers, "Human Personality in the Light of Hypnotic Suggestion",[2] is not relevant to our inquiry except for the fact that in it Myers stated without qualification in the context of the essay, i.e. the "higher phenomena" of the hypnotic state, that "telepathy, or the transference of thought and sensation from mind to mind without the agency of the recognized organs of sense, has, as I hold, been already achieved".[3] The paper also made it clear that Dr. A. T. Myers was working closely with his brother and Gurney on these problems. F. W. H. Myers's following paper, immense in its length, "On Telepathic Hypnotism, and its Relation to other forms of Hypnotic Suggestion",[4] amply demonstrated his deep involvement in this branch of the Society's work and its supposed relation with telepathy, and his complete belief in its value and genuineness. The principal contents of the paper were devoted to his visit to Havre in April 1886 to observe the work of Dr. Gibert and Professor Pierre Janet with the French somnambule Léonie. The author stated that he was accompanied by Dr. A. T. Myers.

In April 1887 Gurney produced yet another long paper "Peculiarities of Certain Post-Hypnotic States",[5] describing further long series of experiments in Brighton. The hypnotist was, of course, G. A. Smith and the subjects were "W– – –s" (clearly Fred Wells, for he was described by Gurney as a young baker in Brighton) "S– – –t" (described as an intelligent young mechanic) and "P– –ll", a "sturdy young fellow" who was a light porter by trade. The tests seem to have involved Gurney and Smith in no less than six stays in Brighton; from 25 to 28 February, 1 to 3 March, 16 to 18 March, 21 to 27 March and two further periods

---

[1] *Op. cit.*, p. 455.

[2] *Proceedings*, S.P.R., 1886–7, iv, pp. 1–24.

[3] *Ibid.*, p. 20. This published statement by Myers, his joint paper with Gurney, "Some Higher Aspects of Mesmerism" and his own paper "On Telepathic Hypnotism, and its Relation to other forms of Hypnotic Suggestion" demonstrate how completely he was publicly committed to the genuineness of the Brighton experiments, as was Dr. A. T. Myers.

[4] *Ibid.*, pp. 127–88.

[5] *Ibid.*, pp. 268–323.

around the dates of 7 and 20 April. This illustrates my remark early in this book that there is no doubt that Gurney had been a constant visitor to Brighton during the years preceding his death for the purpose of experiments with Smith's friends, and that he was invariably accompanied by Smith. As in all the experiments discussed in this chapter, the results depended entirely upon the integrity of Smith and his group of paid young male acquaintances.

Shortly afterwards, in the same year of 1887, Gurney produced yet another long paper "Stages of Hypnotic Memory".[1] This was a further commentary upon the long series of experiments in Brighton in February, March and April. For some reason Gurney felt it necessary to point out in this report that he had no doubts about the integrity of Fred Wells and his two friends. There was, Gurney remarked, not "the slightest sign of trickiness or evasion" in their demeanour.[2] He clearly regarded Smith as his trusted fellow investigator in this immense mass of experimental work to which, in a condition of ever-increasing nervous exhaustion, he devoted the last tragic phase of his life. He seems to have been completely tireless in his application to the work in Brighton with Smith and the youthful subjects. How much of this obsession was due to the disintegration of the results of most of the rest of his labours for the Society we shall never be certain, but it clearly was an important ingredient.

During the autumn and winter of 1887 Gurney was back once more in the familiar surroundings of the seaside town to carry out "a long course of hypnotic experiments at Brighton, with the invaluable assistance of Mr. G. A. Smith (designated in this paper as S.) who was throughout the hypnotizer", as Gurney wrote in his subsequent essay "Recent Experiments in Hypnotism".[3] The tests concerned themselves with so-called "intelligent automatism" but were in the main a continuation of the finger experiments where, as we have seen, Gurney had already conceded that in view of the proximity of operator and subject and the resultant ease of collusion, complete reliance upon Smith's integrity must be assumed. No less than nine subjects were used and amongst the youths named was the now very experienced and favourite Fred

---

[1] *Proceedings*, S.P.R., 1886–7, iv, pp. 515–31.
[2] *Ibid.*, p. 527.
[3] *Proceedings*, S.P.R., 1888–9, v, pp. 3–17.

Wells. Other boys mentioned in the report were Kent, Parsons, Tigar, Hull and two cousins, A. and H. Nye. It was during these experiments, as the reader will recall, that Gurney reported the complete cure of the youth Parsons' toothache and headache by means of hypnotic suggestion by Smith. It is again of interest that the report reveals that both F. W. H. Myers and Dr. A. T. Myers were involved in some of the tests.

Gurney's final contribution to the literature of this subject which, as I have tried to demonstrate as briefly as I can in this chapter, completely dominated the last years of his life, was his paper "Hypnotism and Telepathy",[1] published in S.P.R. *Proceedings* in the spring of 1888. It was the culmination of his indefatigable efforts to prove the existence of what he believed to be the "higher phenomena" of the hypnotic trance since he had first actively interested himself in the subject in 1882. No further experiments were described, but the paper is of considerable interest from three points of view. First, Gurney made it abundantly clear that he regarded the conveyance of hypnotic suggestion from the operator to the subject as an example of thought-transference. He believed that the communication, as he put it, was *psychical* and not *physical*. Secondly, as he now considered that the results of his experiments in hypnosis supported his work on thought-transference and telepathic hallucinations, he said that he had complete confidence in the solid establishment of the contents of *Phantasms of the Living*. He was not to know in this, his penultimate contribution to the literature of psychical research, that his final brief two-page article in *Proceedings* was to be his admittance that the Creery sisters had been caught cheating, and had confessed to using a code in the early experiments upon which so much of the theme of *Phantasms of the Living* depended. Finally, in discussing the various possible explanations of the "phenomena" of the finger experiments, he left no doubt whatsoever in the mind of the reader that by this time he had entirely shut his mind to even the possibility that Smith and the subjects might be in collusion. We may suppose, moreover, from their deep involvement in the experiments and the published accounts of them, that F. W. H. Myers and Dr. A. T. Myers were equally convinced.

[1] *Proceedings*, S.P.R., 1888–9, v, pp. 216–59.

CHAPTER TWELVE

THE S.P.R. AND THE BRIGHTON BOYS

AFTER his revelation of the trickery of the Creery sisters in the late spring of 1888, Gurney's tragic death in Brighton in June soon followed. At a meeting of the Council of the S.P.R. on 16 July, 1888, at which Henry Sidgwick took the chair with F. W. H. and A. T. Myers, W. F. Barrett, F. Podmore and H. A. Smith present, Gurney's duties as honorary secretary were assumed jointly by F. W. H. Myers and F. Podmore.[1] No mention of the position of G. A. Smith brought about by Gurney's death was made in the Society's literature at that time, and we can therefore only assume that his later statement that he had been appointed private secretary to F. W. H. Myers after Gurney's death was correct, and that for the remainder of his period of engagement by the Society he was thus employed.[2]

Mrs. Henry Sidgwick attempted to continue Gurney's work on thought-transference in hypnotic trance with Smith and the Brighton boys in June, July and August 1889,[3] her place being taken by her husband when she was unavoidably absent. F. W. H. Myers, still apparently vitally interested in the subject, also took part in the experiments. It was of these trials that Mrs. Margaret de G. Verrall told Miss Alice Johnson on 7 December, 1908, that she believed that G. A. Smith and the subjects were cheating, and that she herself had guessed some of the numbers from audible indications given by him, adding that Smith talked a great deal to the subjects, that his phrases varied suspiciously and that she was under the impression that there had been some unspecified manipulation of the numbers drawn from the bag by Smith. The reader can judge the accuracy of these comments for himself to some extent by what follows. The principal interest of these trials lies in the additional information they offered on the question of

[1] *Journal*, S.P.R., October 1888, p. 305.
[2] *Journal*, S.P.R., October 1911, p. 121.
[3] H. and E. M. Sidgwick and G. A. Smith, "Experiments in Thought-Transference", *Proceedings*, S.P.R., 1889, vi, pp. 128–70.

the integrity of Smith and his friends, the conditions of S.P.R. experiments in those days and the attitude of mind of the investigators.

Two of the Brighton youths employed were described as "W", a clerk in a shop[1] and "a normal and healthy young man", and "T", a clerk in the telegraph office, aged nineteen "with whom many of Mr. Gurney's experiments described in *Proceedings*, Vol. V, were tried". "T" was clearly Tigar. Tigar had evidently been previously employed by Mrs. Sidgwick in some attempted thought-transference tests in the winter of 1888–9 and the spring of 1889 "but the success of these was not very marked" and it had been decided not to report them.

"P", a clerk in a wholesale business aged nineteen, who had, it was said, been very frequently hypnotized by Smith and used by Gurney in his work in 1887 and 1888, was also employed. He was "a lively young man, fond of jokes" and was obviously Parsons, for it will be recalled that Gurney's "P--ll" was a light porter by trade. A "Miss B", a shop girl, also took part in some of the experiments.

The tests with the youth "W" were very simple in character. He was hypnotized by Smith, who sat in front of him armed with some coloured cards. Mrs. Sidgwick wrote "Mr. W's eyes were apparently [!] closed; Mr. Smith sat in front of him, facing him and holding the card up with its back to him. We feel practically certain that Mr. W. could not see the colour normally. After each guess Mr. Smith said, 'Now we'll do another', whether the colour was changed or not."[2] "W's" guesses were generally successful, at which the reader will probably not wonder. Discussion seems superfluous, when the much superior feats of amateur conjurers are considered.

The next experiments with "W" were done with two-figure numbers written down by Mrs. Sidgwick and handed to Smith, who then conveyed them telepathically to the hypnotized "W". To provide supposedly fraud-proof conditions, Smith moved to a position behind "W's" chair. The divination by "W" of the number 32, for example, as recorded by Mrs. Sidgwick in *Pro-*

---

[1] Clearly "W" was not Fred Wells, who was a young baker. It is distinctly odd that Wells, Gurney's favourite subject, seems to have disappeared from the scene after the latter's death.

[2] *Op. cit.*, p. 129.

ceedings is worth reproducing for the reader's enlightenment. It is not easy to offer any temperate comment upon it, if the probability of a verbal code is suspected.

"*32*   S.   'Now then, Mr. W., here's another one.'
       W.   'Where?'
       S.   'Here it is.' (W. dropped off into a deeper state.)
       S.   'Mr. W., don't go to sleep.' (Roused him.)
       W.   '12, isn't it?'
       S.   'Which figure looks the most distinct?'
       W.   'The 2, I think.'
       S.   'Yes. Then look again at the other. Are you sure it is a 1?'
       W.   'I can't see.' (Pause.) 'I think it is a 3.'
       S.   'Well, then, what's the number?'
       W.   'Why, it's 32.' "

The experimenters next obtained a bag full of wooden numbers used in the game of "loto". These were small circular blocks of wood, and the double numbers from 10 to 90 were used. Smith hypnotized the subject Tigar, and then himself drew numbers from the bag and invited Tigar to guess them. Completely free conversation was allowed between Smith and the subject. When Tigar guessed 21 as 23, for example, the experimenters did not object to Smith saying "Sure about the 3?" Similarly, when the subject said that 59 was 29, the "conditions" did not preclude Smith from inquiring "Are you sure about the first one?"

The same uninhibited dialogue was allowed in similar tests with "P", whose correct guess of 17, for example, was somewhat laboriously made after the following chat with Smith.

"*17.*   S.   'Now then, P., here's another.'
       P.   'Put it there at once.' (Then, after some time): 'You've only put a 4 up. I see 7.'
       S.   'What's the other figure?'
       P.   '4. . . . The 4's gone.'
       S.   'Have a look again.'
       P.   'I see 1 now.'
       S.   'Which way are they arranged?'
       P.   'The 1 first and the 7 second.' "

"Miss B" was said to have been hypnotized before by Smith on three occasions, and was described as a remarkably good subject. She was able to guess numbers as successfully as "W" and "P". Her divination of the number 50 is of especial interest, as Mrs. Sidgwick evidently felt that it was necessary for her to give a helping hand on this occasion, whilst Smith literally told her what the number was.

"50.   S. 'Here's another one, Miss B.'

Miss B. 'Another! I don't see it.' (After a pause.) 'I think I can see something.'

S. 'What does it look like?'

Miss B. '5.'

S. 'Yes?'

Miss B. 'I don't see anything else just yet.' (Then, after a pause.) '5 and a round.'

Mrs. Sidgwick. 'Is the round round the 5?'

Miss B. 'No, after it; beside it.'

S. 'Then it's 50.'

Miss B. 'Yes, 50.'

It would weary the reader to discuss this nonsense,[1] to which Mrs. Sidgwick devoted no less than forty-three pages in *Proceedings*, in any further detail. It is perhaps sufficient to say that she conceded that whilst Smith's position relatively to the subject "so long as both were in the same room", did not affect the success of the experiments, "with Mr. Smith outside the room our success was poor", an admission which the reader may think was remarkably confirmed by the figures. In all 872 guesses were made, of which 140 were correct, although it was admitted that a guess was counted as correct even if the two digits were in the wrong order. Of these 140 notionally correct guesses, 9 only were obtained when Smith was out of sight and sound of the subject.

One's legitimate suspicion that the figures show beyond reasonable doubt that Smith was in collusion with his friends to deceive the experimenters would seem to be confirmed by a most

---

[1] It seems incredible that Frank Podmore, writing of these tests at a later date, could have said, "The conditions of the experiment were rigid, and it is certain that the percipient could not have gained any information by sight or touch." (*Telepathic Hallucinations*, London, 1909, p. 51.)

enlightening remark, made quite casually by Mrs. Sidgwick on pp. 128–9 of the report:

> "It was clear that the power of divining the numbers was exceedingly variable, but whether the difference was in the agent or the percipient or on what circumstances it depended we have so far been unable to discover.
>
> Eight persons, at least, besides Mr. Smith, tried to act as agents, but either failed to hypnotize the percipients, or to transfer any impression. Nor did others succeed in transferring impressions when the hypnotic state had been induced by Mr. Smith."

It seems truly remarkable that the S.P.R. leaders did not attach suspicion to the complementary and damning facts (a) that the earliest reports of the Committee on mesmerism had shown that no thought-transference or other "higher phenomena" were obtained until Smith was allowed to introduce his young Brighton friends as subjects, and (b) that even with the Brighton subjects, no "higher phenomena" occurred with any operator other than Smith, although as many as eight were tried.

A final point illustrates the degree of observation possessed by the experimenters. If the reader turns to p. 153 of the volume of *Proceedings* quoted, he will see that the left-hand column of the table shows the numbers that were drawn from the bag. On 27 July, 1889, in experiments with "P", the number 91 is recorded as so drawn, referenced to a puzzled footnote at the bottom of the page, "This must be wrongly recorded, as there were no numbers above 90 in the bag". If the reader will turn the page upside down he may think that there is a simpler solution to this mystery than that suggested by Mrs. Sidgwick.

One is entitled to speculate why the investigators could be sufficiently credulous to bother further. The reader may think that Mrs. Sidgwick, like F. W. H. Myers, was so consumed with a passion to prove telepathy at any cost, as a step to the proof of survival, that she was quite blind to the obvious facts. Possibly she hoped, with W. F. Barrett, that psychical research with her help might become "a handmaid to religion", as the latter once said to Dr. E. J. Dingwall.

Be that as it may, this time without the aid of Professor Sidgwick, and at various times from January 1890 to July 1892, Mrs. Sidgwick and Miss Alice Johnson, assisted at times by F. W. H. Myers[1] and W. F. Barrett, conducted what seems to have been the last of the Society's substantial inquiries into the subject which had so greatly interested Gurney.[2] Their report covered over sixty somewhat indigestible pages of *Proceedings*. Among the tests attempted were further series with the two-figure "loto" numbers, the transmission of diagrams and pictures and more of the finger experiments. Three of the previous subjects, Tigar, Parsons and Miss B., were used together with, surprisingly enough, three young men, Whybrew, Major and Adams, who had previously been employed by a travelling hypnotist who had been giving shows in Brighton. All the experiments took place in Brighton, sometimes in the investigators' lodgings, but more often in a beach dwelling occupied temporarily at the time by Smith, who by this time was no doubt making the preliminary arrangements, which were to fructify in 1892, to earn his living again in show business in Brighton.

G. A. Smith, as always, was the principal operator. Professor W. F. Barrett hypnotized Tigar one evening, and a Miss Charlesworth was able to hypnotize several of the subjects on a number of occasions without, however, the slightest trace of the alleged "higher phenomena" occurring. The highly suspicious conditions favourable for the production of any of these wonders seem to have been that Smith was the agent, that one of his Brighton friends was the subject and that they were in the same room. As in the case of the previous experiments, the results can be judged by the reader on what the authors of the report themselves wrote:

> "Mr. Smith was in all cases—of success at least—the agent, and when agent and percipient were in the same room the success was very marked. With agent and percipient in

[1] I shall suggest later that Myers had a strong personal motive for maintaining that all the Brighton experiments were genuine, even after Gurney's suicide, completely committed as he was to published belief in them. It is important in this connexion additionally to notice that his immense paper "The Sublimal Consciousness" (*Proceedings*, S.P.R., 1892, viii, pp. 333–535) depended entirely for its validity upon Myers's own experiments in Brighton using Smith as the sole hypnotist and Tigar and Parsons as the subjects. If these young men were suspected of trickery, then Myers's paper was rendered valueless.

[2] Mrs. H. Sidgwick and Miss Alice Johnson, "Experiments in Thought-Transference", *Proceedings*, S.P.R., 1892, viii, pp. 536–96.

different rooms there was some slight success when P was percipient, but none with T., and with Miss B. it was scarcely tried."[1]

It seems quite clear from the tone of the authors' comments in the report that Smith was regarded as a trusted fellow investigator and was subjected to no control. They said, for example (p. 545), that two of the subjects, Parsons and Tigar, "cannot be regarded as responsible for the *bona fides* of the experiments in the same way that Mr. Smith and ourselves are".

Another damaging feature of the report is that the reader is obviously not presented with all the facts, and that some of the omissions seem to be highly relevant. For example, on pages 593–4 the authors said, quite casually, that "various persons not mentioned in our paper" some of whom were "quite good hypnotic subjects" were mesmerized by Smith, and produced no thought-transference or other example of the "higher phenomena" whatsoever. The reader is entitled to wonder who these unidentified persons were, for it may well be suspected that if they were neither friends nor acquaintances of Smith there is a very good reason why they were unable to produce any results. Suspicions on this point are heightened by the disclosure (p. 594) that although Whybrew was a good percipient when Smith acted as the transmitting agent, he failed completely with Miss Charlesworth although she was, apparently, genuinely able to hypnotize him. The authors of the report said (p. 593) with probably more truth than they themselves suspected, "that the possibility of telepathic communication depends on both agent and percipient, and perhaps on a relation between the two".

In 1892 Smith seems to have given up his employment with the S.P.R. and returned permanently to Brighton to earn his living by activities far removed from psychical research. He remained, however, an honorary associate of the Society, and seems on occasions to have been willing to assist in various ways, although his interest in the subject clearly diminished quite rapidly. Whether he was paid for his services is not stated. In 1893, for example, the S.P.R. formed a committee for the systematic investigation of hypnotic phenomena and among the members were Dr. J. M.

---

[1] *Op. cit.*, p. 536.

Bramwell, a physician noted for his interest in hypnotism but who appears to have had little faith in the "higher phenomena", Dr. A. T. Myers and G. A. Smith.

In February 1894 the committee reported that they regretted the dearth of subjects, which had hindered their inquiry, as they did not like having to employ "young men, generally uneducated, who are accustomed to being hypnotized, and have to be paid for their time". These young men were not identified, but it is reasonable to assume that Mr. Smith's circle of acquaintances in Brighton were evidently still willing to accept reward for their services. In 1894 the subjects were becoming fewer, and none who could demonstrate the "higher phenomena" were to be found except in a single isolated case where the operator happened to be G. A. Smith. By May 1894 the committee had discovered nine persons, five of whom evidently were paid for their services. No details of any paranormal phenomena being observed were given.

The reader may think that these developments suggested rather strongly that as Smith's efforts to re-establish himself in show business in Brighton from 1892 onwards became more profitable and by degrees he severed his long connexion with the S.P.R., so the "higher phenomena" of the hypnotic state showed concurrent signs of dying a natural death. In 1893, by coincidence, moreover, Dr. Ernest Hart, a London medical man, published his book, *Hypnotism, Mesmerism, and the New Witchcraft*, formidably challenging the claims of the investigators of the "higher phenomena" and stating that in his opinion the whole subject was suspect. He declared that in his view all the alleged "higher phenomena" were either fraudulent, or due to self-deception on the part of the experimenters.

In their report for 1894–5 the S.P.R. committee stated that eighteen subjects had been hypnotized, that experiments in thought-transference had been attempted but that all the results were negative. The names of the hypnotic operators were not disclosed. In May 1896 the Society, discussing the work of its committee, stated lugubriously that they had been working with twelve subjects but no evidence whatever for telepathy in the hypnotic state had emerged. No details regarding the operators or the subjects were given. The 1897 report was meagre in detail, with no identification of the operators, and again it would seem that the "higher phenomena" were non-existent.

In December 1896 Dr. J. M. Bramwell, who had been an original member of the committee, had contributed two long papers to the *Proceedings* of the S.P.R.[1] The first dealt with hypnotic phenomena observed by the author in the course of his wide practice as a medical practitioner. The significance of this paper in regard to the matter before us is that Dr. Bramwell made no mention whatever of any of the so-called "higher phenomena" being observed by himself during his inquiries. His second paper, which provided possibly the best summary of the various views on hypnotism which had appeared up to that date, again failed to discuss, or even to mention, any of the "higher phenomena". He stated that nowhere had he observed more excellent subjects than among his own patients, and yet he apparently failed to produce in a single one of them any trace of thought-reading, clairvoyance or community of sensation. The fact that he declined even to discuss in print the marvels allegedly produced by G. A. Smith under the scrutiny of F. W. H. Myers, Professor and Mrs. H. Sidgwick and Miss Alice Johnson suggests that Dr. Bramwell had no belief in them.

In 1898 the S.P.R.'s hypnotic committee seems to have been finally dissolved, and the experiments abandoned. It appeared that the Society had now given up all hope that hypnotic subjects would ever again demonstrate with any success the existence of the "higher phenomena". Just as the "golden age" of alleged full-form spirit materializations, popularized by Florence Cook and William Crookes in the 1870's, had come to an end, so it seems true to say that the impetus given to the supposed para-normal manifestations in the hypnotic trance given by the profitable activities of G. A. Smith and his Brighton boys had finally died out. By the close of the century in England there does not seem to have been a single subject who was able to exhibit the "higher pheno-mena" of the mesmeric state in satisfactory conditions, and interest in the subject had permanently evaporated.

I have examined the S.P.R. reports upon the "higher pheno-mena" experiments with Smith and his friends after Gurney's

[1] J. M. Bramwell, "Personally Observed Hypnotic Phenomena", *Proceedings*, S.P.R., 1896, xii, pp. 176–203, and "What is Hypnotism?", *ibid.*, pp. 204–58.

death in 1888, because I think that these revealing accounts throw much additional light upon the work Smith did for Gurney from 1882 to 1888. I am also of the opinion that further insight into the whole matter is to be obtained by a brief examination of Smith's life after Gurney's death.

In the first half of 1888, as we know from the certificate of Smith's marriage in June of that year, Smith had been living in lodgings in London at 54 Beauchamp Place, close to Gurney's house in Montpelier Square, having moved there from Dulwich. In December 1888, however, his address in the S.P.R. membership list was given as Manstone Cottage, St. Lawrence, Ramsgate, on the coast of Kent where he was apparently still residing in 1890. As he married Miss Laura E. Bayley, the daughter of a saddler in Ramsgate, it seems possible that he found it convenient to make his home with his wife's parents for a time. He was, however, undoubtedly working for the S.P.R. in London at this period, as is demonstrated by a letter from Dr. A. T. Myers to Henry Sidgwick after Gurney's death. This letter, in the library of Trinity College, Cambridge, is undated, but is labelled "1888" by the cataloguer.

In this communication, in which Dr. Myers was suggesting to Sidgwick an appointment to discuss Smith's position with the Society, Smith's railway season ticket, for which, among other items, Smith was evidently asking the S.P.R. to pay, was mentioned. "He is rather anxious to have the season ticket", Dr. Myers wrote, "for he thinks he will often want to be with Podmore[1] and wants to do as much as he can to work up hypnotic subjects in London as well as Brighton." As Smith does not seem to have been living in Brighton at this time it seems likely that the proposed season ticket was to bring him from Ramsgate. Be that as it may, he ultimately moved from Ramsgate back to London, and his last address before returning to Brighton in 1892 was 2 Howletts Road, Herne Hill, London, S.E.

The reader is already aware of my opinion that Smith's real interest was in show business. His period of employment with the S.P.R. was a fortuitous interlude in his life which, as a young man,

[1] It is curious that despite Smith's anxiety to be with Frank Podmore Dr. Myers concluded his letter in regard to the suggested talk with Sidgwick to discuss Smith's affairs by saying "I have not asked Podmore to come, thinking it may be better without him".

he obviously welcomed, enabling him to rub shoulders for several years with men of social and intellectual distinction and to marry and live in comfortable security at an early age. But the preference and capability of his extroverted and obviously charming personality lay in the field of entertainment, and in my view it is against this background that his successful performances with the Brighton boys for the S.P.R. leaders should be judged. I am convinced that Smith had some skill as a hypnotist, which Blackburn himself frankly conceded, but I do not believe that Smith read a thought in his life, or that he and his circus of Brighton youths ever produced a single paranormal phenomenon of any kind for Gurney, Myers, Mrs. Sidgwick or anybody else. I think, not intolerantly, that Smith regarded himself as hired by the credulous S.P.R. leaders to produce the results they so obviously wanted, and he on his part was willing to give them value for their money. These assertions can fairly be judged, I fancy, by a consideration of the facts, (a) that Smith was a paid seaside entertainer before he joined the S.P.R. leaders, (b) that the thought-reading demonstrations with Blackburn were obviously trickery pure and simple, (c) that the subsequent demonstrations of the "higher phenomena" of the hypnotic state were unsuccessful even with the Brighton boys if Smith was not the agent, and also failed with Smith as the operator with subjects not recruited from his young friends and (d) that Smith reverted to type when he returned to Brighton in 1892. The first three of these suggestions are, I venture to think, proved by evidence assembled earlier in this book, and only the assertion in regard to Smith's activities in 1892 and subsequent years remains to be examined.

According to his son, Smith became a theatrical agent in Brighton for a short period in 1892, but the venture was evidently not successful. On 24 December, 1892, however, Smith announced in the *Brighton and Hove Herald* that he had taken a lease of the St. Ann's Well pleasure gardens at Furze Hill, Brighton. He added that he would be known to many by reason of the "highly successful hypnotic demonstrations he gave in Brighton a few years ago", and by "his lengthy association with the Society for Psychical Research". By April 1893 Smith had been able to "supplement the many natural attractions" of St. Ann's Well by the addition, amongst other things, of a monkey house, a gypsy fortune teller, swings and see-saws for the children and by popular lectures and demonstrations by himself.

In May 1894 Smith announced that St. Ann's Well had become one of the most popular amusement resorts in Britain. He claimed that "close to 3,000 visitors" had paid 3d. for admission on Whit Monday. The attractions now included captive baboons, an exhibition of dissolving views "by means of long-range limelight apparatus" and juggling and trapeze artists.

Smith's advertisements in the *Brighton & Hove Herald* and the *Brighton Gazette* on 7 and 9 June, 1894, announced a "BALLOON ASCENT AND THRILLING PARACHUTE DESCENT by Neil Campbell, Australia's 'Demon of the Air' ", on the following Saturday, augmented by trapeze, juggling and balancing acts. "The Demon of the Sky", it was said, "will perform his wonderful leap from the sky from a height of over one mile by means of a parachute." We may perhaps think that a mile was an exaggeration. However, in the event, Smith created more of a sensation with his "Demon of the Air" than he could have anticipated. "Half of Brighton", apparently, "was wild with excitement", because during the ascent of the hot-air balloon the Demon had been unable to free himself to make his spectacular parachute descent. After drifting over the town the balloon, with the Demon still attached, crashed into Brighton cemetery. The Demon, it was stated, broke a tombstone by the force of his descent, but was miraculously uninjured.

No doubt encouraged by this excellent publicity Smith placed a large advertisement in the *Brighton Gazette* on 16 June, 1894:

"SPECIAL ANNOUNCEMENT.
Owing to the brilliant success attending Mr. Neil Campbell's skilful and daring Ascent, Mr. G. Albert Smith has arranged for another
BALLOON ASCENT AND PARACHUTE DESCENT
to take place at St. Ann's Well and Pleasure Gardens, This day, June 16, at 6 or 7 o'clock in the evening.
Sole Lessee, G. Albert Smith."

One must admire Smith's audacity in thus advertising the "brilliant success", which had resulted in the unhappy aeronaut being blown willy-nilly over the astonished town, and then dragged igno-miniously among the tombstones. However, on this second occasion there was, according to the *Brighton Gazette*, "not the slightest hitch" and the intrepid Demon "descended without mishap, gracefully waving his hat on the way", landing, not in the macabre surroundings of the cemetery, but in the branches of a tree some little distance from St. Ann's Well. All the arrangements for the complete success of the occasion, it was said, had been made by "Mr. G. Albert Smith, the genial lessee of this charming resort".

Many amusing pages could be written on the basis of Smith's advertisements of his proprietorship of St. Ann's Well pleasureground, all redolent of his skilful and profitable showmanship. But sufficient evidence has been placed at the disposal of the reader, I fancy, to demonstrate that the Smith of thirty (in 1894) was the same public entertainer as the eighteen-year-old Smith of 1882, performing first by himself and then with Blackburn in the musichalls of Brighton. Can we really believe that his personality and outlook was any different during the intervening years?

Smith remained at St. Ann's Well until 1905. Some time between 1894 and 1897, however, he added to his activities and income by becoming a photographer, and developed an interest in another branch of show business, the new and exciting subject of the cinema, possibly inspired by the experiments of Lumière in Paris in 1895. When, in 1946, he was interviewed by Roger Manvell and Rachel Low, the film historians, he told them of his first interest in motion pictures:

> "He showed us the little notebooks in which he kept his first accounts. He had been a portrait photographer who in 1897 began to make simple record films of the streets and beaches at Brighton. The account-books showed columns with small amounts in shillings and pence for outlay and receipts during the first months of his work, but he showed us that by 1900 his profit from the sale and exhibition of his films had amounted to £1,800."[1]

In 1900, according to his half-page advertisement on p. 24 of *Modern Brighton*, published in that year, Smith was still offering the services of Mrs. Lee, the "Famous Gipsy Fortune Teller" in her caravan at St. Ann's Well, and selling grapes and cucumbers from the glasshouses there, but there can be no doubt that he knew

[1] Roger Manvell, *The Film and the Public* (London, 1955), p. 17.

where his future lay. Before 1900 Smith and another Brighton pioneer, James Williamson, had produced many short comic films which were immensely popular with music hall audiences in England, and both, as their catalogues show, were interested in amusing trick photography.[1]

Williamson, who like Smith had been a seaside photographer, built a studio for his film work in Brighton in 1902 as he became increasingly successful. In 1905 Smith followed suit. He sold his interest in St. Ann's Well and took a house in Roman Crescent at Southwick, between Brighton and Shoreham-by-Sea, Sussex. He built there a workshop and studio, naming the house (with his irrepressible showmanship) "Laboratory Lodge", where he worked for three years on the two-colour process for film photography, which he called Kinemacolour, financed by Charles Urban and later by Sir Alfred Butt, the well-known impresario and showman, and which Smith patented. His realization, as an experienced public entertainer, of the immense possibilities of the film industry, then in its extreme infancy, was undoubtedly the financial turning point in his life. As Roger Manvell reiterated in his book:

> "When George Albert Smith, the pioneer film-maker who began work in Brighton in 1897 showed me his account-books some years ago, the shillings and pence of his first entries against the cost of raw materials soon blossomed into three- and even four-figure entries as his business turnover rapidly increased."[2]

The patenting of Kinemacolour brought Smith success and moderate fortune. He was elected an Hon. Fellow of the British Kinematograph Society for his "services to colour Kinematography and his development of the first commercially successful colour system" and was awarded the silver medal of the Royal Society of Arts. Both Queen Victoria and King Edward VII saw some of his work, and on the death of the latter Smith took colour films of the funeral procession entering St. George's Chapel at Windsor.[3] In 1955 he was elected a Fellow of the British Film Academy. When the National Film Theatre was opened on

[1] Stanley Reed, *The Cinema* (London, 1952), p. 39.
[2] *Op. cit.*, p. 185.
[3] *Brighton Herald*, 23 May, 1959.

London's South Bank in 1957, the Academy invited the now ninety-three-year-old Smith as a guest. He was presented to Princess Margaret, met Gina Lollobrigida and other stars of the film world and was given a picture of the theatre by Lord Hailsham.[1]

Smith spent the years of his retirement at 18 Chanctonbury Road, Hove, Sussex. His daughter by his second marriage kept house for Mr. and Mrs. Smith at Chanctonbury Road, where he was visited by Dr. E. J. Dingwall in 1954. Dr. Dingwall did not take notes of the conversation, but has told me that Smith was in excellent health, and looked no more than seventy-five despite his ninety years. He was, indeed, about to mow the lawn when Dr. Dingwall called! It was on this occasion that Smith said that Gurney never suffered from neuralgia, and that obviously he, Smith, as his secretary, would have known about it if he had. Asked about the Brighton subjects, Smith said surprisingly, in what Dr. Dingwall understood to be a homosexual connotation, that these were "Mr. Podmore's young men". Smith offered no further explanation of this remarkable statement. He claimed that the earlier thought-reading demonstrations with Blackburn, however, were genuine, since neither knew anything about codes. When asked by Dr. Dingwall how he could explain why Blackburn's book and articles showed detailed knowledge of the technique and psychology of trickery, however, he had no answer and changed the subject, saying that he really must ask to be excused, as he had to mow the lawn.

Smith died on 17 May, 1959, at Brighton General Hospital of myocardial degeneration and generalized arteriosclerosis. He was ninety-five. A short obituary appeared in the *Brighton Herald* of 23 May, 1959. It is tragic to have to record that within six months of his death both his wife and daughter also passed away.

I am happy that it has fallen to my lot, within the covers of one book, to trace, however briefly, the careers of George Albert Smith and Douglas Blackburn from the days of their short partnership when they so thoroughly tricked the Society for Psychical Research. Both were resourceful and attractive men, energetic and formidable in all they undertook. Small wonder, perhaps, that together and separately they were rather more than a match for the S.P.R. leaders.

[1] *Evening Argus,* 19 October, 1957.

CHAPTER THIRTEEN

THE REVELATION

IT is now our final task to turn back to the account of Gurney's death and the inquest, and try to answer the questions I asked at the end of Chapter II. Why did the happily married, socially accomplished and wealthy Gurney, free from physical disease, affectionately regarded by all who knew him and energetically immersed in work in which he was intensely interested, take his own life behind that locked door in the Royal Albion Hotel in the small hours of 23 June, 1888? Why did the leaders of the S.P.R. go to such lengths for so long to hide the fact that death was self-inflicted?

In Appendix I I have discussed the theory that has been held in some quarters for forty years that Gurney was secretly engaged in homosexual practices in Brighton, and that discovery or black-mail was the cause of his suicide. I fancy that the sensational quality of this idea has more to do with its attraction for some, than its likely truth. There is certain evidence that suggests the possibility of some rather curious goings-on in which Frank Podmore may have been involved, but none, I believe, to connect Gurney with them. But that apart, I do not think that anyone who has studied the events of Gurney's life can doubt for a moment that his suicide was for a reason connected with his work. In the first place, if this were not so the S.P.R. leaders would scarcely have gone to such lengths to conceal it.

More importantly, it is obvious that Gurney's dominant and indeed obsessive interest was his work in psychical research, especially towards the end of his life when his labours were sufficiently compulsive to bring him to the point of nervous exhaustion. His extreme activity was his sole defence against the demon of despair, for we know from the events of his life that his comfortable financial position and his domestic happiness in them-selves offered no alleviation of the cruel torments of his manic-depressive condition. His work was his fatal point of vulnerability.

I do not think that it can seriously be doubted that when, at the persuasion of F. W. H. Myers and against his own initial inclination, Gurney agreed to devote his immense energy and great intellectual powers to the subject of psychical research he realized, either then or later, that a failure in this, his fourth attempt to establish himself in intellectually rewarding work, would be his final tragedy. That is why, I think, he persevered for so long as six years in the face of so much disillusionment. That is why he spoke to Myers, and probably to Margot Asquith, Henry Sidgwick and others, of his recurrent wish "to end all things", a desire kept at bay only by his immersion in his labours and the hoped-for proof of survival through the establishment of thought-transference.

When music failed Gurney he was thirty, and he was only thirty-five when he had finally given up first medicine, and then the law. But when he died he was in his forty-second year. At that period of his life a man of Gurney's psychological structure and case history would have good reason for unbearable despair if he discovered that the whole of his work in psychical research was valueless. Keats wrote that "there is no fiercer hell than the failure in a great object",[1] but the tragedy which faced Gurney in 1888 was more formidable still, if this be possible.

He had, as we have seen, suffered a considerable and bitter disillusionment over many aspects of psychical research, culminating in the Creery sisters' confession. Yet despite so many demolitions of his published work (or more probably because of them), we find that he was more active than ever in the last phase of his life. The reader may think that Gurney toiled feverishly on with his experiments with Smith and the boys in Brighton because the hoped-for proof of the "higher phenomena" of the hypnotic trance was all to which he could now cling. When he was not in Brighton he was writing, amidst his daily duties as Hon. Secretary and Hon. Editor of the S.P.R., the long and laboriously detailed papers that have been listed in earlier chapters. He was, in those final months, as Lady Battersea said of him, devoting not only his time and his pen but also "alas! his strength, to that which seemed always evading his grasp".

[1] In the "Preface" to *Endymion*, written in Teignmouth in 1818, seventy years before Gurney's death.

His beautiful and devoted wife, as Lady Battersea has also told us, suffered much from enforced loneliness as Gurney spent more and more of his time away from her. If proof were needed of the obsession that drove on the weary Gurney during the last phase of his life, I do not think we need look further than his neglect of Kate. He was, as we know, normally an intensely sympathetic and understanding man, unusually sensitive to the sorrows of others, and this causing of distress to his own wife seems highly significant.

Kate Gurney, according to Lady Battersea, remained devoted to him to the end. Although powerless to help him, she seems to have understood the manic-depressive element in her brilliant and beloved husband's personality, which forced him along the path he had chosen with ever increasing momentum during those last few months. It seems also that on that last night he spent at home on 21 June, 1888, Mrs. Gurney knew that he faced a catastrophe in his affairs.

It was a path full of menacing hazards for Gurney because, as we know, he had entirely shut his mind to the possibility that Smith and the Brighton youths might be deceiving him. Was Sir Oliver Lodge right in his recollection that Gurney had caught Smith in trickery in 1883, a recollection which we may think is confirmed by the otherwise inexplicable omission of the Smith–Blackburn experiments from *Phantasms of the Living*? Did Gurney, as must inevitably follow, accept Smith's explanations and assurances of complete future integrity, and employ him as a trusted colleague in that belief? If the answers to these questions are in the affirmative, then we need no further explanation of Gurney's curious repeated insistence in his later writings of the certainty of the *bona fides* of Smith and the boys. He was reassuring himself, against probability and against the evidence, that all was well. He was reassuring himself, not only in regard to the genuineness of the Brighton experiments, upon which the whole of his later work and writing depended, but also in connexion with his faith in his fellow-man. We may recall that Podmore wrote that he had never met anyone who had such an absolute belief as Gurney in "goodness and truth as common human attributes", and in "the goodness and honour of others, of all whom he knew". Gurney's very nobility of character made it easier for Smith to deceive him.

We may be quite certain, I think, that if Gurney discovered that the "higher phenomena" at Brighton relied on trickery, and that the trusted Smith had deceived him again for five years for financial gain, no other reason for his suicide need be sought. That, in my opinion, is what happened in June 1888. Both his work and his faith in human nature were destroyed by one mortal blow. This was the sudden catastrophe of which Mrs. Gurney became aware, without knowing its nature. No other explanation fits the facts so adequately, and in particular the mysterious circumstance of Gurney's solitary journey to Brighton where the experiments had all taken place, and his death there, during the absence of Smith on his honeymoon.

In what form did the tragic revelation come? I think that this question can be answered with reasonable confidence by an examination of the evidence. Gurney died in the small hours of Saturday, 23 June, 1888. On Sunday, 17 June, he had visited Lord Rayleigh's home at Terling Place in Essex. Lord Rayleigh was a Vice-President of the S.P.R. Lady Frances Balfour was a fellow-guest, and wrote to F. W. H. Myers on 26 July to describe her meeting with Gurney. She said that the latter spoke of his work in psychical research "with a force and vividness which at the time I felt most impressive", from which it is clear that during that last week-end before his death Gurney was unaware of the impending catastrophe.

On Tuesday, 19 June, Gurney met Professor and Mrs. Sidgwick, and Henry Sidgwick narrowed the gap further when he wrote later in his "Journal":

> "I myself have had painful doubts;—but the evidence is very strong that he was making plans vigorously up to almost the very day of his death. We saw him last on Tuesday 19th; he seemed to be well and in good spirits."

On Thursday, 21 June, Gurney dined at the House of Commons with his friend Cyril Flower, later to be Lord Battersea, who the reader will recall wrote a letter over the fatal week-end for Dr. A. T. Myers to produce at the inquest, describing Gurney's health as good and his conversation brilliant. Whilst I think that his letter may have overstated the matter of Gurney's health (when the contrary opinions of Lady Battersea and Professor Croom Robertson are considered) for not unworthy reasons and possibly under persuasion, it is nevertheless conclusive enough as regards the matter before us. If the blow had already descended Gurney would not have been in the mood for dining with Cyril Flower or anyone else. What unexplained or significant incident occurred in Gurney's life, then, after he parted from Flower at the House of Commons?

The reader will have foreseen the obvious answer to this question. We know that when Gurney arrived home that night he found a letter awaiting him. We may presume that it was delivered earlier in the day, and the reason why he had not read it before is clear enough if a map of London is consulted. The S.P.R. rooms in Buckingham Street, W.C.2 (the Society had moved from Dean's Yard in 1887) were much closer to the House of Commons than Gurney's home in Knightsbridge. He would clearly be on duty as the S.P.R. Secretary in Buckingham Street on that day in view of Smith's absence, and it would obviously be more convenient to go direct to his meeting with Flower rather than make the longer journey to Montpelier Square, S.W.7, and then return to Westminster.

Mrs. Gurney never knew who wrote the letter, but she did know (clearly from the postmark) from where it came. Its provenance was of significance, and the reader may think of sinister significance, for it came from Brighton and asked Gurney to go there. Either the invitation itself was urgent, or Gurney himself regarded the contents of the letter as not brooking any delay, for he went straight off to Brighton on the following day and Mrs. Gurney never saw him alive again.

If the hypothesis that the letter was very far from being an everyday communication is doubted for a moment, let the reader ask himself the following questions. Why did Gurney conceal from his wife who the letter was from, a circumstance strongly suggesting that it was of an extremely confidential nature? Why did Mrs. Gurney think, presumably from her husband's demeanour, that the letter heralded a catastrophe? Why did Gurney find it necessary to set off alone for Brighton on the following day, which seems a certain indication that the contents of the letter were urgent and important? Above all, why did the unknown writer of the letter not come forward at the inquest, on the irresistible assumption that Gurney went to Brighton to meet his correspondent, and that therefore he or she was the last person to talk with Gurney apart from the staff of the Royal Albion Hotel?

CHAPTER FOURTEEN

THE INFORMANT

So far we have been dealing with facts and what seem to be irresistible inferences from them, and it may be urged that it is not necessary to take the matter further. But what I believe to be the certainty of Gurney's suicide and the reason for it, coupled with the hitherto unknown fact of the letter from Brighton, makes the temptation to try to deduce from whom it came overwhelming, with the obvious qualification that the reader's guess could be as good as my own. As I have said, I believe that Gurney went to Brighton in response to the summoning letter to meet someone who knew and who could prove that Smith and his friends had been deceiving him by trickery from the beginning. Who was this mysterious correspondent who indirectly caused Gurney's death and was therefore too terrified to come forward after the tragedy?

One inevitably thinks first of one of the Brighton youths, for they would be fully aware of the fraudulence of the experiments. My friend Mr. A. S. Jarman, who has long been interested in the history of psychical research, thinks that we need look no further for a solution. Mr. Jarman, I may say, is in convinced agreement with me (a) that abundant evidence has been assembled to show that Smith and his friends were deceiving Gurney and the other S.P.R. leaders, (b) that Gurney committed suicide because the deception became known to him, and (c) that the fact that the tragedy occurred during the very period of Smith's absence on his honeymoon is highly significant.

Mr. Jarman concedes that as the Brighton youths' motive for joining with Smith in the deception, like that of Smith himself, was obviously the simple financial one that they were paid for their work by the S.P.R., it seems unlikely that they would seek themselves to interrupt this comfortable arrangement. Mr. Jarman agrees, too, that it is difficult to believe that Gurney would accept the word of a youthful and confessed trickster in regard to the lack of integrity of the trusted Smith, unless irrefutable documentary evidence was additionally available.

Mr. Jarman is of the opinion that Smith's absence on his honeymoon was in itself the cause of Gurney discovering the documentary proof of trickery himself, and that this is the explanation of the striking coincidence of Gurney's solitary and fatal journey to Brighton having been made at this very time. Mr. Jarman thinks that since a code was undoubtedly used, Smith would possess a notebook or other memory aid with the details of the signals written down, possibly with a duplicate in the possession of a particularly trusted associate like Wells. Mr. Jarman believes, additionally, that there may well have been secret correspondence taking place between Smith and his chief associate in Brighton, arranging the week-by-week details of the deceptions, arrangements which it would have been very difficult to make on the spot as Gurney and Smith always went to Brighton together. Mr. Jarman is of the opinion that in the special preoccupation and excitement of the preparations for his wedding in Ramsgate on 10 June, Smith may have forgotten to take his usual precaution of destroying an incriminating letter, or may have left his code book in an unlocked drawer at the S.P.R. rooms, or in his lodgings at 54 Beauchamp Place, close to where Gurney himself lived.

Mr. Jarman thinks it probable that on Tuesday, 19 June, after seeing the Sidgwicks in Cambridge or in London, Gurney took the opportunity to do some written work in connexion with the Brighton experiments, or some routine S.P.R. paperwork. His secretary was away, and as so often happens in these circumstances, he was unable to find some necessary notes, letter or other document he needed and had occasion to rummage amongst Smith's papers and drawers, or possibly even in his secretary's lodgings where Gurney was no doubt an entirely trusted and familiar figure. To his horror he found the irrefutable evidence of Smith's guilt. His reason told him that he must accept the fact of Smith's deceit, but his emotions demanded an immediate seeking out and confronting of Smith's confederate in Brighton. He wrote at once to the Royal Albion Hotel for a room and according to Mr. Jarman's theory the letter which awaited Gurney when he reached home during the evening of Thursday, 21 June, was simply a confirmation from the hotel of his booking for the night of Friday, 22 June.

Mr. Jarman's reconstruction envisages that Gurney went to Brighton urgently to see Smith's principal associate, who would probably be Wells. Confronted by the documentary proof that Gurney had brought, the sheepish youth poured out the whole sorry story in circumstantial detail that more than confirmed what the horrified Gurney had already discovered in London. If the informant was Wells, then we need seek no further explanation as to why the person whom Gurney met in Brighton did not come forward after the suicide was discovered, and why the facts of Gurney's death have remained a mystery to this day. Wells, seeing the desperate state to which Gurney had no doubt been reduced by the revelation, would know that his share in the deception was partly responsible for Gurney's death. His lips would be sealed forever. I have conceded to Mr. Jarman that it is a remarkable coincidence that Wells vanished from the literature entirely, and seems to have withdrawn from any further contact with the S.P.R., after June 1888.

Mr. Jarman's views carry great weight with me, and his solution of the mystery of the identity of Gurney's informant may well be correct. The fact that I am in amiable disagreement with him is based upon a number of considerations to which the reader may or may not attach importance. First, if the letter from Brighton was from the Royal Albion Hotel in answer to a letter from Gurney requesting accommodation, it is difficult to understand why the authorities had to rely upon the unposted letter found in Gurney's pocket when his body was discovered as the only available information regarding his identity, and in consequence urgently communicated with Dr. A. T. Myers rather than with Gurney's home. Secondly, the timetable of the suggested events in Gurney's life on Tuesday, 19 June, when he appeared cheerful and reasonably well to the Sidgwicks, seems to me possible but uncomfortably tight. It allows only one day for Gurney to have (a) met the Sidgwicks, (b) subsequently discovered the damning documentary evidence, and (c) decided to go to Brighton immediately and written post haste to the Royal Albion Hotel. Thirdly, I find it hard to accept that if on 19 June he knew the worst and his suicide was in consequence imminent, he would have dined with Cyril Flower on the evening of Thursday, 21 June. My view, in short, is that the first intimation of the revelation was in the letter which awaited Gurney at his home after the dinner engagement with Flower.

In the early days of this inquiry Mr. Jarman and I discussed the possibility that the writer of the letter might have been Douglas Blackburn, who of course knew that Smith was a fraud and was later to say so in detail twice in print, without Smith taking any action in regard to what was clearly a libel. As we now know, however, Blackburn was no longer living in Brighton, nor indeed in England, in 1888. He had gone to South Africa.

Who else did Gurney know well in Brighton, who was also intimately acquainted with G. A. Smith and had detailed knowledge of the experiments? It could not be anyone who *officially*, so to speak, took part in the later trials, for according to the published accounts the participants were limited to Gurney and his S.P.R. colleagues, Smith himself and the Brighton youths. There is, however, one person (and, I think one person only) who was in a position to know exactly what was going on, and had almost certainly been involved in the earlier frauds. Who was it?

We know that Smith and Gurney had always stayed in lodgings in Brighton, which is indeed one of the facts which gives Gurney's death in the large impersonal Royal Albion Hotel some of its curious significance. Smith's widowed mother kept a boarding house in Brighton, first in Grand Parade and later in nearby George Street, and I cannot think in the nature of things that Gurney and Smith would stay anywhere else. Whatever else we have discovered about Smith we know that he had, in moden parlance, an eye to the main chance. Had this not been so he would scarcely have bothered to sell cucumbers at St. Ann's Well in 1900, when he was already making a good deal of money in other directions.

Smith was also persuasive, as was demonstrated by his ability to utilize the fraudulent experiments with Blackburn for the creation of a job for himself with the S.P.R. The stays of himself and Gurney in Brighton were regular and frequently out of season, and would be a most welcome source of business to any boarding house. Can we believe that Smith would not suggest, as a matter of course, that they lodged with his mother and that Gurney would not agree? An additional and compelling advantage which Smith could legitimately urge is that his mother would raise no objection, as some landladies might, to having groups of working-class youths continually on the premises, and that she would be able to offer facilities for the privacy which the experiments would demand. If this is accepted, it follows that over a period of five years of constant visits to Brighton Gurney would come to know the members of his secretary-cum-hypnotist's family extremely well.

Smith had two sisters, Frances Anne (always known as "Fanny") and Alice, both of whom were older than their brother. Alice never married. Both are now dead. In the days of the Brighton experiments they assisted their widowed mother in the running of the boarding house, which would include the provision of Gurney's creature comforts. One wonders, in parenthesis, what they thought of this brilliant and charming man, whom Jane Harrison considered to be the most lovable and beautiful human being she had ever met, and whose good looks so fascinated George Eliot that for days she could think of nothing else?

Can it be shown that one of Smith's sisters was familiar with the secrets of her brother's hypnotism, telepathy and all the rest of it? Is there any information available which demonstrates that either Fanny or Alice had actually been involved with Smith and the S.P.R. in this kind of activity? We are fortunate in that such evidence does exist, albeit only in a single tantalizing published reference, and in two unpublished entries in the diary of F. W. H. Myers, for which latter information I am indebted to Dr. Alan Gauld. Neither of these sources indicate which of the two sisters was concerned in the affair.

Myers and Gurney first met Smith and Blackburn and saw the earliest demonstrations of the alleged thought-transference in November 1882. Myers, whose diary entries are annoyingly laconic, recorded that it was on Wednesday, 15 November, that they initially journeyed to Brighton to meet the hoaxers. It is, however, the entry for the following day, 16 November, that is of intense interest to the investigator of this complex mystery. Of that day's meetings and activities Myers wrote simply "Miss Smith and Smith", which means that one of Smith's sisters was at his side on the occasion of his first meeting with the S.P.R.

leaders. The fragment of published evidence, to which I shall shortly turn, makes it certain that "Miss Smith" was Smith's sister and not an aunt or even some unrelated person. At the beginning of December 1882 a second visit to the seaside town was made and the diary entry for the first day, Saturday, 2 December, reads "To Brighton. Smiths seances." On Sunday, 3 December, Myers wrote "Blackburn. Smiths. E. G."

To my mind these entries in a diary over eighty years ago, brief though they are, demonstrate beyond doubt that one of Smith's sisters was importantly involved in some way with her brother and Blackburn in the fraudulent thought-reading experiments from the beginning. These meetings in Brighton were not social occasions; the interest of Myers and Gurney in these young people was their claim to be able to demonstrate mind-reading, and if Miss Smith was present from the first, and indeed given precedence over her brother in the order of names in the diary we may, I fancy, be quite sure that she was very much in the trick. It may of course be urged that in the S.P.R. accounts of the tests no mention of Miss Smith is made, but we are entitled to reach the melancholy conclusion that this is of no significance. The reader will recall that Sir James Crichton-Browne revealed that the Society's published descriptions of the later Smith-Blackburn experiments at Dean's Yard in early 1883 omitted some highly relevant details, the most important of which was the presence, in an otherwise exclusively male gathering, of a young lady who seated herself in an ideal position to pass signals from Blackburn to Smith.

It seems clear, this time from a published source, that Miss Smith was not only in some sort of discreet partnership with Smith and Blackburn in connexion with the bogus mind-reading, but also claimed to be a hypnotist. In the "First Report of the Committee on Mesmerism", published in April 1883, it is stated "Mr. Wolferstan had been brought into the mesmeric state by Miss Smith, sister of the Mr. G. A. Smith above-mentioned, in the presence of Dr. Myers and Mr. Podmore".[1] I have read through every subsequent report in *Proceedings* up to and beyond Gurney's death, and I can find no other mention whatsoever of Miss Smith. Now this is very curious, for the Committee on Mesmerism had great need of hypnotic operators in addition to Smith, both from

[1] *Proceedings*, S.P.R., 1882-3, i, p. 221.

the point of view of convenience and because the employment of nobody but Smith made the experiments vulnerable to criticism on the grounds of collusion. Yet after this single appearance in April 1883 demonstrating her skill to Dr. A. T. Myers and Frank Podmore, Miss Smith is never heard of again. Why?

In trying to answer this question one cannot help but wonder about the mysterious young lady who appeared at Dean's Yard to assist Smith and Blackburn in the bogus thought-reading experiments in April 1883 and who, it seems, was almost certainly Miss Smith. At one time I thought that a claimant for that role could be Blackburn's mistress Mrs. Parsons, but I now have reason to alter that opinion. In the first place Mr. Jarman has since drawn my attention to the fact that the Brighton newspaper accounts of the Parsons divorce case suggest that the liaison between Blackburn and Mrs. Parsons did not begin until August 1883. Secondly, I have only recently been informed (March 1964) by Dr. Gauld of the Myers diary entries, demonstrating the vital fact of the major involvement of Miss Smith in the affair from the beginning.

It is true that Sir James Crichton-Browne, writing more than twenty years after the event, assumed that the mystery woman of Dean's Yard was Blackburn's wife. He was clearly wrong about that, for Blackburn never married, although equally clearly he could not be mistaken at any period of recollection about the striking presence of one young woman in a group of middle-aged men. One answer to the problem of Sir James's mistaken idea that Blackburn and Miss Smith were man and wife could be that he remembered that the young couple were upon familiar and affectionate terms, which might well have been. Blackburn would obviously know Smith's sister extremely well, and who can tell what their relationship at the time might have been, on the assumption that Blackburn's liaison with Mrs. Parsons did not start until four months later?

In this connexion, modern evidence is most fortunately available from Mrs. Ford, the daughter of Fanny, which seems to point conclusively to the fact that the Miss Smith involved in the affair was Alice. Fanny married the late William H. Attwick of Brighton, and according to Mrs. Ford's information her father was courting Fanny in the 1882–3 period with which we are concerned. Mrs. Ford has said that Douglas Blackburn and Alice were "walking out" together at this time, making up a foursome with Attwick and Fanny. Both Blackburn and Attwick, who were contemporary in age, were constantly at the boarding house in Grand Parade. I think that this information establishes beyond any reasonable doubt that the young lady of Dean's Yard, who in January and April 1883 was mistakenly remembered as Blackburn's wife, was Alice, when the facts are considered in conjunction with the Myers diary entries demonstrating that one of Smith's sisters was involved in the trick from its inception. Alice, moreover, by irresistible inference, was clearly the bogus lady hypnotist "Miss Smith" mentioned once in S.P.R. *Proceedings*.[1]

In parenthesis, it is of great interest to discover that Letty, the central character in Blackburn's later novel *Love Muti*, was a girl of outstanding sexual attraction, whose supposed activities as a hypnotist formed an integral part of the plot. I have shown that Blackburn's books abound in material upon conjuring, pseudo thought-reading and similar activities, all clearly based on his early adventures in Brighton. Is it possible that in similar fashion the character and physical charms of Letty were drawn to some extent from Blackburn's memories of Alice?

An inference that could reasonably be made from the dates of these events suggests that Alice and Blackburn acted in concert upon at least one occasion. Alice's single appearance in *Proceedings* as a hypnotist, consorting with Dr. A. T. Myers and Frank Podmore, coincides precisely with the Dean's Yard experiments, for the "First Report of the Committee on Mesmerism" and the "Third Report on Thought-Transference" were both published on the same day, 24 April, 1883, and appeared side by side in the first volume of *Proceedings*. Neither Alice nor Blackburn were ever mentioned again in *Proceedings*, and seem to have disappeared from the S.P.R. scene together. One wonders why.

Whatever the answers to these secondary questions may be, it is clear that Alice Smith, with Blackburn, was in her brother's confidence as regards the earlier frauds. It seems probable, too, that Alice withdrew from further participation in the bogus experiments at the same time as Blackburn, who later published the

[1] According to Mrs. Ford, neither Fanny (her mother) nor Alice (her aunt) had any hypnotic ability whatsoever. When shown the account of Miss Smith having hypnotized Mr. Wolferstan, Mrs. Ford said emphatically that this must have been "just a bit of fun".

details of the fraud. I cannot think that these facts, hitherto undiscovered, can be lacking in significance. Did Alice, in a private statement to Gurney, with what would obviously be a prior condition of absolute confidence, anticipate Blackburn in revealing the truth? We are without information in regard to the personal relationships existing between the persons concerned, and so it is impossible to determine what Miss Smith's motive may have been.[1] Was it spite against her brother, or his new wife, or fear over Smith's ever-deepening involvement in deception for the purposes of gain? Had she herself something to confess?

One thing seems certain, and that is that such a revelation about her brother, followed by the suicide of Gurney (however unexpected this may have been so far as Alice was concerned) would have grave repercussions in regard to her relationship with any member of her family who knew what Alice had done. We may also think that neither Alice nor any confidant she may have had would thereafter speak of the matter to another soul. It would seem to be, therefore, of considerable significance to know from Mrs. Ford that at this time Alice, for some reason not disclosed by either, became completely estranged from her mother, the two never speaking to each other again. This may be confirmed by the fact that in 1889, the year after Gurney's death, the Brighton directories of the period show for the first time a Miss A. Smith as running a boarding house at 39 Marine Parade.

Wherever the truth of the matter may be, it seems quite certain that Alice would be fully aware of the real nature of the alleged thought-reading which Smith claimed as part of the "higher phenomena" of his hypnotic operations. She would be well acquainted, too, with the Brighton youths associating with Smith, some of whom had been involved in his stage performances before the fraudulent demonstrations to the S.P.R. in conjunction with Blackburn and his sister. It seems certain that Alice was in her brother's confidence as regards the deceiving of the S.P.R. in 1883, and it is therefore reasonable to suppose that any letters passing between them after he left Brighton to live in London would be uninhibited on this subject. If she was indeed the secret

---

[1] Mr. H. E. Pratt thinks that a possible motive for Alice's action may have been a sentimental regard for the attractive Gurney, whom she could not bear to see deceived further.

correspondent in Brighton envisaged by Mr. Jarman as necessary to Smith in arranging the deceptions with the boys, we need look no further for the source of the postulated documentary proof of Smith's guilt that was produced to Gurney.

If the reader is of the opinion that Alice probably was the writer of the letter from Brighton, he will have anticipated the reason why she wrote it at the date she did. It would be very difficult for her to communicate with Gurney upon a secret matter concerning her brother without an acute risk of Smith finding out. Smith was always with Gurney during the visits to Brighton, whilst any attempt to get in touch with Gurney in London, by letter or otherwise, would be just as dangerous in view of Smith's position as Gurney's trusted private secretary. Her opportunity came in June 1888 when her brother was on his honeymoon in the Isle of Wight and the coast was clear. The reader may think that the coincidence of the letter and Gurney's hitherto unexplained and solitary visit to Brighton during Smith's absence from the English mainland can be accounted for in this way.

It would be idle to speculate upon the possible terms of the letter. All we know about it is that Gurney did not let his wife know who it was from, or what it was about, but that he set off for Brighton the following day where, according to the theory here advanced, he kept an appointment with Alice Smith. I think it reasonable to suppose that even if Alice merely wrote to say that she was acutely anxious about something connected with her brother and the genuineness of the experiments, which she wanted secretly to discuss with Gurney in Brighton, he would go. He would realize that such a sinister intimation coming from Smith's own sister, whom he knew well, could not be trivial.

I have already suggested that Alice would almost certainly be in a position to give Gurney absolute proof, probably documentary, of what she had to tell him. If this were not so she would scarcely have suggested the meeting. I think also that before the full revelation, she would obviously extract a promise from Gurney that he would not reveal what she was about to tell him to another living soul. She had been acquainted with Gurney for some years, and she would know that in the case of a man of his character an undertaking given by him would be honoured to the letter. Her object would presumably be attained if Gurney ceased to employ her brother in future hypnotic experiments with his friends in Brighton, and it may well have seemed to her that Gurney, once convinced by her that he was being duped, could do this without insuperable difficulty and without revealing the true reason. But can we, knowing more of Gurney's psychological situation at the time than did Alice Smith, adequately imagine his emotions as he walked away, alone, from that rendezvous in Brighton during that afternoon of 22 June, 1888?

CHAPTER FIFTEEN

THE LAST NIGHT

CAN we doubt the effect upon Gurney of the discovery of this second example of Smith's trickery? A single stroke had shattered both his belief in human nature and the published work of five laborious years. To the emotional and unhappy Gurney, who had said to F. W. H. Myers (and seemingly to Margot Asquith, Henry Sidgwick and to others) that only the fervour for his work for the Society for Psychical Research overcame his "wish to end all things", the craving now for personal extinction must have been overwhelming. Relief could only come to him from a sleep from which he would never awaken. In those final hours of 22 June, 1888, however, another aspect of the painful revelation must have occurred to Gurney. He would realize that, did he continue to live, he must endure an impossible dilemma.

He would know that, whatever undertaking of secrecy he had given to his informant, the new and disastrous circumstances must become public knowledge. He could not continue his work for the Society. The prolific papers which he had contributed to the first five volumes of *Proceedings*, all based upon Smith's integrity, must be withdrawn. Already he had done this in the cases of Sir Edmund Hornby, Mr. X.Z.'s haunted house, the Creery sisters and so on. Such a further wholesale withdrawal would make the S.P.R. a laughing stock amongst the scientific men who already regarded its work with open and understandably hostile criticism.[1] The Society's brief life of six years would end in disaster, and even men of the great academic reputation of Henry Sidgwick would not emerge unscathed from the débâcle. Both F. W. H. Myers and A. T. Myers, who were Gurney's friends, were closely associated with the Brighton experiments and were publicly

[1] Professor Simon Newcomb, the astronomer, for example, later said that twenty-seven years of the *Proceedings* and *Journal* of the S.P.R. had produced no proof of telepathy, nor, indeed, anything whatever that one would not expect to find in the ordinary course of nature. ("Modern Occultism", *The Nineteenth Century*, January 1909, pp. 126–39.)

committed to belief in them. Gurney, who had a strong inclination to accept blame even for the mistakes of others, would feel himself entirely responsible for the agonizing situation which now faced both himself and his associates. He may have thought that the catastrophe stemmed largely from his own enthusiasm and misplaced trust in Smith in 1883.

If he lived to meet his friends again, he could not conceal the devastating news that would certainly invite the complete ruin of the Society. At the same time, he would betray any promise that he had given to his informant. Death, upon which he was now determined, offered at least a partial solution of his intolerable problem. So far as the Society was concerned, he could appease his conscience by sending a significant warning that he no longer believed in the validity of the Brighton experiments.

I believe that, with considerable subtlety, Gurney did communicate such a warning to Dr. A. T. Myers. That it failed in its purpose was not the fault of its anguished sender. In my opinion, it was the pride and obsessive belief of F. W. H. Myers, who had publicly identified himself with the Brighton experiments, coupled with a fear of ridicule and the exposure of the now largely rotten fabric of the Society's work, that led to the successful masking of the whole tragic fiasco.

Once Gurney had decided to end his life, he would consider the practical and humane aspects of his grim intention. He would wish to protect his wife from the painful shock of the certain communication from the police and from the distressing duty of identifying his body. This could be accomplished by three moves. These we know he made. He would end his life that night in Brighton in a large, impersonal hotel where he was unknown. He would remove from his person all identifying papers, thus to ensure that the inevitable telegram did not go to his wife. The complementary device of the unposted letter in his pocket would lead the police to communicate with the addressee. Who could be more suitable than Dr. A. T. Myers, a physician who daily dealt with death and who could be relied upon to break the news gently to Mrs. Gurney? Gurney would also remember that Arthur Myers had taken part in the Brighton experiments and he would thus be an appropriate person to warn of the trickery of Smith.

I have little doubt that Gurney implied obliquely to Dr. Myers that he was about to take his life. Whether he also hoped that the physician might seek a verdict of accidental death I do not know. It seems probable, for Gurney would wish to save his cherished wife and daughter from the stigma of his suicide.

Is it possible to reconstruct, at least in outline, the letter that Edmund Gurney wrote, probably in the small hours of 23 June, 1888, before he embraced the oblivion for which he now longed? We know a little about its probable contents. Basically, it asked Dr. Myers to join Gurney at the Royal Albion Hotel, which was, ironically enough, its real as well as its ostensible intention. The tragic subtlety was that Gurney knew that he would be dead when his friend responded to the summons. The letter contained no open statement that Gurney was about to destroy himself. Conversely, we know that it offered no evidence that Dr. Myers could use at the inquest to demonstrate that Gurney did not intend to commit suicide. We may think that it contained implications plain to Dr. Myers but not apparent to the authorities. It might have been phrased thus:

"Royal Albion Hotel, Brighton.

22–vi–1888

My dear Arthur,
  I shall be grateful if you will join me at this hotel as soon as you can tomorrow. It may be inconvenient for you to leave London at such short notice, but you will be doing a great service to an old friend and colleague if you can do so. I need your assistance urgently, for I now doubt the validity of our work in Brighton, and have decided today to bring it to an end.

Yours ever,
EDMUND."

Such a letter would acquaint Dr. Myers with the essence of the calamity, but could plausibly be explained in quite different terms to the authorities. Unlike the Myers brothers, the Coroner and the police would not appreciate the catastrophic effect upon Gurney of his sudden disbelief in the validity of all the work at Brighton. Dr. Myers could convincingly explain that the value of any scientific inquiry might well become doubtful at any time for a variety of reasons, and the trials be discontinued in consequence.

In spite of his private knowledge, he could stress that Gurney's declared intention to terminate matters in Brighton referred to nothing but his work there.

In parenthesis, it seems extraordinary that this letter, known to be the last written by Gurney, was not produced in evidence at the inquest. We know that Dr. Myers had consulted with the authorities before the inquest, and that he even visited the Stipendiary Magistrate immediately upon his arrival in Brighton on the Monday. Were the actual contents of the letter suppressed at the inquest at the persuasion of Dr. Myers, supported by the testimonies written by the eminent Henry Sidgwick and Cyril Flower, and by the "short memorandum" prepared in Cambridge on the previous day? Was this successfully urged upon the Deputy Coroner, on the grounds that the letter contained ambiguities possibly suggesting suicide to anyone unfamiliar with Dr. Myers's "version of the story" and which he claimed might mislead the jury?

It seems clear that a verdict of suicide, in the case of the death in the midst of his work of the Hon. Secretary of the S.P.R. and Editor of its publications, for no reason connected with his domestic or financial circumstances, or his physical health, could arouse the most dangerous and critical speculations regarding the Society's work and methods. For this reason, it seems clear that the two Myers, well knowing that Edmund Gurney had taken his life, were determined to conceal the fact if possible. I believe that this decision was taken, and the operation planned, at the home of F. W. H. Myers in Cambridge on Sunday, 24 June, 1888.

Dr. Myers saw Gurney's letter on his first visit to Brighton, when he went to identify the body on the Saturday. It seems highly significant that, despite his indisposition, he then found it urgently necessary to go to Cambridge next day to see his brother. It will be recalled that after the inquest, the doctor wrote to F. W. H. Myers that he had given his "version of the story" to the Stipendiary Magistrate, and he referred to the effectiveness of the "short memorandum". This suggests that there was a version of the story that differed from the one Dr. Myers was determined to advance, and which had been prepared in written form beforehand. Presumably this was the tale of Gurney's alleged neuralgia and of his supposed addiction to various opiates. The first reference we have to these matters comes in the story that Dr. Myers had prepared for the Coroner. It is an odd coincidence that Dr. Myers was almost certainly using similar drugs himself to alleviate his epileptic condition.

If the purpose of the Cambridge conference was not the preparation of this "version" to be given at the inquest the following day, then what was it? As I have written previously, if no camouflage was to be devised, a simple letter from Dr. Myers to his brother would have sufficed. Why the additional tiring journey to Cambridge between his visits to Brighton on the Saturday and Monday? Why the telegram immediately the inquest was over?

I do not think that Sidgwick was involved in the plot. He had, as we know, "painful doubts" about Gurney's death; he had to be talked out of the idea of suicide by Myers. The call upon Sidgwick, after the brothers had arranged matters between themselves, was to persuade him to write the letter, supporting that obtained from Flower, which rebutted the theory of suicide.

If the reader is satisfied that the two Myers went to considerable trouble to obtain a verdict of accidental death, he can decide for himself on whose behalf it was sought. We know that little anxiety was shown for Mrs. Gurney. The day after her husband had died in the service of the Society, his closest colleagues were not comforting her in London, but were conferring amongst themselves in Cambridge. It is noteworthy that in the lengthy letter to his brother following the telegram after the inquest, Dr. Myers made no reference to his dead friend's widow or to the relief that the verdict may have brought to her. The satisfaction over what had been achieved was confined to a small circle of the S.P.R. leaders. It was they who had been saved from ridicule, from the critical speculation and from the disaster that could follow the startling revelation of the self-destruction of the Society's most active member in the midst of his work.

It is impossible to say with certainty whether the Myers brothers believed that Gurney had positively discovered Smith in further trickery. It seems unlikely, on the face of it, since Smith's employment was continued and two further series of experiments were conducted with him before the whole business of the "higher phenomena" was allowed to fade into decent oblivion. Even so, we may suspect that if Gurney's letter aroused suspicion at the

S.P.R., Smith would talk his way out of it and that his persuasions would fall upon willing ears. He had managed it before. He could legitimately maintain that Gurney had been suffering from nervous exhaustion, and that his judgment was impaired. We have already seen how F. W. H. Myers, at heart a spiritualist, was only too ready to believe in Miss Wood and Miss Fairlamb after they had shown every evidence of fraud.

It may be thought, too, that a threatening situation could have developed if Smith, who had just married on the strength of his employment with the S.P.R., had been dismissed. F. W. H. Myers, who, with Frank Podmore, had assumed the position of joint honorary secretary immediately after Gurney's death, would fear that an angry Smith could have precipitated the exact calamity that he and his brother had taken so much trouble to avoid. It seems not without significance that F. W. H. Myers gave Smith a job as his own secretary. If he remained dependent upon the Society for his living, he could cause no trouble and everything could continue as before. The Society and its leaders were safe, and the death of the man who had given to it the last six years of his life would soon be forgotten.

In his letter to his brother, Dr. Myers referred to the short obituary which F. W. H. Myers had written on Sunday, obviously to be given to the press after the inquest if all went well. It was possibly that published in the *Sussex Daily News* on Tuesday, 26 June, 1888. If this is so, it is a curious reflection upon Frederic Myers's loyalty and upon his supposed friendship for Gurney that, when writing the obituary the day after the latter's body was discovered, the co-author of *Phantasms of the Living* seized even that opportunity to excuse himself from the criticisms which had been directed against the evidence collected in the book.

> "Mr. Gurney worked up himself the enormous mass of material which is contained in this book; and whatever opinions may be held as to the soundness of the view expressed in the work, everyone must be struck by the extraordinary grasp and subtlety with which the intricate theory of evidence is treated."

The reader may think that there is some similarity between Myers's attitude to Gurney and his treatment of Anne Marshall, whose tragic story has been briefly told on pp. 51–2. Be that as it may, I believe that just as Myers, plagued by remorse, ultimately revealed the truth about his involvement with Mrs. Marshall, so I think that similarly he betrayed his uneasy knowledge of Gurney's suicide.

As already mentioned, in 1893 Myers prepared for private printing, in twenty-five copies, his *Fragments of Inner Life*, the contents of which were to remain secret until after his death in 1901. Even at this later date, the circulation was limited to six friends. The booklet consisted of a somewhat rambling autobiography and a score or so of poems in Myers's lush and rather turbid style, mainly concerning his affair with his cousin's wife, which ended in her suicide in 1876. One poem of three verses, however, which appears on pp. 33–4, seems entirely different in theme and emotional involvement from anything else in the book.

It bears the simple but, to my mind, highly significant title "Brighton". No less an authority on Myers than W. H. Salter told me, in his letter of 28 July, 1962, that he had always supposed that this poem, so clearly personal in tone, was written by Myers with Gurney's death in mind. One is bound to agree, for what more momentous event for Myers could have occurred in Brighton than the suicide of his colleague? If this is accepted, together with the interpretation of the lines which follows, then Myers was revealing another secret as intimate as those relating to Anne Marshall, which are contained in the other poems of *Fragments of Inner Life*.

The first two verses of the poem portray the promenade at Brighton at night as "the long-lit pavements gleam" in the lamp-light, and the "gay groups" of visitors pass to and fro. It will be recalled that the Royal Albion Hotel is on the front at Brighton, and that the imagined scene might therefore exactly depict that of the latter part of the evening of 22 June, 1888, when Gurney went up to his room and locked his door on the world for the last time. It will be recalled that Gurney retired about 10 p.m., when the gas-lamps on the promenade would be lit but visitors would be strolling below.

But now "dark midnight deepens", and the sea, "which kissed at morn the children's play", becomes melancholy and sinister. The atmosphere is transformed in the depths of the night (when Gurney took his life) to one of impending tragedy:

"O starless waste! remote despair!
Deep-weltering wildness, pulsing gloom!
As tho' the whole world's heart was there
And all the whole world's heart a tomb."

It is the sombre final verse, however, which seems so clearly descriptive of suicide:

"Eternal sounds the waves' refrain;
'Eternal night,'—they moan and say,—
'Eternal peace, eternal pain,
Press close upon your dying day.
Who, who at once beyond the bound,
What world-worn soul will rise and flee,—
Leave the crude lights and clamorous sound,
And trust the darkness and the sea?' "

Although Gurney is not named, the meaning seems fairly obvious. The soul, weary and "beyond the bound" (or driven beyond the limit of endurance, as Gurney was) seeks refuge in flight (by self-destruction) from an unmerciful world. Fleeing from the now insupportable cruelties of life (symbolized by "the crude lights and clamorous sound") it entrusts itself in ultimate despair to the darkness of death, and the unknown, eternal sea of oblivion.

If this melancholy poem is written of Edmund Gurney—and there is no evidence to suggest that any other suicide in Brighton had affected Myers—then the latter had known from the beginning that his friend had died by his own hand. One may think that he was troubled again by his conscience, as he was when composing the verses about Anne Marshall, in whose tragic death he was also closely involved. He knew that he had imposed upon the vulnerability of his kindly but reluctant colleague; that he had persuaded Gurney, against his inclination and good judgment, to devote his life to psychical research. To this labyrinth of fraud and frustration, Gurney had given six years of his life—and finally had yielded that life itself.

It is curious to contemplate how Frederic Myers, that ardent lover of life, and the Society which his obsessive enthusiasm had largely founded, were encompassed by a dark aura of violent death. When *Fragments of Inner Life* was written Anne Marshall, deserted in her extremity by Myers, had already drowned herself in Ullswater, and his co-author and close friend had destroyed himself behind a locked hotel door in Brighton. His brother and colleague, Dr. A. T. Myers, succumbed a few months later to an overdose of drugs (and who better than a physician would know the border-line between a safe and a fatal dose?), whilst his other co-author, Frank Podmore, was to be found drowned in mysterious circumstances in a small lake near Malvern.

Was the poem "Brighton" a threnody to the dead Gurney? In the light of the context, and of the knowledge that we now have, it is difficult to believe otherwise. Edmund Gurney, sickened to his soul and past the bounds of suffering, had sought the sanctuary of death on that June night those many years ago. And thus it fell to the conscience-stricken Myers to compose both his epitaph and elegy.

APPENDIX I

IN the nineteen-twenties, a rumour became current in certain psychical research circles that Gurney and other S.P.R. leaders of the period had been secretly engaged in homosexual practices in Brighton, involving G. A. Smith and his circle of youthful working-class hypnotic subjects. This suggestion, which had its origins in Brighton and has persisted over the years, included the hypothesis that discovery or blackmail was the cause of Gurney's suicide.

I have not found any evidence whatever to confirm such a rumour, except in the case of Frank Podmore.[1] The knowledge that he was an active

[1] I do not think that this submission is made invalid by the disclosures in Dr. Phyllis Grosskurth's *John Addington Symonds. A Biography*, which was published on 29 June, 1964, some weeks after my book had gone to the printer. This biography is based upon Symonds's MS. memoirs, to which Dr. Grosskurth has been allowed access. The memoirs themselves cannot be printed until 1976 because of a fifty-year embargo upon their publication by Symonds's literary executor, H. F. Brown.

J. A. Symonds (1840–93), the author and translator and one of the first members of the S.P.R., is revealed as a practising, and indeed a proselytizing, homosexual. Dr. Grosskurth's book shows that a number of his friends in the Society during its earliest years actively shared his proclivities. These included Arthur Sidgwick (the brother and joint biographer of Henry Sidgwick) whose lifelong friendship with Symonds, Dr. Grosskurth tells us, "had strong erotic undertones". (*A Biography*, p. 76.) Symonds considered that Sidgwick's love affair with a boy at Rugby exposed him to "external danger". (*Ibid.*, p. 109.) Another S.P.R. friend was Oscar Browning, who was dismissed from his position as a master at Eton in 1875 because of his alleged intimacy with some of the boys (*Ibid.*, p. 76). H. Graham Dakyns, whose liaison with Cecil Boyle, a pupil at Clifton College, is revealed in the biography (*Ibid.*, pp. 108 ff.), was Symonds's lifelong friend and an early S.P.R. member. The Hon. Roden B. W. Noel, "handsome, feminine in manner, and inordinately vain", frequently tempted Symonds "to succumb to homosexuality". (*Ibid.*, p. 119.) It was when Noel came to stay with him that Symonds "abandoned himself to sex". (*Ibid.*, p. 177.) When the S.P.R. was founded Roden Noel became one of its first Vice-Presidents.

Although Henry Sidgwick was a close friend of all these persons, and was especially intimate with Symonds and Noel, I can find nothing in Dr. Grosskurth's book to confirm the suggestion in Mr. Raymond Mortimer's review in *The Sunday Times* (London), of 28 June, 1964, that Sidgwick was inclined towards homosexuality. More importantly, the name of Edmund Gurney is nowhere even mentioned in the biography, which unquestionably would have been the case had he been involved in any way whatsoever in these activities. Nor, so far as I am aware, did the S.P.R. members named by Dr. Grosskurth as active homosexuals take any part in the experiments with the Brighton boys, if the accounts in *Proceedings* can be relied on at all.

The single possible exception is F. W. H. Myers, who Dr. Grosskurth tells us was "a close friend of Symonds who suffered the same sexual problems as Symonds in early adulthood". (*Ibid.*, p. 125.) It was whilst Symonds was staying with Myers at Cambridge in 1865 that the latter suddenly read to him the section extolling homosexuality from Walt Whitman's poem "Calamus", a section omitted from the later editions of *Leaves of Grass*. (*Ibid.*, p. 119.) Writing to H. G. Dakyns in 1866 Symonds said that he, Arthur Sidgwick and F. W. H. Myers were "three of not the least intellectually constituted members of our Universities assailed by the same disease". (*Ibid.*, p. 115.) But there is no mention in the biography of any incidents involving Myers in active homosexual practices, as is the case with every one of the other persons named. It is fair to point out, moreover, that Myers, born in 1843, homosexual is traditional in the Society for Psychical Research. A former President gave me this information, which has been confirmed to me during the past year by the present President. Neither of these informants suggested to me that there was any connexion between Podmore and the Brighton youths, but others with whom I have discussed the mystery of Gurney's death have done so.

My opinion is that this vague rumour arose simply because of what seems to be positively known about Podmore, and the fact that he was a close colleague of both Gurney and Myers on the Council of the Society for Psychical Research, and collaborated with them in the preparation of *Phantasms of the Living*. Another ingredient is no doubt the fact that the S.P.R. leaders spent so much time in Brighton in constant association with G. A. Smith's large circle of young male acquaintances, most of whom were uneducated working-class youths. The Cleveland Street scandal, which shocked London in 1889, the year after Gurney's death, and the trial of Oscar Wilde in 1895, both affairs involving the association of educated and eminent men with just the type of youth used in the hypnotic experiments, may have provided a circumstantial background for these suspicions.

In disposing of this story in connexion with Gurney, it is helpful that in this book I have assembled the evidence which demonstrates beyond reasonable doubt that F. W. H. Myers was, by the time of his affair with Mrs. Marshall in 1873 to 1876 at latest, actively heterosexual in his tastes. I think, therefore, that his many visits to Brighton and his contacts with Smith's young men in the 1880's were wholly for their ostensible purpose of psychical research. If this was true of Myers, who was as close a colleague of Podmore as Gurney, then clearly any argument based merely on Gurney's own collaboration and friendship with Podmore breaks down. Gurney was, moreover, happily married and, as I have shown, seems to have been as much attracted to women as they were to him.

There remains the problem of Frank Podmore himself, his homosexuality and his possible connexion with the Brighton youths. This must be briefly examined, because of the very curious statement made by G. A. Smith to Dr. E. J. Dingwall, that the Brighton boys were "Mr. Podmore's young men". My own view is that this oddly casual remark, which is supported only by tenuous fragments of evidence, can safely be ignored by any student of the Brighton affair. However, the reader must judge for himself, and I will set out such facts as there are which relate, however circumstantially, to Podmore and Smith's friends.

Podmore was employed as a senior clerk in the Secretary General's Department of the Post Office in the headquarters building at St. Martin's-le-Grand in London. Some of the youthful hypnotic subjects, such as the favourite Tigar, were employed by the Post Office. Blackburn, in one of his accounts of how the deception was accomplished, referred to "the lad Murphy, a telegraph messenger, and a young fellow who was a sort of learner, or something of that kind, at the Brighton telegraph office".[1]

The department of the Accountant General of the Post Office was housed in the same building at St. Martin's-le-Grand where Podmore worked. In 1889, the year after Gurney's death, London was shocked by the scandal of

was in his forties (and therefore well past "early adulthood") at the time of the activities in Brighton.

[1] *John Bull*, 9 January, 1909, p. 39.

the male brothel at 19 Cleveland Street.[1] The Earl of Euston and Lord Arthur Somerset were involved, the latter being forced to resign his offices in the Royal Household and flee to France. Five of the male prostitutes at the house in Cleveland Street, Swinscow, Wright, Thickbroom, Perkins and Barber, were telegraph boys. Henry Horace Newlove, who introduced the boys to the brothel and was sentenced to nine months' imprisonment for assisting to keep a disorderly house, was a clerk in the Accountant General's Department of the Post Office.

Any connexion between Podmore and the youths at Brighton which has been argued on the basis of the preceding paragraphs is limited to the following slender and what seem to me unrelated circumstances. At the relevant time there was some homosexual activity involving junior Post Office employees, and this activity was connected with a clerk who worked in the same Post Office building as Podmore but in a different department. Some of the boys at Brighton were telegraph messengers. Against this must be set the fact that nowhere in the long accounts of the Cleveland Street affair is the name of Podmore mentioned so far as I am aware. None of the names of the Cleveland Street telegraph boys correspond with those in Brighton.

Other evidence to which my attention has been drawn is equally tenuous. On 5 December, 1908, Sir Oliver Lodge wrote a letter to J. G. Piddington, a fellow Council member of the S.P.R., in regard to Smith and Blackburn. This letter has never been published by the S.P.R. The first paragraph of the letter referred to Lodge's recollection "that the code or deception practised by Smith and Blackburn" had been detected by Gurney. Lodge went on to say (in development of his theme that Smith could nevertheless hypnotize "however fraudulent he might be") that Blackburn had not been involved in the published hypnotic experiments "with the boys and Smith". The word "boys" occurred at the beginning of a line. Very oddly, the one word "street" was added in the left-hand margin against the word "boys", presumably after the letter had been completed. It has been argued that since this addition was clearly deliberate, its meaning must be significant. What were "street boys"? Were they identical with the "boys on the Boulevard"[2] with whom Lord Alfred Douglas asserted Oscar Wilde notoriously associated during his last years in Paris? It must be conceded that the youths at Brighton seem to have been gainfully employed in various ways, and could therefore not in any sense have been regarded as urchins or street-arabs. So the expression "street boys" cannot, it would seem, have been intended in this sense. On the other hand, such dictionaries and compilations of slang of the period as I have seen offer no suggestion that the expression meant youthful male prostitutes.

The only other information of which I am aware relating to Frank Podmore's mode of life and his mysterious death has been briefly mentioned by Dr. E. J. Dingwall in his Introduction to *Mediums of the 19th Century* (New York, 1963), a reprint of Podmore's *Modern Spiritualism*. Podmore's body was found in a lonely pool in Malvern Wells on 19 August, 1910. The information offered by Dr. Dingwall is limited to a fairly short account of the inquest, but includes the comment of the coroner that the case presented

---

[1] For details of the case see the *North London Press* from July 1889 to January 1890.
[2] H. Montgomery Hyde, *Oscar Wilde* (new and enlarged edition, London, 1962), p. 312.

an unsolved mystery. Dr. Dingwall also reveals that no member of the Society for Psychical Research attended the funeral, and that amongst the dozen or more wreaths none was sent by the Society. This omission is curious when it is remembered that Podmore was almost, but not quite, a founder member of the S.P.R., had served on its Council and had been joint Hon. Secretary with F. W. H. Myers for eight years after the death of Edmund Gurney in 1888.

There were other absentees from the funeral. Podmore's wife Eleanore did not attend, and sent no wreath. Podmore, moreover, had spent twenty-eight years in the service of the Post Office until 1907 when, in the words of a letter limited to a single sentence from the Personnel Department to the present writer, "he left without the award of a pension, not having reached pensionable age". No representative of the Post Office came to the funeral and no wreath was sent.

Miss Edith S. Hooper, who was responsible for the short life of Podmore in the *Dictionary of National Biography*, said:

> "In 1907 Podmore left London for Broughton, near Kettering, a parish of which his brother, Claude Podmore, was rector."

The year 1907 was a significant one for Podmore, as is demonstrated by his entries in *Who's Who* for the years 1907 and 1908, which were of course compiled by himself. The particulars given in 1907, which would be written in 1906, showed Podmore, in common with earlier entries, as having married Eleanore Bramwell in 1891, as being in the service of the Post Office and an active member of the Society for Psychical Research. The entry for 1908, written by Podmore in 1907, and the subsequent entries during the few years of life remaining to him, completely omitted all reference to his wife, the Post Office and the S.P.R., the other particulars remaining as before. It would seem almost as if Podmore started a new existence in 1907, leaving London for ever and obliterating from the public record of his life the three connexions which had previously been of most importance to him.

Miss Hooper said, "In his later years Podmore lived apart from his wife; there was no issue". On the evidence of the *Who's Who* entries it seems fairly evident that Podmore and his wife parted in 1907. This likelihood is supported by the fact that in the S.P.R. List of Members prepared in March 1907 Podmore changed his address from 6 Holly Place, Hampstead, London, N.W., to the Secretary's Office, G.P.O., London, E.C. In the same year, as we already know, he left the service of the Post Office without a pension and moved from London altogether. It is difficult to believe that these events were not connected, just as it seems obvious from the absence of a wreath at the funeral, that Podmore's break with his wife was bitter and permanent.

An examination of Podmore's financial affairs throws a somewhat curious light upon the matters under scrutiny. Podmore joined the staff of the General Post Office in 1879. By 1907 he was a first class clerk with a salary range of £550–650 per annum, which was fairly substantial remuneration in those days. Podmore was, moreover, fourth in order of seniority in his grade, and he could have assumed that promotion to a higher position was probable in a year or two. 1907 would seem, in other words, to have been a singularly inappropriate time for Podmore to resign from the Post Office and relinquish his pension, after twenty-eight years' service.

Podmore made his will in March 1893. He left the sum of £300 to any surviving parent or parents, and the residue of his estate to his wife, who was the sole executrix. It is reasonable to assume from this that in 1893 Podmore's estate was very considerably in excess of £300, the bequest to his parents, and was indeed of such an amount that a payment from it of £300 would not significantly affect his wife's financial security in the event of his death. In fact, probate of Podmore's entire estate was granted to his wife in 1911 at an amount of £155 6s. 4d., which presumably would go to his parents. Mrs. Podmore was left destitute and was granted, through the influence of friends, a civil list pension of £60 per annum.

Against the background of the fact that Podmore was virtually penniless when he died in 1910, it is interesting to consider the two possibilities in regard to his financial situation during the years 1907 to 1910. If he was almost without means in 1907, as he was three years later, then any suggestion that he voluntarily relinquished his excellent position at the Post Office and his pension is clearly nonsense; obviously he was asked to resign. On the other hand, if in 1907 he possessed a private fortune sufficient to enable him to retire and sacrifice his pension, then this fortune mysteriously disappeared during the last three years of his life. As Podmore was living modestly with his brother in a country rectory, and spending his time writing, it is difficult to imagine an everyday explanation. It would be incredible folly for a man who had retired from a gainful occupation at the age of fifty-one voluntarily to spend the whole of his capital in three years.

Podmore's death occurred in mysterious circumstances, suggestive of suicide. The information which follows has been taken from *The Times* of 20 August, 1910, the *News of the World* of 21 August and the *Malvern Gazette* of 19 and 26 August.

On Wednesday, 10 August, 1910, Podmore arrived at 2 Ivy Cottages, The Wyche, near Malvern Wells, to stay, as a paying guest, with Mr. Henry Cross. It was not his first visit to the house of Mr. Cross, who said in evidence that he believed that Podmore had arranged for an unnamed male friend to stay with him, but that this unknown person did not arrive. On Sunday evening Podmore went out alone for a walk, returning to the cottage at eight o'clock. He brought with him a young man, whom he had met during his walk, and whom he had invited to have supper with him. After the meal Podmore and his casual acquaintance, as the *Malvern Gazette* called him, went out for a further walk together, from which Podmore returned alone some time afterwards, as it had started to rain. He asked that his coat and boots be dried, and evidently started to write a letter to his mother in his room.

Mr. Cross went to bed shortly afterwards, and a light was left burning on the landing. Between 12.30 a.m. and 1.00 a.m. Mr. Cross and his wife were awakened by a thunderstorm and noticed that the landing light had not been extinguished. On investigation it was found that Podmore had gone out for a third time that night, locking the door behind him. He never returned, and the following day he was reported to the police as missing. Mr. Cross's son-in-law, Mr. George Smith, who lived next door, gave evidence that he had seen Podmore leaving the house about 10.30 p.m., and that he had said "Good-night" to him.

Inquiries, said the *Malvern Gazette* of 26 August, 1910, "were actively prosecuted, and parties of men and Boy Scouts systematically searched the hills, but all these efforts failed to disclose any trace of the missing visitor". According to the police, the young man who had supper with Podmore said that he had parted from his host about 9.00 p.m., before cycling back to

Worcester. Presumably because after this incident Podmore had returned to the cottage, and had been seen by Mr. and Mrs. Cross before going out into the night for the third and last time, the young man was not asked to give evidence at the inquest.

Podmore's body was not discovered until Friday, 19 August, five days after his disappearance. John Harvey, a farming pupil, said that he observed what appeared to be a human head just above the surface of the water of New Pool, described as a silent lakelet near the Wyche rarely visited in the summer, about half a mile from Podmore's lodgings.

Podmore's body bore no marks of violence and had been in the water several days. Death was due to drowning. The body was fully clothed, and the pockets contained, amongst other things, a gold watch and £4 in cash. The watch had stopped at 11.23. Podmore's walking stick was found about a yard from the bank. A juror asked if it would be possible for anyone to slip into the pool from the footpath at the side of the pool. The police evidence was that a most careful examination of the bank showed no marks such as would have been caused by anyone slipping in, and that at the point where the walking stick was found it was only at some distance from the bank that the pool became deep.

After this fairly clear indication that the police considered that the facts pointed to suicide, Mr. and Mrs. Cross gave evidence that Podmore was of "a cheerful and jolly disposition". Podmore's brother George, who stated he had not seen the dead man since April, said that it was inconceivable that Frank would have any desire to put an end to his life. Asked by the coroner whether Podmore had any troubles, "financial or otherwise", the witness replied firmly that his brother had no troubles at all. Another brother, Austin, offered similar evidence, and said that Podmore was the last man in the world to contemplate suicide.

The Coroner, in his brief address to the jury, said that there was really no evidence which might assist them to penetrate the mystery of how Podmore met his death. Possibly he had been affected, the Coroner said, by the brilliant lightning which accompanied the heavy thunderstorm which occurred in the Malvern district on the Sunday night. The Coroner emphasized that the evidence showed an entire absence of any motive whatever for suicide, although the reader may wonder if the Coroner would have made the same observation had he been aware of the facts assembled in the foregoing pages.

Podmore's watch stopped at 11.23 p.m., unless the unlikely assumption be made that Podmore met his death the following morning in broad daylight thirteen hours after he left the cottage. In this connexion it is pertinent to point out that although rain had fallen earlier in the evening and some pretty lightning effects had been observed, the thunderstorm did not break until about midnight, according to the newspaper accounts. So even if Podmore's watch had stopped immediately it was immersed in the water, which would be unusual, it seems doubtful whether the incidence of the storm could have caused him to slip accidentally into the pool, leaving out of account the police evidence in regard to the shallowness of the water at that point, the total absence of any marks of slipping on the bank, and the fact that his stick was left beside the pool.

The unfinished letter to his mother offers no proof either way of suicide or accidental death. Podmore was greatly attached to his mother, and the letter may have been designed to remove any intolerable thought from the old lady's mind that her son intended to take his life when he left the cottage for the third time that evening. On the other hand, the reader may consider that it demonstrates that Podmore intended to return to the cottage alive. A third possibility is that the decision to end his life was taken by Podmore after he left the cottage for his third expedition during that rainy evening. Whether he went out secretly to meet and talk with someone after Mr. and Mrs. Cross had retired to bed we shall never know, but it may not be lacking in significance that he left the cottage at 10.30 p.m., that his watch stopped at 11.23 and that his body was found no more than half a mile from his lodgings.

The facts of this very curious case are now before the reader. If he accepts the opinions of Podmore's brothers George and Austin (it is odd that his brother the Rev. Claude Podmore, with whom he had been living immediately before he came to Malvern, neither gave evidence at the inquest nor attended the funeral), together with the evidence given at the inquest other than that of the police, he will doubtless conclude that Podmore's death was accidental. In this connexion, however, he will no doubt have regard to the fact that the verdict was an open one of "found drowned", presumably because the Coroner emphasized to the jury that on the evidence they had heard there was no motive for suicide.

On the other hand, if the reader attaches weight to the police evidence and the strange circumstances of Podmore's life which have been assembled in these pages he may reach the conclusion that Podmore, faced that night with a final crisis in his affairs from which no escape presented itself, decided to end his life.

APPENDIX II

ON p. 118 I remarked upon the surprising fact that there are two issues or "editions" of Part III of the first volume of S.P.R. *Proceedings*, recording different results of experiment No. 41 in the final series of tests at Dean's Yard in April 1883. I can find no mention in either the *Journal* or the *Proceedings* of the Society of any admission of error in the original printed report of the experiment. According to the S.P.R. *Journal*, it was simply resolved on 30 December, 1884, to reprint Part III because the stock was "nearly exhausted".[1]

Part III consisted of 84 pages, of which no less than 56 were devoted to the "Third Report of the Committee on Thought-Transference", i.e. the experiments with Smith and Blackburn at Dean's Yard. The remaining 28 pages contained three short reports on the activities of the Committee on Mesmerism and the "Reichenbach" Committee, together with a paper by W. F. Barrett on alleged phenomena associated with abnormal conditions of the mind. There seems to be no doubt, therefore, which was the important section of the contents of Part III. An interesting secondary mystery is that the original drawings which illustrated the report were kept by the Society on the file, but the accompanying text is no longer available.

It will be recalled that the last test of "telepathy" between Smith and Blackburn utilized an arrow drawn on a sheet of paper, which was shown to Blackburn with the arrow pointing either up, down, left or right. Smith had, of course, a simple one in four chance at each trial of guessing correctly.

It was stated by the authors of the "Third Report on Thought-Transference" (p. 166):

> "After the 37th trial, Mr. Blackburn was obliged to leave; but we continued the experiments, one or two of the Committee taking Mr. Blackburn's place, and with fair success. Counting these last, we made in all 42 trials. In these the arrow was held in a perpendicular position, up or down, 23 times; and of these cases 20 were guessed rightly, 3 wrongly. It was held in a horizontal position, right or left, 19 times; and of these cases 7 were guessed rightly, 12 wrongly. The three wrong guesses when the arrow was in a perpendicular position occurred after Mr. Blackburn had left us."

This comment in the text is identical in both the first and second issues of Part III.

On the same page of *Proceedings*, above the statement quoted in the previous paragraph, the results are set out in a table, and the following are the last ten experiments as printed in the "first edition" of 1883.

	True position of Arrow	Position as stated by Smith
33.	Pointing to right.	Pointing to left.
34.	„ down.	„ down.
35.	„ up.	„ up.
36.	„ to right.	„ to right.

[1] *Journal*, S.P.R., January 1885, p. 223.

True position of Arrow		Position as stated by Smith
37. Pointing	down.	Pointing down.
38.	„ to left.	„ down.
39.	„ up.	„ to right.
40.	„ down.	„ to right.
41.	„ right.	„ right.
42.	„ up.	„ up.

The results of the preceding 32 experiments were printed in the same form. The final 10 results only have been reproduced here, apart from the question of space, because (*a*) it was among these last results that the alteration in the "second edition" was made and (*b*) these results show that in the last five tests with Blackburn as the "transmitter" (Nos. 33 to 37) Smith made only one mistake (No. 33), whilst in the final five tests without his confederate (Nos. 38 to 42) Smith scored only fractionally over probability.

In the statement in the text six positive comments were made by the writer or writers of the report. A comparison with the 42 results in the printed table shows that only four of these observations were correct, and indeed that a point has to be stretched to admit the first of these:

Text	Results as shown in table (First edition)
(1) "After the 37th trial, Mr. Blackburn was obliged to leave; but we continued the experiments, one or two of the Committee taking Mr. Blackburn's place, and with fair success."	Correct only if 2 correct guesses out of 5, or fractionally above probability, are counted as "fair success".
(2) "The arrow was held in a perpendicular position, up or down, 23 times."	Correct.
(3) "Of these [perpendicular] cases 20 were guessed rightly, 3 wrongly."	Incorrect. 21 were guessed rightly, and 2 wrongly.
(4) "It was held in a horizontal position, right or left, 19 times."	Correct.
(5) "Of these [horizontal] cases 7 [were] guessed rightly, 12 wrongly."	Correct.
(6) "The 3 wrong guesses when the arrow was in a perpendicular position occurred after Mr. Blackburn had left us."	Incorrect. Only 2 wrong vertical guesses (Nos. 39 and 40) were made.

The most obvious mistake was of course in the last, or sixth statement, for in this single case the error could be readily observed without going through the table and counting the correct and incorrect guesses. Whether a reader of the *Proceedings* drew the attention of the S.P.R. leaders to this mistake I do not know, but it was evidently decided to make an alteration to the table in the "second edition" of Part III. Experiment 41 was amended to show the "True Position of Arrow" as "Pointing down" instead of "Pointing to right", the "Position as stated by Smith" being left as in the "first edition". This alteration produced three incorrect vertical guesses

(Nos. 39, 40 and 41) in the five experiments "after Mr. Blackburn had left us" (Nos. 38 to 42) and thus made it fit with the statement in the text.

The alteration must have been done with a reckless lack of care, for the amendment of Experiment 41 actually increased the overall crop of mistakes in the textual statement (which remained unaltered in the "second edition") when compared with the table, from two errors in the "first edition" to no less than five in the "second edition"! The amendment of the table to fit the last of the six comments in the text produced, in fact, the following extraordinary result:

Text	Results as shown in table (Second edition)
(1) "After the 37th trial, Mr. Blackburn was obliged to leave; but we continued the experiments, one or two of the Committee taking Mr. Blackburn's place, and with fair success."	Incorrect, instead of marginally correct as formerly. 1 correct guess out of 5 is not "fair success", being fractionally below probability.
(2) "The arrow was held in a perpendicular position, up or down, 23 times."	Incorrect, instead of correct as formerly. A total of 24 perpendicular guesses was now recorded in the altered table.
(3) "Of these [perpendicular] cases 20 were guessed rightly, 3 wrongly."	Still incorrect. 3 incorrect guesses were now recorded by reason of the altered table, but 21 correct guesses were still tabulated.
(4) "It was held in a horizontal position, right or left, 19 times."	Incorrect, instead of correct as formerly. The amended table now showed only 18 horizontal guesses.
(5) "Of these [horizontal] cases 7 [were] guessed rightly, 12 wrongly."	Incorrect, instead of correct as formerly. The altered table now recorded only 6 correct guesses.
(6) "The 3 wrong guesses when the arrow was in a perpendicular position occurred after Mr. Blackburn had left us."	Correct, instead of incorrect as formerly.

It may, of course, be urged that what may have been the earliest example of the adjusting of the record in experimental parapsychology was a printer's error, but I doubt whether such a submission could be justified. It would be necessary for the printer to re-set the type in the forme to make the alteration, a procedure which could scarcely be accidental. It may be presumed, moreover, that some attempt was made, however inept, to examine the proofs.

It may be argued that what was done was so clumsy, in that whoever was responsible failed to realize that the alteration of the table to fit the text in one particular reduced the remaining five-sixths of the text to nonsense, that it could hardly have been intended to deceive. If this is so, it can only be pointed out that if the chaotic result of the alteration has been noticed during the intervening eighty years, no comment upon it has been made in the S.P.R. literature. It occurred, moreover, in a report which was already crudely evasive in that Podmore, who I think was responsible for it, had already resolved the problem of the embarrassing visit to Dean's Yard of Sir James Crichton-Browne and his friends by simply omitting all reference to the incident in the account. This omission was even coupled, it will be remembered, with the reckless assertion that the authors of the report had been "minutely careful and conscientious in recording the exact conditions of each experiment".

It is for the reader to judge the implications of this ludicrous affair for himself. Few copies of the first issue of Part III seem now to be extant, but the reprint, containing the five mistakes, is available in many libraries and private collections where the interested reader can examine it for himself.

INDEX

INDEX